LANDSCAPES
OF
ABANDONMENT

SUNY series in the Sociology
of Culture

Charles R. Simpson, editor

LANDSCAPES OF ABANDONMENT

Capitalism, Modernity, and
Estrangement

Roger A. Salerno

STATE UNIVERSITY OF NEW YORK PRESS

Published by
State University of New York Press, Albany

Cover art: *Melanconia*, 1912 (oil on canvas) by Giorgio de Chirico (1888–1978)
Estorick Collection, London, UK / Bridgeman Art Library © 2003 Artists
Rights Society (ARS), New York / SIAE, Rome.

For information, address State University of New York Press,
90 State Street, Suite 700, Albany, NY 12207

Production by Diane Ganeles
Marketing by Anne M. Valentine

Library of Congress Cataloging in Publication Data

Salerno, Roger A.
    Landscapes of abandonment : capitalism, modernity, and estrangement /
Roger A. Salerno. p. cm. — (SUNY series in the sociology of culture).
    Includes bibliographical references and index.
    ISBN 0–7914–5845–8 (alk. paper) — ISBN 0–7914–5846–6 (pbk. : alk. paper)
    1. Social integration. 2. Marginality, Social. 3. Capitalism—Social aspects.
4. Alienation (Philosophy) I. Title. II. Series.

HM683.S25 2003
302.5'44—dc21

2002042636

10 9 8 7 6 5 4 3 2 1

For Sandi, with love and hope

Contents

Acknowledgments

The inspiration for this book has come from many sources, chief among these has been a misguided public agenda to achieve total security in an inherently insecure world. The personal wellspring for this work has been my connection to and separation from those who have been important to me. I am especially grateful to Sandra Salerno for her inspiration, patience, and assistance in just about every aspect of this project. In some ways, this book is a product of the loss and desolation we both shared. I am thankful to Frances Exler for her belief and faith in what I was doing, and to Theresa Aiello whose assistance enabled me to re-examine my past and bring this project to closure. Among my colleagues Pam Smith, Laura Hapke, Steve Goldleaf, Amy Foerster, Robert Chapman, Walter Levy, and Michelle Fanelli have all provided important assistance. The Dyson College of Arts and Sciences at Pace University and the Scholarly Research Committee supported me with release time. I am particularly appreciative to those affiliated with SUNY Press, especially Charles Simpson and Ron Helfrich, for welcoming this enterprise and to Diane Ganeles for her production assistance. I also want to thank June Rook and Kate Wilson for their contributions to improving the manuscript and book. Finally, I am grateful to Carlos Rojas who entered my life and gave me an opportunity to better understand the consequences of early abandonment. I wish him luck wherever he might be and hope that he finds the happiness he seeks.

Introduction

The Landscape of Abandonment

Abandonment has been a powerful cultural motif. The biblical account of the banishment of Adam and Eve from Eden, Moses' abandonment to the bulrushes, the casting of Remus and Romulus into the Tiber and the parental surrender of the infant Oedipus testify to its powerful cultural iconography in the west. Its significance as a theme in literature, in Goethe's romantic tale of *Young Werther*, in Flaubert's *Madame Bovary*, in Conrad's *Lord Jim* speak to the dramatic power of abandonment. A list of artistic works dealing with abandonment and its existential manifestations can fill volumes. In a sense, it has often shaped our path to human understanding.

From Hegel to Marx, from Nietzsche to Foucault, from Freud to Lacan, abandonment makes its way into much of the intellectual discourse we characterize as modern. It forms a contraposition to modernity's frequent emphasis on social control. It is this relationship between attachment and abandonment, authority and anarchy, constriction and release that is the pulse of modern discourse and the focus of this book.

This is an exploration of the significance of abandonment and its phenomenological currents in modern life. It is an examination of abandonment as both discourse and as a consequence of political and social forces. As a broad freewheeling survey, this study raises many more questions than it answers. Among these are how does abandonment inform modernity? How is it manifested in our thinking? How does it color human interaction? And how does it affect civic life?

1

Abandonment is viewed not only as phenomenology, but it is also examined as iconography. In viewing it in this way, I have subscribed to Raymond Williams' formula for a sociology of culture.[1] Abandonment is both a factor of production, in a deeply Marxian sense, as well as an object of that production. Through the system of capitalism we become both alienated and abandoned, objectified and commodified.

Throughout this book I assert that abandonment is central to modernity. I do not mean by this that the dread of abandonment is specific to modern societies alone. The fear of abandonment is primal. While forms of abandonment and reactions to it vary from society to society, it appears to have taken on enormous social and cultural importance in modern life and characterizes not only our superficial relationships, but also many of our most intimate ones. It has become a significant part of our artistic expression and serves as an important influence on the production of contemporary culture.

Our anxieties, as Freud noted, are central to modern life. However, I see these anxieties as culturally produced in societies wherein the power of the few is based on the insecurity of the many. In modern life, anxieties often emerge out of inequitable class relations generated by capitalism. While not alone in this respect, capitalism promotes an emotional sense of aloneness and vulnerability.

In capitalistic society, it is our class system that frames even our most personal perceptions of the world. Our awareness of these power inequities produces within us a sense of anxiety, and imbues us with a dread of abandonment.

I propose that such socially induced anxieties frequently become manifest in a retreat not only from self-actualization, but also from social progress. Anxieties associated with abandonment often induce what Erich Fromm once called an "escape from freedom," and an overemphasis on security. Often there is a desire to insulate oneself from the dangers and chaos inherent in modernity. Thus, by restricting spontaneity and overemphasizing security and ritual (whether religious or commercial) people run the risk of closing themselves off to change. The gating of petty bourgeois communities, the excessive nourishing of the police apparatus, record levels of incarceration, large military budgets, and excessive surveillance are some manifestations of totalitarian societies where security becomes a way of life. The retreat into unquestioning faith in patriarchal authority is also symptomatic of this escape.

While I offer no programmatic solutions to such dilemmas presented in this book, I believe that the first step is an understanding—an appreciation of abandonment and its role in modern life. Like many of the critical theorists, I do not view modernity as a force of liberation. I do not romanticize it, nor do I demonize it. Modern life provides us with the possibility for both severe human oppression and significant personal liberation. How we struggle with these potentialities in the face of abandonment is the subject of this book.

ABANDONMENT AS A SIGNIFIER

Before presenting a brief etymology of abandonment it is important to indicate that the word has many uses, both positive and negative. It has become an increasingly powerful signifier of modern life and as such deserves special consideration.

According to the *Oxford English Dictionary*, the word "abandonment" encompasses several distinct definitions, but these are often oppositional. The word first appears in the Middle French (eleventh to thirteenth centuries) as *metrè à bandon*, meaning to put under anyone's jurisdiction or domain; to proscribe; to release from proscription; to banish.[2] *Ban* is an important root of the word and denotes a restriction or obligation under feudal or church law. Originally, it was an interdiction, sometimes a proclamation or edict; frequently an excommunication. There is a close association between a*ban*donment and other derivatives of ban, such as the French *au ban*, meaning to outlaw, or the English "band" meaning something that binds, fetters, or restricts; or bandit—one who is outside the law, unrestricted.

In the beginning of the thirteenth century, abandonment's earliest uses described submission to authority, control, or jurisdiction of another. It sometimes described individuals who gave themselves or their children into bondage. It denoted submission of the serf to his or her master, the priest to his church, and other ties of servitude—often complete and utter surrender. But by the fourteenth century, while retaining the various uses related to human subjugation and alienation, the meaning of abandonment also came to signify an abdication of one's rights or obligations to another person, place, value, or thing. Thus, abandonment could mean the surrender of someone or something to another, or the total disregard of one's personal, familial, religious, or civil obligations. The abandonment of children, for example, was frequently considered abdication of one's rights to them as possessions, but later came to mean the relinquishment of one's personal responsibilities in the eyes of community, church, or state.

Historian John Boswell, in his research on the abandonment of European children in the Middle Ages, conceptually located the root of abandonment in the Greek ἔκθεσις, and in the Latin root as *exposito*.[3]

Both words meant "to put outside," "to expose," "to throw out." Both convey the risk of harm or exposure to danger. They reveal an affinity to an older signifier, exile, which corresponds to the banishment and alienation associated with abandonment. However, Boswell's etymology is contextually confined and his focus is exclusively on abandonment of children. In contrast, late medieval and early modern usages of abandonment imply a tension between attachment and separation—bondage and freedom. In fourteenth century England, the typical use of abandonment stressed its material and practical applications to property and insurance law. When new land-tenure arrangements and enclosure policies forced tens of thousands of peasants from commonly open farmlands, abandonment denoted an alienation of property and corresponding homelessness. The expulsion of peasants and the commodification of property produced new forms of separation. In order to survive, children of this new laboring class were frequently sold into servitude for several years and were forced to live away from their families. Women were left behind by their husbands who migrated in search of work.[4] Abandonment had come to represent the severing of feudal ties and a separation from the land. It represented a loss of a fixed place in the world.

With major challenges to traditions of manorial life brought on by structural changes inherent in market capitalism, the Reformation, and the Enlightenment, abandonment was accorded a variety of other more modern uses that stressed liberation: "at one's own discretion," "at one's own will," or "without interference." These were eventually joined by "unrestricted freedom," and "free without responsibility," which clearly illustrated a perceived degeneration of medieval fealty, familial and patrimonial loyalties in the face of the ascent of personal self-interest.[5] Abandonment, therefore, may be linked to *laissez-faire* capitalism and the sense of freedom that seemed to characterize the lives of the emerging bourgeoisie.

Abandonment is used in its broadest sense here as an all-encompassing term. That is, abandonment is viewed as constituting a variety of forms of material and nonmaterial detachments, relinquishments, banishments, and separations. It may range from infant/caregiver separation and personal individuation to worker alienation and social anomie. On a psychological level it might even constitute repression and denial. It is my goal to explore its many diverse renderings in the social sciences and to show its importance in the iconography of modern life. Furthermore, it is my purpose to interpret its significance to modernity and postmodernity.

THE LANDSCAPE OF ABANDONMENT

The use of the term landscape is borrowed from a number of sources, but most obviously it is derived from the word developed in sixteenth century Europe to describe a particular type of art that isolates a scene in nature from both the painter and the adjoining panorama. Robert Nisbet must be credited with the first full application of the concept of landscape to sociology.[6] It was Nisbet who suggested that landscapes in sociology were individual perspectives on any particular sociological terrain or social phenomenon isolated from the rest of society for the purpose of description and study. Geographer Denis Cosgrove presents the idea that landscape is more than the isolation of a natural scene in pictoral representation; it is also an ideological perspective influenced by history, class, and culture.[7] And Sharon Zukin notes: "Today the concept landscape is almost less likely to refer to a genre of painting than to a sociological image."[8] I use the term here in both an aesthetic and sociological sense. Landscape art is predicated on separation, and particularly isolation from nature. As Georg Lukács noted, it is only when one stands apart from the scene, outside of nature, that one can even fathom a landscape.[9]

This book has been divided into two parts. The first part is an examination of the theoretical and conceptual elements that have brought about an intense focus on abandonment in modern life. These are perceptual paradigms through which abandonment is discussed and described. The second part constitutes vistas of abandonment—how we have come to see it manifested in conscience, community, nature, and globalization.

Thus, the first chapter is an attempt to understand abandonment's modern significance as rooted in historical and social forces, primarily capitalism, modernity, romanticism, and consumerism. I have confined my investigation to these areas because I believe that they constitute salient categories of contemporary life. Each of these imbues a distinct meaning into the concept of abandonment, and each assigns to it a uniqueness, represented as a theme in the social sciences, the arts, and the humanities. Presented in this chapter is an exploration of how these forces can be interpreted as agents of abandonment.

The second and third chapters also deal with theoretical constructs that shape modern notions of abandonment. In the second chapter I examine social theory that helps to articulate the sense of abandonment in modern life. Beginning with a brief survey of the relevant ideas of Hegel and Kierkegaard, and examining the pertinent contributions of Marx, Freud, Heidegger, and the Frankfurt theorists, this chapter explores the theoretical roots of abandonment as an essential feature of modern life captured in philosophical discourse. Secondarily, a survey of a variety of diverse philosophical and social scientific perspectives on the notion of abandonment are reviewed here including poststructuralism, postmodernism, and feminism. This survey lays the foundation for the further development of theoretical approaches to abandonment that will be presented throughout this book. In chapter 3 I draw upon early childhood experiences of modern writers and artists such as Kafka, Poe, and Munch to provide an overview of psychological theory of abandonment, separation, and loss. The classic work of Bowlby, Ainsworth, and Mahler on separation anxiety is scrutinized. In this chapter I explore the place of abandonment in object relations theory, including the work of Klein, Winnicott, and Kohut and connect these ideas to critical sociology and Marxian analysis. I review the work of Sartre and Lacan and attempt to unveil the importance of abandonment to existential and poststructural theory. The social pathology of abandonment anxiety and its connection to capitalism and consumerism are assessed.

Fragmentation and abandonment are the subjects of chapter 4. I provide a survey here of how the forces of modernity, but more particularly modern capitalistic societies, undergo a process of social and cultural disintegration. In doing this I make use of contributions of a variety of theorists including Simmel and Lukács. Marcuse's notions of the "happy conscience" and "one-dimensionality" are related to the problems of modern consciousness. Relevant ideas of Habermas, Fromm, Goffman, and MacIntyre are also assessed. The focus of this chapter is on problems relative to reification, false consciousness, doubling, and desensitization associated with modern capitalistic societies.

Chapter 5 deals with abandonment of community. I examine the classical conceptualizations of community as well as more contemporary ones. Community romanticism is contrasted to more critically modernistic conceptualizations. The impact of capitalism, privatism, and globalization on communal life is assessed. I explore how the idea of community undergoes transmutation from a sense of authentic relationship to an empty, artificial construct of propinquitious or networked individuals; how some of the forces of modern life and particularly market capitalism have undermined human associations; and how community has given way to a synthetic, commodified Disneyfication of the landscape. The abandonment of community is seen as contributing to the weakening of a socially constructed self-concept resulting in a deepening of anxiety and fear of otherness.

The sixth chapter examines the abandonment of nature. It is an attempt to understand the brutalization of the natural environment emanating from the forces of modernity and capitalism. I commence this chapter with an assessment of Mary Shelley's *Frankenstein* and the notion of nature. By comprehending how nature was conceptualized by early modern scientists, philosophers, and romantics, and by challenging some of their assumptions, I hope to provide a better understanding of the material and symbolic significance of nature. While this chapter examines the consequences of eradicating the spiritual importance of nature, especially wilderness, it also proposes that segmentation, manipulation, and commodification of nature have been important to both modernity and the Enlightenment project. The bifurcation of nature and self, that is the abandonment and alienation of nature, is viewed as contributing to an overall sense of human/environmental dissociation resulting in a heightened sense of aloneness.

Finally, chapter 7 concludes with an analysis of abandonment and globalization. It is suggested here that the forces of capitalistic development including neocolonialism, privatization, and consumerism have radically altered the natural and cultural landscapes around the world. Globalization, as a stage of capitalistic development, presents new problems and cultural challenges. Yet, abandonment remains an underlying feature of both the new postfordist strategies of production and global consumerism. It is global change that presents the greatest challenge for personal identity and the greatest hope for community.

SIGNIFICANCE OF THIS WORK

In this work I examine the essential features of abandonment and human disconnection associated with it from a variety of theoretical perspectives. Attempting to understand the modern significance of abandonment, I provide an analysis of the historical, social, and psychological dimensions of detachment embedded in our contemporary culture. Abandonment permeates not only our social and familial arrangements, it forms the basis of our deepest self-awareness. While it always has been a means through which people reluctantly dealt with their personal dilemmas—the unwanted child, the intolerable mate, the ill parent, the oppressive community—with the advent of market capitalism it has become more central to our social lives. Capitalism accelerates the rate and intensity of abandonment behavior and the level of anxiety we feel relative to it. That we find millions of abandoned children in cities of countries undergoing intense economic development and modernization should not be a surprise; nor should our own record number of abused, deserted and abandoned children and adults. The power of the market system to forsake and displace is enormous. Under commodity capitalism, abandonment has become institutionalized; it is represented not only by the culture of perpetual consumerism, but also by those billion-dollar industries that now warehouse the homeless, the prisoner, the mentally ill, and the disenfranchised elderly. These institutions of legitimized abandonment contribute

to our own feelings of loss of control. Thus, the narrative of social disengagement forms the basis for much of Marxist analysis, psychoanalytic
theory, and existential philosophy. The motif of abandonment permeates
much of our art, literature and social science; it colors modern, postmodern, and feminist ideas.

In concentrating most exclusively on capitalism as the dynamo of
modernistic change, I have excluded a discussion of those systems of
socialist modernity. This is not because I see these systems as less connected to processes of modernization. I join Zygmunt Bauman in his
position that both capitalism and socialism are outcomes of the
Enlightenment and have much in common in this regard.[10] Joseph
Stalin's brand of socialist modernity was a powerfully destructive force
in the world. So-called utopian-socialist Enlightenment has a blood-
stained history; and much done in the name of progress has produced
inhuman outcomes. Rather, I choose to discuss those forces that dominate the world today. While there are many versions of capitalism at
work, ranging from Singapore capitalism to New York capitalism, it
remains a protean force influencing and often determining the content of
expanding consumerist culture.

In conducting this survey I have relied more on ideas than on data.
Therefore, this is not a typical social science monograph replete with
charts and graphs. I have always believed that some of the best sociology
comes to us from artists, writers, and poets. To this end, I locate the value
in Marx, Weber, Simmel, and Goffman not in their compilation of data
(for which I can forgive them) but in their exquisite narratives and complex discourses that help us to better understand the human condition. It
is the purpose of this work not to contribute to the ongoing quantitative
expression of the world, but to pause and take stock of some of the most
powerful imagery and ideas concerned with abandonment. I have
attempted to weave these ideas together as an abandonment montage.

I cannot deny that this venture may appear to be exceedingly ambitious. Its integration of several disciplines and disparate analytic modal-
ities affords only casual expositions of important topics warranting
much greater attention. I realize I thereby open myself to criticism of
those who might view much of this work as superficial; however, this
book is intended merely as a survey of the abandonment terrain and as a
possible way of opening up avenues for further exploration. Still, I
believe that part of its strength rests in ascribing to abandonment a
position of critical social and cultural importance not only by calling
attention to its significance in everyday life, but also in revealing its role
in the process of globalization.

Chapter 1

Capitalism, Abandonment, and Modernity

The cultural significance of abandonment in modern life is rooted in the disruptive historical forces generated by market capitalism. By spawning a system of social destabilization capitalism invents a form of modernity characterized by perpetual insecurity, alienation, and dread. The culture of modern capitalism is conveyed through abandonment motifs in a vast assortment of intellectual and artistic narratives. These motifs are repeated in modern literature, art, philosophy, and the social sciences. Through an examination of some of these narratives a clearer understanding of abandonment's role in modern life is gained.

CAPITALISM AND ITS DISCONTENTS

As social discourse, capitalism's history is relatively short. We are told that the word "capitalism" did not appear in print until 1854.[1] Used neither by Adam Smith nor Karl Marx, capitalism and all that it has come to mean as an ideology and method of production, is still a relatively recent signifier and very much in the process of evolving.

Adam Smith is recognized as having formalized a narrative of what we now regard as the early modern capitalistic economy, even though he did not use the term "capitalism." For him economy was a subject of moral, social, and intellectual inquiry. As he saw it, the moral imperative of capitalism was free markets, unbridled access to them, and the free flow of resources (supply and demand) guided by an "invisible hand." The social manifestation of capitalism was heightened individualism. As an Enlightenment thinker his intellectual agenda was to discover the natural laws that kept the machinery of the marketplace operating with efficiency and effectiveness. His economic paradigm comprised moral and natural processes, which ultimately would result in the advancement of societies and the material well-being of people everywhere. He understood, as did other eighteenth-century commentators, that he was looking at a newly emerging world market system. His credentials in moral philosophy and his ability to describe capitalism in positivistic terms drew considerable attention to this work. Thus, Smith can be credited with the reification of what we now term "modern capitalism"—giving it both an internal and eternal life.

Adam Smith provides not only a particular representational image of the capitalistic system wherein the employer and employee engage in a highly rational exchange of specialized labor for money, but he also depicts a system of markets characterized by a human propensity to "barter, truck and exchange" goods and services. This is a pattern in which all supply and demand perfectly intersect and determine a fair price. The individual participant is central to Smith's work. Given that *The Wealth of Nations* was produced at the very beginning of the industrial revolution, his industrial landscape is almost pastoral—void of smoking factories, violent labor movements, and corrupt corporate ventures. It all seemed to be running smoothly as the last quarter of the eighteenth century drew to a close. Still, in his description of economic life we cannot find reference to one labor abuse—none in the mines of Durham, not one in the pin factory, none in the workshops of Glasgow. He sees little of the excesses, such as the exploitation of children for cheap labor, and he praises the benefits of the factory system without much concern for its destabilizing influences on social life.

Smith sees a society driven by market demand, competition, and acquisitiveness. His work predicts a modern bourgeois liberalism that raises capitalism to the position of secular veneration, imbuing it with naturalistic powers while ignoring many of its abuses. In that he posits capitalism, like nature, to be inherently rational, he establishes a strong intellectual link between Enlightenment thought and capitalistic enterprise. Therefore, he presents capitalism within a specific ideological context.

Bourgeois freedom from avarice is seen as essential to capitalism's success and to the social progress that is dependent on it. Smith embraces the *laissez-faire* proposed by François Quesnay and the French Physiocrats. For Smith the unregulated market, guided by competition and profit, produces the most benefit for the whole of society. Civil society and economy must be segregated from the state. It is the free market, not the state, that creates wealth and civility. Accordingly, the state needs to be kept clear of the natural ebb and flow of the market. Trade barriers must necessarily come down, except in cases where this flow is restrained by monopolistic practices. More than merely possible, capitalistic expansion on a global scale is desirable.

Accepting Hobbes' assumption that greed and sloth are qualities inherent in the very nature of people, Smith firmly believed that individual self-interests can produce an overall social good.[2] He postulates that many of the more brutish, egoistic drives could be put to a nobler purpose. While this idea of harnessing the vile, egocentric, and lustful nature of people and putting it into the service of the general public good dates back at least to St. Augustine, it was popularized by Bernard Mandeville in his classic text *The Fable of the Bees* in 1714. Smith refines it and advances this idea in *The Wealth of Nations* by integrating it into the narrative of modern capitalism. Although Mandeville had used the terms "vice" and "passion" in his book, Smith neutralizes these problematic signifiers and converts them into pleasure-seeking drives—"interests" and "advantages." Economist Albert O. Hirschman proposes that there was a "semantic drift" in the seventeenth century wherein highly charged terms such as greed, lust, ambition and avarice were converted into more neutral words such as "interests." And Smith, in the late eighteenth century, contributes to the shift in semantics by making material self-interest—at the expense of other destructive passions—a respectable part of capitalism.[3]

Hirschman contends that a principle of countervailing passion had a long tradition in western social thought, but it was most notably adopted by Enlightenment thinkers such as Montesquieu, Vico, Smith, and other moralists. In developing this idea they proposed that highly destructive and dangerous human desires could be restrained and less dangerous interests unleashed in their place, acting as surrogate passions.[4] These interests could be let loose in the marketplace and, hopefully, might be used to quell the festering indeterminate pool of more dangerous human desires, including drives for power, sex and destruction. In fact, these deleterious passions could be submerged, and perhaps subsumed, by the desire for material things. Thus, at the base of Smith's capitalistic narrative is a process similar to sublimation to be identified by Freud more than a century later.

While conservatives expressed concern that these innate drives of the rabble could be dangerous if released, Smith pronounced that the primary purpose of civil government was to keep the wealthy safe from the poor. Still, many saw a significant danger in the lack of formal constraints on market appetites. Edmund Burke, a strong supporter of private property and the market economy, was quite skeptical of freedom without some form of centralized control. For him and for others the unleashing of avarice could become a nightmare leading to further cravings. The Marquis de Condorcet in France and William Godwin of Britain, both liberals, opposed the abuses they saw connected to unbridled capitalistic ventures for other reasons. Like Smith, they supported the Enlightenment's precept that reason and market could be used to address social concerns. Unlike Smith, Condorcet saw problems stemming from unbridled capitalism that encouraged asymmetrical concentrations of wealth.[5] Smith was more concerned with the consequences of damming-up of avidity.

Although Smith's work was produced at the beginning of the industrial revolution, he clearly understood the social importance of the newly emerging market system. The division of labor and the emergence of monetary and credit systems were changing not only the enterprise of business, but the nature of human relationships. For Smith, individualism and human acquisitiveness were emerging as central features of modern egoistic culture. This could produce positive consequences since the masses would be forced to resort to rational, self-serving calculation. Unrestrained passions associated with the poor would be put into the service of building a civil society. While the division of labor made people narrow and dull, the money economy made people cold and calculating.

In *The Wealth of Nations*, men and women are Hobbesian pleasure-seeking machines, lazy and unreflective. There is no hint of utopianism here, no glimmer of human compassion, no allusion to personal loyalty, or to bonds of community. There is no meaningful communal life in the capitalism he describes. There is only increasing human atomization resulting from the intensification of the division of labor and an ever-expanding pecuniary network of interests. As specialization intensifies, the work itself becomes increasingly meaningless. Capitalism, as he envisions it, sets into motion the commodification of all factors of production. He clearly recognizes that the laborer is but one more commodity. A life under capitalism is one of getting and spending. The future is to be judged primarily by economic growth and the accumulation of wealth.

The Wealth of Nations is an exemplary modernistic narrative. It helps to establish our essential understanding of an abstract system we now refer to as capitalism. It is both a powerful political and philosophical tract without ever identifying itself as such. While its underlying values are not obtrusive, it nevertheless is openly supportive of an ever-emerging bourgeois system of human greed and exploitation. It celebrates the power of capital accumulation to uproot the past while generating conditions of poverty and promoting an expansion of wealth. Still, as a living system guided by sacred natural laws, Smith views it as remaining outside of our sphere of control and guided by a Calvinistic predestination. People need only surrender to the prerogative of the invisible hand.

For laborers, the landscape of capitalism presented by Smith in this work is frequently bleak. Smith knows this system is based on the workers' fears of losing their means of providing the necessities of life for themselves and their families. This should force the laborer to redirect negative drives into constructive, productive outlets. He acknowledges that as the world shifts to dependencies on capital production, the continual fear of starvation and homelessness drives labor to become more mobile and productive, frequently bidding down its own wages in the process. The volatility of the marketplace, the depressions, recessions and collapses, further promote worker perturbation and docility. He proposes that there can be no escaping the inevitable dependence on the market mechanism for one's very survival. He shows clearly that mortality rates are fixed to wages, which are frequently determined by colluding employers who prefer healthier profits to salutary working conditions. While Smith asserts that greater profits would eventually result in higher salaries for workers (something he supported), he is not very confident of this occurring.

Smith makes no conscious connection between capitalism and abandonment. Still he does suggest that capitalism disrupts the traditional social order. In his emphasis on the importance of the division of labor, he seems to indicate some of its inherent problems such as the dumbing-down of labor and overall worker desensitization;[6] his focus on the factory or central workshop as the nexus of commerce speaks of the collapse of a home-based familial life associated with more agrarian societies. Throughout Smith's discourse there are indeed signs of humanistic sensibility. Among these is his recognition of a drive that unites all: the desire on the part of everyone, rich and poor alike, to be connected to others, to be respected, to be desired and loved. In *The Theory of Moral Sentiments*, Smith asks:

> For what purpose is all the toil and bustle of this world? What is the end of avarice and ambition, of the pursuit of wealth, of power, and pre-eminence? . . . From whence . . . arises the emulation which runs through all the different ranks of men and what are the advantages which we propose by that great purpose of human life which we call bettering our condition? To be observed, to be attended to, to be taken notice of with sympathy,

complacency and appreciation are all the advantages which we can propose to derive from it.[7]

The desire to be wanted and respected by others, in a Hegelian sense the
desire to be desired, seems to be the overriding force at work here.
Capitalism is viewed as repressing the more base human drives and converting them into pecuniary interests through a simple process of coer-
cion. But the trade-off for work is not merely material reward. For
Smith, the quest for human acceptance is the compensation for all this
bartering, trucking and exchanging. And behind this rests the fear of
destitution, disconnection, and aloneness, which is the essence of capitalism itself.

Following Smith were others who contributed to the conceptual
landscape of this developing system. Numerous historical narratives
compete for dominance in explaining capitalism's emergence. Smith did
not venture to elaborate a detailed account of capitalism's development
in *The Wealth of Nations*, since he viewed capitalism as inherent in
nature. Nevertheless, Karl Marx and Max Weber both followed with
socially grounded historiographies. Both traced the origin of modern
capitalism to feudalism and its eventual demise. Political and ideological
lines were drawn whereby the more ardent defenders of capitalism
viewed it as a natural evolutionary force, which had no particular origin
in time; others saw it as having distinctive social institutional begin-
nings.[8] While there are still controversies raging over what exactly constitutes capitalism and when specifically the modern European version
began, it is clear that this system holds an important place as both an
object of discourse and as a perceived generator of modern life.

The conceptualization of capitalism as a harbinger of modernity was
not the sole purview of social critics and historians. Beginning in the late
eighteenth century, romantic artists and poets contributed greatly to the
overall imagery that would become embedded in western visions of capitalism. Thus Blake's "dark satanic mills" found a place deep in the
hearts of even the most conservative thinkers.[9] The disquieting effects of
the new social order became the raw material of literary and poetic narratives, which were to have a far greater influence than Smith's market
ideology. Literary critic H. G. Schenk notes: "No one, not even Marx
himself, could expose the hollowness of economic liberalism better than
these thinkers have done. Sismondi and Baader, Coleridge and Adam
Müller, were well aware of the fact that the proletarian in the newly
arisen industrial society had only seemingly gained liberty, but had most
certainly lost whatever security he had previously possessed."[10] The literary attacks on capitalism carried great currency because they resonated
as truth. Artists, writers, poets, and painters contributed significantly to

the modern imagery of capitalistic exploitation and dehumanization of workers. But the story of capitalism's evolution as generator of intense social forces was left chiefly to historians and sociologists.

The Marxian discourse on capitalism is sociologically compelling. Unlike Smith, Marx reveals the underbelly of capitalism as a force of social upheaval. Of course the differences in western capitalism between 1776 and 1844 were tremendous. Now there were smoking stacks, polluted rivers, armies of drone-like workers in the service of their own exploitation. These were hard to ignore. There is no invisible hand here, only the imposition of might against the weak. Thus, the capitalistic tableau resonates with human drama and dread. It depicts armies of the poor struggling against oppression and celebrates the coming proletarian revolution. Marx, and to an even larger extent Engels, adds the human face to capitalism. It is Marx who puts capitalism into the context of class and social history. His imagery of capitalism is well known to most of us; it is the version we tend to associate with dark cities, urban hunger, and abusive child labor practices. Marx, not Smith, would inspire the intense scholarship of Max Weber on capitalism and estabilished for succeeding generations of scholars and thinkers a new challenge to classical liberal thought.

TRANSFORMATION NARRATIVES

While Marx and his image of capitalism will be more closely examined throughout this work, it is important to introduce other, more sociologically oriented models of capitalistic development that address its modernistic dimensions. Among these was a model proposed by Karl Polanyi in his 1944 work, *The Great Transformation*.[11] While Polanyi's classic interpretation of history remains a controversial one, it is useful as a frame of reference here. One hundred years after Marx, he connects the development of capitalism to key social institutional changes that we associate with modernization. According to Polanyi, capitalism set into motion what he referred to as the "great transformation" in western Europe between the fifteenth and eighteenth centuries. The uprooting of traditional social arrangements (including methods of exchange) and the imposition of radically new forms of human relationships based upon market principles drastically altered the course of social history.

Polanyi asserts that prior to the coming of industrialization in Europe, the market played a minimal role in economic life. Wherever it could be said to have existed, the market was not central to the primary form of economic organization. Drawing on the work of anthropologists, Polanyi suggests that preindustrial economic behavior was determined by societal needs, not market demands. He introduces the concepts of reciprocity and redistribution, and he posits the notion that people historically produced goods and services for which they were best suited and shared them with those around them. This sharing he calls "reciprocity." Underlying this process was always an unstated agreement that everyone produced what he or she could do best. This did not emerge from the drive to profit, but out of the need to be attached to others, the fear of social ostracism, and the desire for social prestige. In this regard, Polanyi's suggested reasons for the exchange of goods and services are similar to those Adam Smith identified—the need to be desired, loved, connected, and respected. In differing from Smith he sees social relations, not the market, as the central force behind the division of labor. Instead of depicting capitalism as an avenue to individual freedom, Polanyi portrays it as the road to human alienation and social devastation.

Redistribution was the second element in Polanyi's analytic schema. Contrary to Smith, he asserts that historically the redistribution of goods and services was never the product of invisible market forces. Redistribution frequently involved a leader or chief who collected the surplus, maintained it, and redistributed it to members of his group through holding communal feasts, festivals or fairs. These functions served as a means of equitably reallocating resources and reinforcing the social structure. They celebrated one's place in the community and promoted group solidarity. Community festivals were used to forge or to reinforce relationships with neighboring tribes. Thus, the exchange of goods and services had more to do with the promotion of social linkages than meeting egoistic needs. While markets did exist simultaneously with reciprocity and redistribution, they were peripheral to social life. Capitalism, he asserts, did not naturally evolve from such associations; rather, members of the newly emerging bourgeoisie forced their will upon mercantilist states to provide protections for their businesses and, in essence, created capitalism. Thus, Smith's market capitalism is viewed as state intervention—evolving from policies developed by nation states to protect the wealthy. They were not a product of nature.

Finally, Polanyi's central argument is that market economies are relatively new and never accounted for more than a fraction of the systems of exchange that existed in the world at the end of the eighteenth century. These arrangements emerged only with the advent of European modernization and colonial expansion. Traditionally, all economic arrangements and patterns of stratification were determined by the social values inherent in kinship, religion, politics, and community. In modern, capitalistic societies, however, the opposite is true. Here economic arrangements dictate social values.

An excellent counter interpretation of the development of capitalism in the west is presented by Alan MacFarlane who contends that Polanyi's theory is incorrect; the notion that capitalism developed in England between the sixteenth and nineteenth centuries from nonmarket peasant society is wrong. MacFarlane insists that evidence indicates that English individualism was not at all a product of post-sixteenth century capitalistic development and that market society was not something new that transformed society.[12] Many disagree.

Fredric Jameson asserts that there is a vital connection between modernity and capitalism.[13] Jameson, who has gained a considerable reputation in America and Europe as an innovative literary and cultural critic, has been able to synthesize disparate elements of Marxism, postmodernism, and Lacanian analysis into his own hermeneutic landscape. Like Marx, he proposes that if we went back far enough into human history we could see primitive communism as a universal way of life—one that directed all forms of human association. For him, as for Polanyi, the emergence of markets and the development of nation states promoted the appearance of vast social inequities and the decline of a collective consciousness. Jameson believes that the primitive communistic state, as in the pagan myth of the Golden Age of Saturn and the Christian myth of Eden, was one in which there was universal sharing. All property was held in common and all thought was collective. The concept of the individual did not and could not exist. While he admits that such a system today might appear neomythical, he proposes that it can be authenticated from the remnants of history. It still can be found in some tribal societies.

Jameson's interpretation of history, while in keeping with the Marxist tradition, is also divorced from it in some respects. He throws into question the Enlightenment project and the dichotomization that was inherent in it. While his notion of the primal collective conscience is certainly a part of anthropological and sociological tradition, his subscription to it frequently exposes him to charges of romanticizing history and the primitive collective. Still, it remains an important component of his thought, and he insists is essential to Marxism.

Modern alienation, for Jameson, is a product of the evolving market system. It runs counter to tribal communal expression. Modernization forces the loss of the primitive collective mind. By responding to the specialization inherent in capitalism, thought processes are fragmented. Even the senses are estranged from each other and start to function independently. The collective mind is further fragmented and thinking compartmentalized. Under capitalism there is a loss of vividness or color that is an essential aspect of modern alienation. As specialization diminishes perception, there is a real loss of sight, hearing and an overall sense of reality. Under this system of capitalism there is a severing of emotions from reason. Functions of the mind become limited to empirical and descriptive processes. Splitting, in fact, becomes the norm. Modernism evolves from this.

For Jameson, Freud's essential ideas, like those of Smith, reflect a human nature that is isolated in time and place—a consequence of market capitalism. He sees Freud as providing an exemplary method of unearthing that which lays hidden and buried within us. While Freud's model of the unconscious and the psyche are reflective of the alienation and fragmentation brought about by capitalism, they provide important tools for unearthing our political unconscious.[14] We will return to Jameson and these ideas later on in this book.

CAPITALISM AND ABANDONMENT

As an engine of social change, capitalism was an important generator of human abandonment. Historical renditions, both conservative and radical, reveal how it helped to usher in the collapse of feudalism throughout Europe and around the world. These accounts reveal a shattering of relations bound by collective endeavors and ways of life.

The commodification of land through the enclosure movement, accompanied by the forced expulsion of tens of thousands of peasants from commonly farmed lands, produced a rise in both peasant tenancy and in the number of displaced nomads who pursued refuge in overly congested towns. While massive numbers of peasants were forced from public lands between 1570 and 1630, enclosure actually began as early as the thirteenth century and lasted well into the 1800s resulting in a crazy quilt of individually operated farms, each under private management.[15] Along with enclosure was a sudden upsurge in poverty and squalor. Those who found their way into the ranks of tenants also found themselves separated from any control of the means of production. All were powerless and under the direction of new landlords. Each succeeding harvest failure increased unsettlement and insecurity. The severing of feudal ties and a separation from the land marked a new wave of social abandonment. Thus, capitalism undermined systems of communal obligation, reciprocity and redistribution. Capitalism in conjunction with mercantilism and the development of nation states, created enormous wealth for the few. For some it meant the freedom to expropriate the work of others for profit. It was a form of self-expression, a creative venture, and in the eyes of the Protestant Church an act of civic responsibility.[16] For the peasant laborer, however, it meant personal fragmentation as well as social alienation. The worker was commodified in the marketplace, and labor became just one of a number of other commodities to go up for sale. Marx noted:

> Finally, there came a time when everything that men had considered as inalienable became an object of exchange, of traffic and could be alienated. This is the time when the very things which till then had been communicated, but never exchanged; given, but never sold; acquired, but never bought—virtue, love, conviction, knowledge, conscience, etc.—when everything finally passed into commerce. It is the time of general corruption, of universal venality, or, to speak in terms of political economy, the time when everything, moral or physical, having become marketable value, is brought to the market to be assessed at its truest value.[17]

In 1941, Erich Fromm, who examined both the psychological and social consequences of this breakdown of feudal life and the subsequent rise of market forces recapitulates Marx and reinvigorates his sentiments:

> By losing his fixed place in a closed world man loses the answer to the meaning of his life; the result is that doubt has befallen him concerning himself and the aim of life. He is threatened by powerful supra personal forces, capital and the market. His relationship to his fellow men, with everyone a potential competitor, has become hostile and estranged; he is free—that is, he is alone, isolated, threatened from all sides.[18]

Fromm posits that early capitalism engendered these feelings of personal insecurity and anxiety, as well as an estranged form of liberation. They were all necessary for the new system's success. Yet, capitalism also entailed an escape from these feelings of hostility and aloneness by repressing them and converting them into productive energy.

Thus, with the decline of feudalism and the central authority of the Roman Catholic Church, capitalism exerted an enormous influence over the lives of many. The importance of the Protestant Reformation in this transition became the subject of Max Weber's *The Protestant Ethic and the Spirit of Capitalism*.[19] Here he asserts that the Protestant Reformation transformed both the survival anxiety and spiritual dread of workers into a secular work ethic. All of these feelings of worker alienation and economic insecurity were discharged through blind submission to the forces of capitalistic production. Weber proposes that the Reformation helped to make successful the transition from feudalism to capitalism in Europe by providing the necessary ideology that could assist in launching a thriving industrial revolution.[20] The Protestant Ethic's emphasis on individual autonomy, blind obedience to authority, self-sacrifice, and the vocationalizing of work all contributed to capitalism's ascent. Anxious energy, transformed into productive labor power, was now guided by the

Calvinistic piety. Abandonment in the form of relinquishment of the self to another without resistance found its way into the lexicon of the Reformation as Martin Luther preached that there was no sure road to salvation other than complete surrender to God's authority.

John Milton's *Paradise Lost*, written in 1644, became a metaphor for the abandonment generated by the new capitalistic order—a social banishment from a definite secure place to a placelessness haunted by personal insecurity. This was movement away from the center flooded by God's light to the dark periphery characterized by chaos.[21] Thus, the expulsion of Adam and Eve from Eden produced an ontological dread that had to be countered by an emphasis on individual initiative, sacrifice and self-denial. There was no looking back. The sin of enlightened consciousness could only be redressed by hard work and sacrifice.

Capitalism set into motion what Joseph Schumpeter called a process of creative destruction, wherein the new constantly destroyed and displaced the old.[22] Where there was industrial capitalism factories sprung to life, darkening the urban skies with black clouds of smoke. Rivers and streets became sewers. New waves of consumables now dislocated the previous wave. Dangerous machines displaced farmers and manual workers. The primary purpose of the market was not only the satisfaction of wants, but the creation of new desires for the purpose of ever-growing profits. With the advent of the nation states, centralized markets, and currency of exchange, a dynamic system of perpetual change was set into place. This was a pulsating system, seemingly with a life of its own. The impulse to produce and consume became the propelling force. Exploration, colonialism, and imperialism helped to stoke the furnace of human productivity and exploitation around the world while opening new markets and meeting growing European demands for inexpensive and exotic goods. If labor costs became too dear, there was always colonial slavery.

As the dynamic force behind the new social ordering, capitalism provided little hope for security, stability and permanence. Profits became the fulcrum of economic production. To maximize them required, then as now, cheap factors of production. The safest way to assure that profits were not being lavished on workers was to keep them on the brink of starvation. Capitalism required a state of perpetual abandonment—of place, of people, of things—as well as a threat of abandonment. As it generated social instability, periodic booms, and recessions, it inculcated deep-seated feelings of anxiety centered around economic loss both for the capitalist and the laborer. While the quality of living rose for many, for more it fell. But, for the far greater number, it was uncertain.

Statistical data from the seventeenth century onward showed that the fluctuations of death rates corresponded to trade booms and depressions.[23] Infant mortality rates jumped throughout Europe and were connected to economic slumps and growth. Families were frequently forced to reduce their size through measures as extreme as infanticide.

Although the economy of France in the eighteenth century was primarily agricultural, major trade depressions destroyed supporting businesses and shops in many cities. Businesses in Rouen and Lyons, for instance, were financially ruined as a result of the crop failures of surrounding farmlands. Town workers wholly dependent on industry were also affected overnight as people were thrown into conditions of extreme deprivation.[24]

With the advent of more intensified enclosures in the late eighteenth and early nineteenth centuries, rural people were forced into cities and towns where they either worked or starved. A few were able to tenant farm land they occupied. Heilbroner recounts one example: "Thus in 1820 nearly fifty years after the American Revolution, the Duchess of Sutherland dispossessed 15,000 tenants from 794,000 acres of land, replaced them with 131,000 sheep, and by way of compensation rented her evicted families an average of two acres of submarginal land each."[25] Many not as lucky entered into inhumane factory systems of these dark cities, or descended into dank and dangerous coal mines outside of them, working fourteen hours every day, seven days each week, with little to show for their labor but a subsistence wage and deteriorating health. There was no security.

These poor conditions under which workers lived and worked offended many with humane sensibilities. Friedrich Engels in his classic *The Condition of the Working Class in England*, written in 1844, laid out this situation in a blazing protest against human exploitation in Manchester:

> The workers have to live in damp dwellings. When they live in cellars water seeps through the floor and when they live in attics the rain comes through the roof. The workers' houses are so badly built that the foul air cannot escape from them. The workers have to wear poor and ragged garments and they have to eat food which is bad, indigestible and adulterated. Their mental state is threatened by being subjected alternately to extremes of hope and fear. They are goaded like wild beasts and never have a chance of enjoying a quiet life. . . . Every day they have to work until they are physically and mentally exhausted. . . . If the workers manage to survive this sort of treatment it is only to fall victims to starvation when a slump occurs and they are deprived of the little they once had.[26]

According to Karl Marx, the mode of production shaped all other dimensions of society; this included marriage and family. With the advent of market capitalism, children of the poor became either burdens or a means to enhance meager working class incomes. Some were placed into servitude, some were killed, others were deserted. That child abandonment reached record proportions during the industrial revolution is therefore not surprising.

John Boswell, who conducted a masterful study of the abandonment of children in the medieval period, was astonished at figures he discovered for child abandonment in eighteenth-century Europe. Here desertion reached record proportions.[27] In Toulouse, France, for instance, one in four children was known to have been abandoned. In the poor laborers' quarters of that town, the rate reached 39.9 percent. In Lyons, between 1750 and 1789, the number of children abandoned was approximately one-third of the number of registered births; while in Paris for this same period children known to have been abandoned amounted to between twenty and thirty percent. France was not exceptional. In early nineteenth-century Florence, the rate of child abandonment reached forty-three percent, up from fourteen percent in the eighteenth century.[28]

Although a fair number of abandoned children were illegitimate offspring of well-to-do parentage, a far greater number appear to have been children of the very poor—those overtaken suddenly by economic hardship. "Social and economic conditions alone might have induced more parents to abandon children in 1780 than in 1680. . . ," notes Boswell, "or the expansion of public facilities for abandoned children might have inspired more abandonment, as contemporary appeals to terminate state support for foundling homes suggest. But it is also likely that improved public assistance simply made the matter more open and recognizable."[29] Boswell notes that in the second half of the eighteenth century, one in every three or four children was abandoned in many French, Italian, and Spanish cities. In France, particularly, infanticide was a major problem. Bodies of suffocated newborns were found in fields and towns. It was common to find dead infants stuffed into sewers and drains.[30]

The intensity of the industrial revolution also produced a breakdown in the traditional welfare system, including those programs that addressed the needs of foundlings. Promoters of capitalism in Britain, such as Thomas Malthus and David Ricardo, campaigned to put an end to the Speenhamland Law—a public assistance program put into place by the Elizabethan Poor Laws of 1601, which guaranteed everyone a subsistence income in order to prevent starvation during difficult economic periods. They called for an end to all handouts and no more than subsistence wages for workers as they laid out convincing arguments to those in power.[31] Generous wages and welfare programs, they asserted, could only contribute to social problems that were originally wrought by natural population increases in the first place. An excess of children, sex and sloth were viewed as the primary causes of poverty. According to Polanyi, Speenhamland was abolished by the middle classes in order to remove the final obstacle to unbridled capitalism. Speenhamland had prevented the establishment of a ruthlessly competitive labor market.[32] Labor, insisted Polanyi, was the last market to be organized into the new industrial system. There would be no economic safety net.

Cities were now overcrowded, teeming with bands of the homeless poor. Unwanted boys and girls filled streets imposing both an eyesore and a threat to the bourgeoisie. The poor, especially women with children out of wedlock, increasingly became the targets of the state's draconian laws.[33] As an alternative to public relief, asylums were erected throughout industrial Europe. In England, workhouses proliferated after the enactment of the new Poor Law in 1834, which eliminated Speenhamland and most other forms of welfare. These workhouses, as well as some of the lesser notorious "orphanages" of England, became the common methods of state-supported relief and foster care. The only assistance for most poor families was through admission to one of these houses. Small children and the aged who were begging on the streets would be placed here, commingled with the chronically ill, the criminally insane, and the mentally retarded. Mental illness became a significant focus of urban concern. As psychologist Philip Cushman notes, many such incidents of mental disturbances during this time can be linked to problems of economic instability and unemployment.[34]

Workhouses often were run by individual contractors whose primary interest was making a profit—which they rarely did. In return for bad food and lodging, men, women, children, and frequently the mentally ill, would be confined to labor with rare permission to go outside. Mothers, fathers, and children were segregated into separate quarters, and visitations would be granted at the whim of the house officials. Workers who failed to produce their allotted work would not be fed. Many young children who were incarcerated at the age of two or three never saw the outside world again. Historian Roy Porter points out: "The death-rate in the workhouse of St. George's, Middlesex, was one hundred percent. Out of 2,339 children received into London workhouses in the five years after 1750, only 168 were alive in 1755."[35] Engels describes the abusive treatment suffered by children who did live:

> In the summer of 1843 a five-year-old boy, who was an inmate of the Greenwich Union (at Depford) was punished by being locked-up in a

mortuary for three nights and he had to sleep on some coffin-lids. At Herne (Common) workhouse a little girl was treated in the same way because she wet her bed. This particular punishment appears to be very popular in the workhouses.[36]

Thousands of men, women and children were housed in these facilities. Workhouses were rampant with all forms of diseases and inhuman punishments and tortures. Engels recounts incident after incident of wanton abuse of impoverished inmates. "In West London Union workhouse one of the porters suffered from syphilis, with which he infected (three or) four girls. But he was not dismissed. Another porter took a deaf and dumb girl to his room for four days and slept with her. He, too, was not dismissed."[37] From rape to beating to murder, poor working-class children as well as adults suffered enormously under the conditions associated with early industrialization.

The tearing apart of families, particularly in Britain, was the hallmark as well as the legacy of centralized capitalism and the industrial revolution. The eighteenth and nineteenth centuries saw not only the separation of people from the land and the herding of surplus populations into towns and cities, but also the removal of both the worker and work from the home. Cottage systems of production were displaced by factories. With the atomization of family, the alienation of the worker was complete. Impersonal factories and offices beyond the boundaries of family and kinship systems established a new order based on depersonalized production and worker commodification. The functions of family as a source of socialization rapidly deteriorated as the home was emptied of meaningful activity.

Feminist sociologists Michèle Barrett and Mary McIntosh assert that the insulation of the patriarchal family was overall fortified by industrial capitalism. Families that remained intact became more privatized, participating less frequently in communal life.[38] The nuclear family itself, insist Barrett and McIntosh, was a result of early capitalistic development as was the emergence of individuation as the central familial process.[39] This familial function would have a tremendous influence on the future of all relationships. Childhood socialization, aimed at rapid individuation, produces an array of problems connected to issues of attachment and separation that do not appear in tradition-based societies.

The individual in this socioeconomic context found the experience of alienation inescapable. As Marx explained it, commodification and alienation were essential features of market capitalism. Alienation was not simply a feeling of estrangement, but an important societal process that took on special significance during the industrial revolution.

Capitalism and its inherent specialization fragmented everything, including laborers, removing them from their homes and families, assigning identities relative to their place in the production process. Out of this disintegration came a sense of loss, which was manifest in *entfremdung*, or estrangement. According to Marx, it was the commodification of labor that produced these feelings. People lost an historic sense of self and community, were turned against one another, or became tools of each other in their drive for survival. All workers were made into factors of production, instruments for another's wealth. In the *Communist Manifesto*, Karl Marx noted: "The bourgeoisie, wherever it got the upper hand has put an end to all [that was] feudal. . . and has left remaining no other nexus between man and man than naked self-interest, than callous cash payment."[40] This produced an epidemic of interpersonal estrangement. Capitalism as a system could not only destroy meaningful human relationships, but also could produce a fragmented self that lowered the possibilities for future, healthy relations.

Such a portrait of early capitalistic development is quite bleak. Nevertheless it was Marx who saw the power inherent in capitalistic productive technology to change the world for the better in the short-run. Inevitably, the inequities of a capitalism pregnant with its own self-destruction would succumb to revolutionary social change; it would take an awakening of consciousness on the part of the workers to make this happen. Despite the alienation of the laborer and the commodification inherent in the capitalistic system, Marx remained hopeful that reason would triumph over injustice. Capitalism, with all of its flaws, would be crushed by those who were the targets of its exploitation and abuse. He remained steadfast in this optimism: "The proletarians have nothing to lose but their chains. They have a world to win."[41]

Capitalism has been depicted here, and in various discourses, as a powerful social force that set into motion a state of affairs that led to fragmentation, alienation and separation. The separations are frequently associated with the process of creative destruction, which is a constant annihilation of the old to bring about the new in the pursuit of profit. It is a system wherein market relationships displace all others, one in which all value is assigned by the market and all work is oriented toward satisfying market demands. The all-consuming nature of market capitalism with its power defined by its ability not only to organize the means of production in a manner that will materially enrich the lives of those who own them, but also to construct a culture predicated on a seamless production/consumption process, requires a class system to support it. It is this system with its exploitive inequalities that gives life to capitalism's productive enterprise.

Abandonment produced by the capitalistic machine results from two primary sources. The first is the inordinate inequities in power—a class system in which most perceive of themselves as dependent on a very few for their survival. The second is the process of perpetual change generated by shifts in market demand and technologies of production spawning social instability and personal vulnerability. In this regard, capitalistic societies can be identified by an intensity of material and human relinquishment: an abandonment not only of things but of practices, places and people.

MODERNITY AS SOCIAL CHANGE

While the affinity between capitalism and modernity is great, there needs to be a clear distinction between the two. Modernity takes many forms, but as a term it generally describes a type of social landscape arising through a process of modernization. In philosophy it is linked to the ideas promoted by such thinkers as Descartes, Bacon, Hobbes, and Machavelli. It deals with such issues as the nature of knowledge, the uses of science, political individualism, and the essence of modern power. In sociology it describes the rise of industrial cities, secularization, market economies, and democratization.[42] Yet, modernity is a problematic concept for most social theorists. Although it reflects some of the same central concerns of market capitalism—not least of which is its emphasis on fragmentation, objectification, individuation, and rational control—modernity is essentially an intellectual construct of critics, theorists, and philosophers. Its definitions are too numerous, too varied, too abstruse to serve any common purpose. Any discursive treatment of modernity tends to be inherently ideological, male-oriented, and Eurocentric. Modernity shares with capitalism definitional plasticity making it a problematic signifier for social science.

If modernity is an era, as many have suggested, then there is vast disagreement as to when this era began or ended. Some contend that its origins date back to the Renaissance or the sixteenth century, others favor the eighteenth or nineteenth century. Many see a temporal division between modernity and postmodernity, but some do not. Those who praise modernity and defend it from its detractors define it to reflect their own political ideologies, although the same might be said of those who champion capitalism. Yet it is the relationship that modernity has to capitalism that is most troubling for some analysts. Where the conceptual terrain of modernity leaves off and capitalism begins is a matter of extensive intellectualization and speculation. Likewise, there is considerable difficulty, although much less, in distinguishing the central features of modernity from those of the Enlightenment. Great confusion abounds. The differences between modernity, modernization, and modernism seem even more frustrating as various theorists use these terms interchangeably to mean the same thing.

Modernity is associated with the civilization/savagery opposition promoted by the European Enlightenment. In this dichotomy, the "modern" is distinguished from primitive. What is frequently labeled as modern is a particular state of western economic development and intellectual cultivation applied as a universal standard of achievement and progress, a standard frequently used to oppress, control, and sometimes enslave an "underdeveloped world." This Eurocentric brand of modernity is often an ideology imbued with racism, sexism, and a belief that modern life arises out of the natural evolutionary course of events. It is this brand of modernity that became part of a romantic narrative in which what is *not* modern (what is underdeveloped) is typically thought to be a closed primitive enclave. Such a place is thought to be in need of development, requiring modern means of production, transportation, communication, and enlightenment. The "developing world," on the other hand, is one that has begun to open up to outside investment—to the "assistance" of transnational corporations and those already modernized who prepare the way for economic integration into a system of global colonialism. Thus, this sort of modernity shares an agenda with capitalism, which is the absolute undermining of traditional life and the substitution of a nearly complete reliance on the global marketplace. Social historian Rajani Kannepalli Kanth notes:

> Amazingly, the wholesale destruction of local autonomies, and the authoritarian hierarchial organization of all societal institutions . . . , is seen by the modernist impulse as but so many splendid moments in the exciting ascent of (European) man. To alienate, and then to subject to a craven subordination—that in a nutshell, is the modernist way . . . of catastrophic uprooting of social relations.[43]

Defenders and detractors of modernity comprise an impressive cadre of scholars and social theorists. Many early modernists, such as Claude Henri de Rouvroy de Henri Saint-Simon and Auguste Comte, suggest that its potential for good is quite vast. In their writings we have a clear indication of the initial romance with (and contribution to) modernity's narrative of industrial utopianism in post-revolutionary France. In Saint-Simon's early nineteenth-century renderings, we have a technocratic means for integrating a society shaken by revolution and class strife through centralized planning and empirical social science.

Inspired by elements of the Enlightenment, Saint-Simon and his followers formulated principles of civic engineering aimed at achieving equity
and social progress. Both Comte and Saint-Simon called for building a
coalition of public and private interests that would engage inordinate
resources for social benefit through public works. Canals, bridges, railroads, and massive feats of technological innovation are all a part of a
vision in which scientists, businessmen, and engineers will guide social
change. Both men were enthralled with science and envisioned a society
directed by scientific and technocratic elites: priests of reason.
Enlightenment science could be applied to discovering the important
facts about society so it could be more easily controlled. Although the
engine of capitalism would drive the course of modernity, it had to be
guided by an enlightened cadre of bourgeois intellectuals. It was Saint-
Simon's grand vision that the agenda of industrialization would be
exported around the world. Also, it was Saint-Simon, not Marx as commonly thought, who first observed that capitalism was the initial stage in
an evolutionary progression toward socialism. His work set the tone for
other utopian planners such as Charles Fourier and Robert Owen who
attempted to develop and organize industrial societies predicated on a
medley of capitalistic efficiencies and socialistic humanism. For Saint-
Simon, modernity represented human progress predicated on technological advances.

   This romance with modern society was frequently offset by more
pessimistic views of modernity. By the mid to late 1800s social theorists
such as Sir Henry Main and Ferdinand Tönnies described modernity as a
process of communal degeneration wherein society's interpersonal relationships deteriorated from trusting, primary, tradition-based connections to impersonal, superficial, contractual associations. For them,
human belongingness was corrupted by the market system and cost-to-
benefit calculations. In this shift from *Gemeinschaft* to *Gesellschaft* traditional communities guided by human sentiment gave way to
impersonal modern societies. Tönnies observed a decline in the power of
religion, and a near abandonment of family life. According to this perspective, the process of modernization led to increased secularization,
the ascent of the market and weakened communities.

   In the late nineteenth century, social theory became more equivocal.
While Tönnies' work was rejected in many important intellectual circles
as too emotionally laden and reactionary, theory became increasingly
more ambivalent toward the forces of modernization. Emile Durkheim,
who was Comte's intellectual successor and therefore a supposed champion of modernity, espoused the benefits of modern life in his work, but
also sounded a cautionary note. In two of his sociological classics, *The*

Division of Labor in Society and *Suicide*, Durkheim warned of social disorganization—the unraveling of a collective conscience and the decaying of a shared sense of moral order. He referred to this erosion as *anomie*. It was his belief that capitalism had contributed significantly to this process. Tradition, which had held society together in the past, could no longer accomplish this goal since society was becoming more and more heterogeneous. Commercialism eclipsed all else including human intimacy and the personal nature of communal life. Modernity was associated with ever-increasing greed, personal disillusionment, and dissatisfaction. Although industrial capitalism attempted to address this malaise by substituting the promise of a sense of well-being through material consumption for the middle classes, this could not satisfy their thirst for social cohesion. The unending craving for the new, which capitalism helped to promote, often had a disabling effect by hollowing out the self. Thus, materialistic dreams displaced the need for deep human connections as people were caught up in the romance of consumption.

For Durkheim, modernity represents unending cravings associated with an interminable agenda of consumption:

> From top to bottom of the ladder greed is aroused without knowing where to find its ultimate foothold. Nothing can calm it, since its goal is far beyond all it can attain. Reality seems valueless by comparison with the dreams of fevered imaginations; reality is therefore abandoned, but so too is possibility abandoned when it in turn becomes reality. A thirst arises for novelties, unfamiliar pleasures, nameless sensations, all of which lose their savor once known. Hence forth one has no strength to endure the least reserve. The whole fever subsides and sterility of all the tumult is apparent, and it is seen that all these new sensations in their infinite quantity cannot form a solid foundation of happiness to support one during days of trial.[44]

Of course Durkheim was describing the outcome of modern capitalism. In the above passage he delineates the conditions that lead to increasing rates of egoistic suicide. It is Durkheim's contention that egoism is not merely a contributing factor, but a generating cause of human depression and suicide in modern societies. The attachment of individuals to their communities is weakened due to modernity's emphasis on competition and self-gratification. Similarly, the bond connecting the individual to life itself becomes frayed. Thus, *Suicide* illuminates a loss of connection brought on by the process of modernization. The individual attempts to hold on to some new material thing or novelty as a replacement for deeper human relationships, but to no avail.

While Alexis de Tocqueville saw American society as characterized by egocentrism guarded by the Protestant work ethic, Durkheim was among the first sociologists to connect excessive egoism to modernity.

This was later expounded by Georg Simmel, Thorstein Veblen, Daniel Bell, David Riesman, Richard Sennett, Christopher Lasch, Philip Slater, and a host of other twentieth-century theorists. For these theorists, modern capitalistic culture and its inherent consumerism came to dominate social life and helped to construct modern narcissistic patterns of adjustment. Durkheim's concerns for the potential damage resulting from excesses of egoism and consumerism associated with modernity holds an important place in the history of modern social thought. It not only promoted considerable modern sociological discourse but also helped influence Thorstein Veblen and the critical postmodern agenda of Baudrillard and Lyotard, particularly their concern with the inherent signifying power of consumer goods.

In examining the impact of modernization on human relationships, many social psychologists and psychoanalysts have pointed to emergent problems in the development of a relatively stable sense of self. In the early 1930s, Wilhelm Reich warned that market capitalism was revolutionizing human relationships and undermining the familial and ontological sense of security; in so doing, it was paving the way for the rise of fascism.[45] Borrowing from Marx and Engels, Reich contended that capitalism had made the family into an instrument of social oppression. Children were prepared to take their place in a nonreflexive social machine.

In the early 1940s, Erich Fromm argued that feelings of separation engendered by capitalism's radical social transformations were felt on the most intimate of levels. These feelings of separation exhibited in capitalistic culture corresponded to separation anxiety experienced in early childhood. Separations from caregivers and the push to individualize children altered the child's sense of connectedness to the world. This produced inordinate degrees of anxiety, which frequently promoted an ambiguous relationship to authority—a desire to retreat into blind submission to authority or, sometimes, a drive for complete domination and control over others in order to feel secure.[46] Thus, modern anxiety and feelings of insecurity often prompted self-enslavement, or an autocratic overcompensation. Thus Reich and Fromm prepared the way for Adorno's work on authoritarian personalities, which would come in response to Nazism.[47]

In the work of many theorists, the distinctions between capitalism and modernity are not clearly drawn. Many contemporary social theorists, such as Alex Callinicos, suggest that all modernity is a merely particular form of capitalistic development.[48] But others strongly disagree. Zygmunt Bauman, for instance, suggests that modernity is a much more encompassing concept; it is inclusive of capitalism, fascism, socialism and more. Bauman, like many other social theorists, links modernity directly to the Enlightenment. In his view modernity is a quest for absolute truth wedded to absolute power. Bauman asserts that modernity has been a quest to impose structure on an unstructured, and order on a seemingly disorderly world. Yet, in his view, modernity has come to be represented by the Holocaust—a dream of total unified order at *any* cost. While positing a unique brand of civility and reason, modernity fosters a heightened dependence on bureaucracy and mechanistic reasoning. This is what leads Bauman and others to believe that modernity has something quite sinister within it. In his own search to better understand the Holocaust, Bauman reviews historical records and comes to the conclusion that the Nazi decision to exterminate Jews rather than to relocate them was *"a product of routine bureaucratic procedures*: means-ends calculus, budget balancing, universal rule application."[49] Like Theodor Adorno, he sees the Holocaust as the consequence of crude rationality or instrumental reason. For him this is quintessentially modern. Here, society behaves like a machine, devoid of moral sentiment. In fact it is the same technology that is applied to mass production that is applied here to mass destruction. In this respect, Bauman borrows a chilling modernist image of the Holocaust presented by historian Henry Feingold:

> [Auschwitz] was also a mundane extension of the modern factory system. Rather than producing goods, the raw material was human beings and the end-product was death, so many units per day marked carefully on the manager's production charts. The chimneys, the very symbol of the modern factory system, poured forth acrid smoke produced by burning human flesh. The brilliantly organized railroad grid of modern Europe carried a new kind of raw material to the factories. It did so in the same manner as with other cargo. In the gas chambers the victims inhaled noxious gas generated by prussic acid pellets, which were produced by the advanced chemical industry of Germany. Engineers designed the crematoria; managers designed the system of bureaucracy that worked with zest and efficiency more backward nations would envy.[50]

For Bauman, an essential element of modernity is moral indifference. The Holocaust is viewed not as a modern aberration, but rather as an outcome of the rationalistic ends-means schema that was put to work in the service of a civilizing process maintained through normative order and the rule of law. The Holocaust imagery is emblematic of its inhumanity.

Marshall Berman, on the other hand, posits a much more optimistic view. He finds in modernity "a mode of vital experience," one which in many ways unites humanity. To be modern, for Berman, is to live a life of contradiction and paradox. He sees modernity as unity in disunity, "a maelstrom of perpetual disintegration and renewal," struggle and anguish.[51] This is decidedly *not* Bauman's rigid nightmarish modernity. Berman's use of the maelstrom is decidedly more optimistic and, since it is literary, simultaneously more aesthetic.

The maelstrom imagery is mid-nineteenth-century naturalism. It was Edgar Allen Poe's "The Descent into the Maelstrom," which is in many ways a transcendental tale in which the maelstrom has a life of its own. In the Poe story a Norwegian seaman whose fishing boat becomes trapped in a hurricane finds himself in a "funnel of vast circumference, prodigious in depth and whose perfectly smooth sides might have been mistaken for ebony, but for the bewildering rapidity with which they spun around, and for the gleaming and ghastly radiance they shot forth, as the rays of the moon. . . ." The small craft was trapped in a maelstrom "a smooth, shining, and jet-black wall of water . . . speeding dizzily round and round with a swaying and sweltering motion, and sending forth to the winds an appalling voice, half shriek, half roar, such as not even the mighty cataract of Niagara ever lifts up in its agony to heaven." Its depth is unfathomable. The escape for the seaman was to plunge, attached to a water-cask, into the dark, violent abyss into which he had peered and from which he gained "more hope than terror." Berman uses the maelstrom imagery to capture what he sees as the magic and majesty of change that conditions modern life.

Marxist social theorist Matei Calinescu has proposed that, in the latter half of the nineteenth century, European modernity evolved as two basic types: "a product of scientific and technological progress, of the industrial revolution, of sweeping economic and social changes brought about by capitalism—and modernity as an aesthetic concept."[52] The former modernity was often driven by a pragmatic, empiricist philosophy and social science, the latter by aesthetic concerns. Using this framework it is easy to see where one might classify the work of Bauman or Berman.

On the other hand, Michael Hardt and Antonio Negri make another distinction. For them, European modernity was characterized by two oppositional factors over time. The first was more revolutionary and characterized by an unleashing of thought and experimentation—a radical force that was manifest in culture, science, and politics. The second was a countervailing force of control aimed at channeling this new power and restoring order. This second one was to become the prominent form of modern life because it attempted to end instability brought about through perpetual revolution. It was this, more reactionary form, that was manifest in religious inquisitions, wars against nature and battles between nation states.[53]

The closest we have to a comprehensive theory of modernity as a social force comes from the British sociologist Anthony Giddens in the form of what he refers to as structuration. It is Giddens' vocation to discover the linkages between micro and macro order process, or agency-structure integration. He wants to explore those discrete human activities and social practices that give both meaning and shape to social structures; likewise he wants to better understand the workings of social structures—how they constrain and enable. Thus for him agency and structure operate as a duality in that they are inseparable. Structuration means that all social relations are organized in time and space and are outcomes of this temporality.

Giddens' theory of modernity is more classically sociological. He presents no expansive exposition on the aesthetic of modernity. Unlike Bauman who associates modernity to the Holocaust or Berman who envisions it as a maelstrom, Giddens adopts the symbol of a juggernaut—something he borrows from Hindu celebrations. It means an overpowering force, idea, or set of customs demanding blind loyalty and terrible sacrifice. In his introduction to this metaphor Giddens cites the modern *jagannāth* that takes the form of a statue of Krishna paraded through the streets of Indian towns each year on a huge car where "followers are said to have thrown themselves under, to be crushed beneath its wheels."[54] In describing its relation to modernity, Giddens notes:

> The juggernaut crushes those who resist it, and while it sometimes seems to have a steady path, there are times when it veers away erratically in directions we cannot foresee. The ride is by no means wholly unpleasant or unrewarding; it can often be exhilarating and charged with hopeful anticipation. . . . The juggernaut of modernity is not all one piece, and here the imagery lapses, as does any talk of a single path which it runs. It is not an engine made up of integrated machinery, but one in which there is a tensional, contradictory, push-and-pull of different influences. Any attempt to capture the experience of modernity must begin from this view. . . .[55]

Giddens' interpretation of modernity is indeed an ambitious project. It is aligned with the grand narrative tradition of classical sociological discourse. Over many years, in several volumes, he has mapped out and refined a set of interconnected propositions that attempt to give modernity character and meaning. Not only does he look at the broader institutional mechanisms that have evolved to give shape to this phenomenon, but he also takes his analysis to the level of self-identity and attempts to explain the meaning of modernity for the individual. He begins, however, with identifying those institutional arrangements that appear to give modernity its character.

For Giddens there are several institutional dimensions of modernity. These include capitalism, industrialization, surveillance as social control, and militarism as ultimate power. Embedded within each institution is a host of relational patterns. For instance, capitalism is comprised of such elements as private property, commodity production, propertyless workers, and a resultant class system. Industrialism involves the mechanization of production, the use of administratively organized procedures for commodity production, technologically advanced means of communication, transportation and so on. Surveillance capacities include those myriad activities in modern societies used to closely monitor and examine the day-to-day behavior of individuals and groups. Under the pretext of protection, surveillance denies privacy and gives the state enormous power to monitor private activities in the name of state security. Anyone who opposes a "modern" agenda is an enemy. For Giddens, military power provides a legitimized means of violence directed against those who might oppose the project of modernization. All of these institutional arrangements contribute to or join forces with what Giddens recognizes as key structural changes responsible for the unique social relations inherent in modernity.[56]

The first of these structural changes is what Giddens sees as the separation of time and space or the time-space distanciation. To be modern means that space and time are not connected through place as they were in more traditional societies. In other words, in premodern societies one could only understand time as a function of the place where it occurred. The advent of portable time, or the mechanical clock, did away with this union. Thus, the mechanical clock "emptied space" of much of its meaning. Modernity required and used time for coordinating activities around the globe. The outcome of such coordination has been globalization. This severing of time from space has led to a weakening significance of the latter. As David Harvey has noted: "The reduction of space to a contingent category is implied in the idea of progress itself. Since modernity is about the experience of progress through modernization, writings on that theme have tended to emphasize temporality, the process of *becoming*, rather than *being* in space and place."[57] We can see this in the notion of "the developing world." While this time-space distanciation, has become the focus of physics, aesthetics, and philosophy, it also has very real political, social, and personal consequences.

Among the more significant outcomes of this distanciation is what Giddens describes as the "disembedding of social institutions."[58] By this he means a lifting out of social relations from local contexts. He implies that modern forms of human interaction and exchange are forced to become more impersonal and abstract. In modern societies, as compared to traditional ones, material and barter exchange are displaced by use of symbolic tokens—currency and digital displays come to represent a highly abstract form of value. Technical expertise further compounds the distanciation as unseen experts make important decisions that directly affect the very survival of those living in modern societies. Trust, therefore, emerges as essential to modern life. Yet, given these new levels of abstraction and accelerated flow of information in a compressed amount of time, trust is often difficult to achieve. For Giddens, modernity becomes characterized not only by uneasiness, but also by doubt, dread, anxiety, stress and a constant threat of meaninglessness.[59] Because of this, individuals must become increasingly reflexive. By this he means that the self becomes something to be continuously reflected upon, altered, and modified in order to remain contemporary.

Giddens proposes that the modern individual constantly confronts key dilemmas: fragmentation of self versus self-unification, powerlessness versus appropriation, authority versus uncertainty, the personalized versus the commodified experience. It is how we individually and communally come to terms with these that will determine our success in dealing with the juggernaut of modernity. The key, as he defines it, is in establishing durable ties to others. The delicate nature of these modern self-other relationships speaks to what he envisions as one of modernity's real challenges. This has led Giddens to turn to social psychology in an attempt to better understand modern existence and the fragility of self-identity. He even delves into matters surrounding early child-caregiver separations—looking at issues such as trust and anxiety. For Giddens such circumstances not only condition our self-identity but they represent an important part of "how modernity is done."[60] He sees anxiety emerging from early fears of abandonment or loss of others generated by capitalism's social transformations. How we see ourselves in relation to others is connected to what he terms as ontological security—something difficult to establish in an ephemeral and modernistic society.

The personal consequences of modernity—how one experiences it, processes it and finally comes to terms with it—are essential to understanding the prospect of an integrated self in the face of increasing fragmentation. For Giddens, as well as for most theorists of modern life discussed here, modernity fosters perpetual segmentalization and personal separation from family, home, community, work and self. Modern existence becomes a series of efforts to overcome the atomization characteristic of modernity.

Inherent in all renderings of modernity are powerful oppositions: domination and submission, oppression and freedom, order and chaos, connection and separation. A discourse on the struggle of the self to be distinguished from other forms a basis of modernity's most important conceptualization; it creates a foundation for a wealth of modern philosophy and social theory. In both capitalism and modernity there is a simultaneous quest to free people and to enslave them. The ethos of modernity is ambivalence.

This connection between modernity, control, and freedom is central to most contemporary sociological analyses. Frankfurt school theory as well as the more contemporary hermeneutic theories have examined both modernity and capitalism not only as systems of change and markets, but as schemes for establishing order through mechanisms of dominance and submission. Foucault's notion that all knowledge is directed toward control is typical of these more recent interpretations of modernity. Many critical feminists understand modernity as a masculinist-ideology directed toward the domination and control over women and nature. Its rationalistic modeling, its romance with positivist science and its inherent impositions of dualisms on a fluid world, appear far too patriarchal. Even sociology itself, which is rooted in positivism, must be called into question. As feminist sociologist Anna Yeatman notes:

> Sociology is an intellectual enterprise structured by the dualism of the modernist perspective. Its own particular versions of these dualisms—for example, structure/agency, social structure/culture, social/psychological, family/society—are logically derivative of the basic dualistic structure of the modern consciousness. . . . Sociology cannot change this modernist framework of reference which has governed it as a specific intellectual enterprise without abandoning its whole tradition and approach, that is, becoming something other than itself.[61]

While many feminists have found greater affinity for postmodernity, which offers less structure, greater flexibility and is without the historical baggage associated with modernity, this position is not without problems. The overriding emphasis on the subjective and the interpretative in the postmodern landscape requires constant defense from attacks of more traditional modernists who see in its pragmatic pluralism a lack of substance and an abandonment of critical reason. However, in the final analysis postmodernity, like modernity, is as progressive or reactionary as its proponents. Like most great debates in the social science, it is the particular definition of the term that constructs one's understanding and use of it. Great debates still rage over the meaning of postmodernity.[62]

Modernity will be used here to suggest a quality of life that is associated with modernization, and in particular Euro-American modernization. Aesthetic modernity shall be referred to as "modernism." Unlike capitalism, modernity is not seen as a social force but rather a set of features that are a result of social forces—the most significant of which are capitalistic development and the Enlightenment project. The values that guide it are parallel to those that govern capitalistic development and those characteristic of the Enlightenment itself: total conquest and control of nature, the dismantling of tradition-based relationships, the veneration of power, the ascent of secular individualism, an intensification of bureaucratization, a heightened emphasis on binary opposition, rationality in the service of personal industry, and a morality governed by competitive self-interest.

Modernism is viewed here as having arisen in response to this type of modernity. Its expression is found in an aesthetic movement and a petty bourgeois way of life that challenged key elements of modernity in the late nineteenth century and continues to do the same today. It houses a vast number of progressive and reactionary artistic perspectives. As an aesthetic narrative, modernism has a number of variations on some central themes it shares with modernity such as the transformative power of science and technology, the social and economic consequences of industrialization, the emergence of individualism, the secularization of society, the dialectic of personal freedom, and the emergence of centralized bureaucratic planning. It has in some cases fostered and nurtured the *avant-garde*, as exemplified in a literary movement broad enough to include the ambivalent freedom of Baudelaire's *The Painter of Modern Life,* or the technologically advanced mode of human oppression and torture depicted in Kafka's *The Penal Colony.*

The landscape of modernism is strewn with the debris of modernity reflecting an abundance of human and materialistic abandonment. It is battered by the storms of constant decimation and creation. Such a disturbing place instills in many the need to connect to something—to find a secure place, a sense of order, and stability. Many view this as a desire to return to some primitive state of oneness. Yet, the relentlessness of the forces of creative destruction makes coherence and unity appear impossible. The modern person is caught between the forces of attachment and separation. Blaise Pascal articulated this feeling in the seventeenth century:

> We sail within a vast sphere, ever drifting in uncertainty, from end to end. When we think to attach ourselves to any point and fasten to it, it wavers and leaves us; and if we follow it eludes our grasp, slips past us, and vanishes forever. Nothing stays for us. This is our natural condition, and yet most contrary to our inclination; we burn with desire to find solid ground and an ultimate sure foundation whereupon to build a tower reaching to the Infinite. But the whole ground cracks and the earth opens to abysses.[63]

To better understand this modernity we will need to examine its associated aesthetic.

FROM ROMANTICISM TO MODERNISM

While modernity is frequently viewed as a set of social characteristics that describe a particular way of life, or even an era reflecting such attributes, modernism, as previously indicated, is more exclusively seen as a cultural movement. Where modernity focuses on philosophical and social discourses, modernism is primarily concerned with issues of culture and aesthetics. Modernism, as a movement in the arts, emerges from the influences of modernity, but it is not the only aesthetic to emerge from it. Romanticism, its precursor, was equally a product of these same forces. Though it proceeded from similar intellectual and social roots, romanticism produced a very different aesthetic, which both anticipated modernism and in some ways preconditioned modernism's development.

European romanticism, as a form of artistic expression, is commonly traced back to the late eighteenth century. It was inspired by the Enlightenment and emerged from modernity's emphasis on the uniqueness of each individual. The romantic movement in the arts has been both complimentary to and antagonistic toward modernity. On the one hand, romantic writers and artists espoused the preeminence of free-will and the creative potential of the individual released from the prison that was feudalism and the servitude of an oppressive aristocracy; they frequently idealized the power of reason, science, and industry as potentially liberating forces. They celebrated personal freedom and the potential of the subjective imagination. On the other hand, many were apprehensive of modernity's alienating and dehumanizing influences. They glorified the medieval and were attracted to the mysteries and gothic symbolism associated with the Catholic Church. While some bemoaned the loss of community and the fealty inherent in the virtues of antiquity, many were thrilled by the unbridled power of the machine.

Some romantics valorized the irrational and praised the unrestrained power of nature, imbuing it with spiritual significance once reserved for religion alone. In their art, some pitted nature against the individual while others recorded the struggle of nature against the machine. Romantics were simultaneously progressive and reactionary, and like the proponents of modernity itself did not subscribe to any unified system of thought. As a group they exhibited great ambivalence equal to that of the modernists. Just as there would be many modernities, there were many forms of romanticism. Arthur O. Lovejoy posited that a central characteristic of romanticism was that it meant different things to different people, often contradictory things.[64] Nevertheless, aside from the great diversity of positions that characterized the European romantics, inherent in their work was an underlying tension between dominance and submission—between total control and complete surrender. While Rousseau asserted the need for the individual to be free, he also believed the individual might need to be forced to be free.

The French romantic, François-René Chateaubriand, shrouded himself in the mysteries of the medieval Catholic Church, idealizing its authority and extolling the pleasures of its morbidity and melancholia. German romantics such as Goethe revealed both a fondness for the power of nature, and an awe of the power of authority. The tension between the need to control and to be controlled is central to much of his work and a driving force in *Faust*. So too is abandonment. In *Faust* the protagonist must leave behind everything he truly values . . . including his soul!

Central to much of the Romantic Movement was an elaborate abandonment motif. Romanticism's contribution to the establishment of an iconography of abandonment was highly significant. In France the romantic poem is said to have begun with Alphonse de Lamartine's "Le lac"(the Lake), which was published in 1820. It became one of the more influential poems of that period. Lamartine's poem is based on his visit to Aix-le-Bains and his meeting of Julie Charles (Elvira in the poem) on the shore of Lac du Bourger where these lovers spent three weeks together. Although they arranged to return to the spot the next year, Julie Charles was too ill to make the trip. The poem commemorates Lamartine's aloneness and sense of emotional abandonment on the shore of the lake—the place of their planned *rendezvous*. Although Julie Charles was not well at the time of the failed meeting, the poet seemed to be anticipating her death. In the poem Elvira was already dead. The lake became the voice of his deceased lover and a representative of the power of nature that extolled their love.

Barbara Johnson, who has written an insightful feminist critique of this poem and its place in French romantic literature, suggests that although the poem can be interpreted as an attempt on the part of Lamartine to bring the woman he loved back to life with the help of nature, it also appears to have emerged "out of a desire to write her into death." Johnson supports her thesis by revealing the author's ambition of writing a collection of elegies. Furthermore, she posits: "It was as though his pen were just waiting for a real death to mourn. Could it be that the death of a woman represents not the thwarting but rather the fulfillment of desire?"[65]

Johnson suggests that romanticism in lyric poetry makes implicit equivalencies between the beloved and the dead. This is especially true throughout the romantic revitalization. We see this not only in the work of French poets, but in Wordsworth, Goethe, and of course Poe when

Johnson quotes: "the death of a beautiful woman is, unquestionably, the most poetical topic in the world."[66] Although Johnson sees this remark of Poe as misogynistic, it is important to understand how the premature death of his mother and later his young wife haunted his life and influenced most of his work. Abandonment resonates from the works of many romantic writers and poets because they found themselves abandoned, banished, and alone. This is critical to our understanding of abandonment as a cultural motif and will be further explored in greater depth later in this work. But it is important to note that as a literary device the death of women is not limited to one genre; it was even more pronounced in tales of gothic romance. The gothic novel that crossed from sentimentalism to romanticism extolling an enchanted world of dark forests, isolated moors, haunted castles, medieval churchyards, and brooding men also idealized the dying young woman. Contemporary criticism frequently draws the figurative connection of nature to women. The control, maltreatment, and abandonment of both was an important social and literary motif of this period.[67]

Death, decay, the macabre, and sadism were essential elements of both the gothic tale and the dark romantic lyric, and came to represent the most profound forms of abandonment that one might be forced to confront. They elicited the most primal feelings of loss. Although death was always important iconography, it came to signify the end of all human attachment. This aloneness and detachment reflected the pronounced cultural emphasis on the isolated individual, void of humanity, whose human relationships were commodified, where people were means to ends. This was made clearest in the darkest work of the Marquis de Sade. It was the imagery of Sade that most clearly represented the nihilism of that era. His writings were expressions of personal entitlement, glory in the pain and humiliation of others, and extreme self-absorption. Throughout his stories the purest and meekest of the characters becomes a victim, an object of personal humiliation, sexual abuse, and torture in order to minimally satisfy the base desires of the aristocratic aggressor. As a true iconoclast, Sade takes the most tiresome sentimentalism of his day—the helpless damsel in distress—and turns it into cutting edge pornography. He makes extensive use of a medieval motif of torture chambers and insidious devices of sexual mutilation as each victim is dehumanized for the lustful egocentric pleasures of the host. His work is a response not only to the banality of romanticism, but also a critique of Adam Smith's rationalistic notion of commodification of labor and the unleashing of human passions. Sade strips away the romance of hyper-individualism exposing the unbridled power of libertine elites; he displays what he sees as at the core of the hegemonic depravity—a lust for the pain and brutalization of others. His victims are helpless pawns, frequently innocents, sometimes paid for but never knowing the extent of debauchery that will be directed their way. The Sadian libertine, highly civilized and rational, corresponds to the most advanced state of Hobbesian individual self-interest. For him there is no meaning beyond personal, sexual pleasure gained through the excruciating pain and physical humiliation of another.

Sade's nihilism and literary emphasis on the total objectification of and control over others influenced the next generation of modern writers. Many elements of sadism helped to establish a new wave of romanticism and strongly influenced modernism. But the fascination with death, torture, and putrefaction was not limited to literature. What Mario Praz called "black romanticism" entered vividly into the works of great visual artists such as Delacroix and Goya.[68] For him romanticism expressed a deep fascination with the abominable. The severed head of Medusa, for example, symbolized universal horror as well as the tempestuous loveliness of terror—an expression of the discord between pleasure and pain.

Swiss born artist Henri Fuseli expressed much of this sentiment in his work that bridged the gap between expressionism and surrealism. *The Nightmare*, painted in 1802, depicts a young woman in the throes of a violently erotic dream while all around her ghostly and grotesquely sharpened images stare from the darkness with eyes ablaze. The unconscious union of forbidden sex and violence, between what Georges Bataille recognizes as the vital connection between transgression and eroticism, will appear again in the work of some of the most disturbing of modernists, including Antonin Artaud and his theater of cruelty.

Throughout the late eighteenth and early nineteenth centuries, abandonment had become a prominent theme in the literature of the romantic era, reflecting both personal tragedy and oppressive social forces. All around was evidence of human abdication: the abandonment of the poor, the abandonment of nature, the abandonment of place, the abandonment of the soul. The personal lives of bourgeois artists often helped to shape their perspectives. Many writers and poets of this period, such as Coleridge, had been orphans or lost a parent at an early age; others were sent off to boarding schools, sequestered, or politically exiled. Chateaubriand, himself, was isolated from members of his family as a small child—locked away in the dark recesses of an enormous castle and left alone where he is said to have developed an intense fantasy life. As an adult he was politically exiled. Sade is said to have been sent away at age four to live with a licentious uncle. Many romantic and modern writers and artists experienced intense personal feelings of emptiness, abandonment and isolation.[69] Some, such as Dickens and Coleridge, lived in intense poverty as children. Others came from wealthy families. Personal life situations reflected and were conditioned by the changes taking place in the societies in which they lived. The romantics frequently valorized aloneness, isolation, and introspection as a response to the social decay that was all around. Thus, romanticism resonated with the various forms of personal alienation and social loss that characterized industrial Europe.

Where modernity and the ethos of capitalism were to emphasize the importance of power, reason, and social order, romanticism opposed these by stressing the critical value of the imagination and the significance of feeling. Rousseau countered Descartes' dictum *cogito ergo sum* with "I *feel* therefore I am." Romanticism frequently glorified the outsider—the bandit, the prostitute, the beggar, the grotesque. Writers such as Victor Hugo and Charles Dickens made an art of elevating those held in lowest esteem to positions of heroic proportions. The outsider became central to romantic art and literature, but also became significant to the modernists as well. Intrinsic to all romanticism, as well as to modernism, was this new cult of the self, elevating the place of the individual above that of culture and society. Romantic novels, poetry, and art reflected this alienation.

Where the period of romanticism ends and modernism begins is often difficult to discern, but certainly romantics helped form an important cadre, perhaps the vanguard, of the modernist movement in the arts. The German romantic philosophers were quite influential in this regard as well. Nietzsche's radical modernism recognized the death of God as both a destabilizing force in the west, and as an opportunity for personal and social growth.

Much of early romanticism was a reaction to the chaos that capitalism and modernity helped to produce. Modernism, however, was coming to terms with both. Modernism was an aesthetic promulgated on the forever-new. While it was also a rebellion against the sentimentalism that characterized much of early romanticism and its retreat into the medieval, modernism shared with romanticism the dark imagination. While celebrating the power of imagination as a tool for heightened awareness, it degenerated into nihilism.

CONSUMERISM AND THE AESTHETIC RESPONSE

Romanticism and modernism were both mindful of the growing power of consumerism in modern life. Nevertheless, romanticism had become the bourgeois brand of entertainment catering to those of wealth, education, and position. It simultaneously insulated them from the real life that surrounded them and allowed them to partake of the exotic novelties the romantics offered-up in their art. Of course, romantic art and literature was becoming a new industry in itself. More than anything else, romanticism represented an escape for the liberal middle classes from their boorish lives—and from the formidable demands of Calvinism. Those who read poetry, read novels, joined salons, or attended concerts, art galleries, and theaters were not the factory workers. Rather, they were the remnants of an aging aristocracy, or the emerging bourgeoisie, or petty bourgeoisie. It was these social classes of the newly educated elites with their discretionary wealth and leisure time won at the expense of those working their factories who consumed these new modes of escape from capitalistic banality. Romanticism announced their boredom, their loneliness, their need for feeling human, and their quest for personal connectedness. It was frequently a release for repressed sexuality.

Modernism, however, went a step further. It was more self-reflexive, more self-conscious of its role in the construction of culture. Modernism promoted an aesthetic revolt against the sentimentalism inherent in romanticism and displayed a critical disdain for its middle class pretensions. Beyond this, it was contemptuous of political life while reflecting considerable insight into the emergence of consumer culture of which romanticism was a part.

This new movement in the arts provided the bourgeois audience with something more radical than could be represented by escapist romanticism. It held up a mirror. It revealed the imperfections, the ugliness associated with superficial beauty. Such modernism first took root in France. Two of the leading literary exponents of this approach were Gustave Flaubert and Charles Baudelaire. Flaubert's work helped challenge romanticism through a heightened sense of realism. He was among the first to viciously attack the vacuousness of romanticism and Victorian society in his novel, *Madame Bovary*. In *Sentimental Education*, he evolved as a true modernist by exposing the unspoken objectification inherent in modern human relationships. It is Flaubert who illuminates the emerging power of consumerism in the nineteenth century and its undermining of personal and communal authenticity. His work constitutes an assault against the suppression of female sexuality and the romantic tradition along with its portrayal of women as either asexual virgins or passionate whores. Beyond this, Flaubert reveals to his readers the process of human commodification and the power of market forces in changing the nature of human relationships. Baudelaire, who shared many of these same sensibilities, emerged as the more central critic of modern urban life and the most modern. Nevertheless, both writers contributed uniquely to this modernist movement and to sociologically relevant fiction. In January of 1857, Flaubert was tried in the French courts for the obscenity of *Madame Bovary*; seven months later, Baudelaire went on trial for his *Les Fleurs du mal*.

In *Madame Bovary*, Flaubert dramatically portrayed the trend in society toward the commodification of human beings, their relationships to one another, and their sense of physical and personal detachment. These elements of self-objectification and alienation, which are found in the writings of Hegel, Fitche, and Marx, eventually became part of a modernist aesthetic. Flaubert masterfully incorporated these elements into the story of Emma Bovary. Emma Bovary is portrayed as a young woman who is not content with her everyday bourgeois existence. She has disdain for reality, holds her own life in contempt, and seeks to live the romantic and adventurous existence depicted in the novels of her day. Such literary works allow her to escape into erotic fantasies and enable her to move from pleasure to pleasure, from luxury to luxury, from one aesthetic gratification to another. Flaubert tells us that she is addicted to romanticism as the drug addict is addicted to opium and illustrates how this addiction (epitomized in her consumerism) will lead to her downfall.

Emma is inclined to relate material gratification to her own self-identity; that is, she seeks fulfillment by surrounding herself with things. She has no allegiance to anyone. She uses people to achieve her romantic fantasies; yet, she finds it shocking that others would use her. She increasingly becomes more detached, ungrounded, and emerges as an object of her own creation. Throughout the novel Emma sees herself as being tossed this way and that by the winds of fate. Yet, she is the quintessential narcissist. In her study, she lounges, dressed in recently purchased attire, and dreams of far off places and romance. "Deep down within her she was waiting for something to happen. . . ."[70]

Flaubert depicts Emma as often looking into a mirror to capture an image of herself. But the image is only a surface manifestation—an artificial construction of her own materialism comprised of make-up and new dresses. For Emma, fashion is everything, and for Flaubert its superficiality has become the essential feature of modern life. Even Emma's child is viewed by her as a possession, something that might complement her appearance—like new shoes or imported furnishings or glassware. Emma lives in a world of objects, and in doing so becomes objectified herself. This small town woman cannot escape the alienating force of capitalism.

There can be little doubt that Emma's fragile self is underdeveloped. There is no real love in her life and, although she wants an authentic connection, she appears incapable of loving anyone, particularly Charles, her husband, who nevertheless loves her unconditionally. Charles is a well-meaning man and a nearly competent country doctor. We are told that the more he loves her, the more contempt she has for him. She is in search of passion, romance, and adventure. Instead of loving her husband, she is attracted to worldly men of culture and personal charm. In her first adulterous relationship with the nobleman Rodolphe, she gives herself to him completely in love-making as women had done time and time again in the romantic novels she had read. Yet, the giving is never mutual; it is always one-sided. Her self-abandonment is accompanied by feelings of alienation and dissociation; and the more she abandons herself to him, the more distant he becomes. He views her love as escalating into a desire to possess him. While escaping her mundane life through fantasy, novels, and passionate love-making, Emma Bovary attempts to prove her value to her lover by giving him material gifts. She spends excessively both on him and on make-up and fashions for herself—going into debt in order to be attractive to him. Clearly, Emma's materialism is ingrained in her romantic sensuality.

Flaubert portrays Emma as a tragic modern woman in search of feelings and love who is a victim of her own romantic delusions and her time—an individual who is deserted by her lovers to whom she has given herself passionately and completely. In the wake of Emma's abandonment by her lovers she often is seen as overpowered by her loneliness and alienation. Several times during the story, Flaubert graphically depicts Emma's dissociative episodes. There is physical as well as psychological disengagement—a type of hysteria common to that era. The attic scene, in which she reads Rodolphe's letter, which terminates their relationship, shows the extent of this detachment and also brings on her subsequent forty-two day illness:

> The beam of sunlight reflecting directly up at her from below was pulling the weight of her body into an abyss. She felt as if the square were swinging to and fro, its ground climbing the walls. The floor was tilting at one end like a vessel in a storm. She was right at the edge, almost hanging out, surrounded by a great vastness. The blue of the sky flooded over her; the air rushed through her hollow brain. All she had to do was to give in, let herself go.[71]

When Leon, Emma's romantic soul-mate and second lover, is incapable of finding the money she needs to keep the bill collector from auctioning her home to pay her debts, she finds herself alone outside their hotel, even while surrounded by a mass of Sunday pedestrians. Here in the busy streets of Rouen she becomes overpowered by sensation:

"Everything, within her and without, was abandoning her. She felt herself lost, rolling beyond control in bottomless abysses. . . ."[72]

Emma's final abandonment is her suicide. She thought frequently of her own death as part of her romantic fantasies. As Flaubert noted: "At one and the same time, she wanted to die and to live in Paris."[73] While sentimental literature was filled with descriptions of lovers' suicides and "beautiful deaths," Flaubert's depiction of Emma's death was meant to de-romanticize this behavior. His account of her suicide is prolonged, detailed, and gruesomely graphic. When Emma takes her life she sets into motion a number of events that culminate in the broken heart and eventual death of her husband, Charles, and the abandonment of her daughter, Berthe, who ends up living with a destitute aunt and is forced into child labor in a cotton mill.

Flaubert's *Madame Bovary* is his reaction to the sentimentalism of his time. It speaks of his understanding of the powerful constraints that had been placed upon women forced into shackles of repressive suburban life with no acceptable outlet for their needs or desires. His portrait of a superficial, decaying middle class society comprised of shallow social climbers desiring to be something they are not is considered the epitome of realism. He displays a masterful ability both to utilize some of the story elements of the romantic novel and to attack the genre simultaneously. The book reflects his disdain for the commercialization of human relationships and the trivialization of a culture that he viewed as associated with romanticism. He is contemptuous of writers' romances with the small town and makes it a point to illustrate the banality of such places. He is equally scornful of the romantic notion of urban life and, therefore, emphasizes its superficiality and phoniness. His biting literary portraits have led many to view his work as nihilistic.

Flaubert was among the first to identify what sociologist Colin Campbell has described as the close cooperative relationship of the romantic ethic and modern consumerism.[74] Flaubert reveals through his characters what now is recognized as the modernistic quest for that indefinite something—an important malaise of the burgeoning modern middle class.[75] In his novels, the middle class can be seen actively pursuing material things in a search to fill an ever-expanding spiritual void. In this regard critic Mario Vargas Llosa has noted:

> A hundred years before her flesh-and-blood sisters and brothers, Emma Bovary in a little Norman town, tries to compensate for a fundamental emptiness in her life by acquiring objects, by looking to commercial products for the help that her fellow humans fail to give her. In Madame Bovary we see the first signs of alienation that a century later will take

hold of men and women in industrial societies (the women above all, owing to the life they are obliged to live); consumption as an outlet for anxiety, the attempt to people with objects the emptiness that modern life has made a permanent feature of the existence of the individual.[76]

Although it can be easily claimed that Flaubert personally lacked much of a social conscience, his work reveals a solid sociological understanding of the outcomes of modern capitalism, particularly its production of alienation, narcissism, false consciousness, anxiety, and self-commodification. Bovary's life exemplifies the gulf between connection and separation and the "desire to be desired." Her life is an expression of insatiable longing coupled with a deep sense of alienation. This desire to be desired, insists Fredric Jameson in his critique of the novel, is central to the modern literary expression, and at the very heart of capitalistic production.[77]

Also there is great ambivalence expressed in the work of Flaubert— another quality closely associated with aesthetic modernism. Such ambivalence is key to understanding the power of capitalistic hegemony and the personal sense of powerlessness as one confronts it.

The sense of disempowerment inherent in modernity was later explored by Frankfurt social theorists, some of whom put much hope into modern art as a challenge to capitalism and the confining rationality associated with the Enlightenment project. Romanticism as an aesthetic movement was viewed a virtual failure in this regard. Walter Benjamin was especially hopeful that modern writers and artists could undermine the world of commodity production and consumption through their innovative approaches to style and structure. Modernism's forms were iconoclastic and disruptive. However, art became one more commodity in the ever-expanding marketplace. Art lost its critical edge as it was co-opted by the commercial world, which turned artists into media celebrities. Thus, much of art, even modern art, becomes counter revolutionary by attempting to reconcile the individual to an oppressive and exploitive economic order.

CONCLUSION

Abandonment stands as central to all that is modern. It is inherent in the most modern of economic systems: market capitalism. It permeates all modern social institutions and is emblematic of consumer societies. It saturates modern culture—the arts, philosophy, and the social sciences. To be modern is to feel disconnected, to be detached, and in a state of constant loss. It is to become accustomed to the evanescent—comfort-able with the instability that is endemic in modern life.

While market capitalism is a generator of the values and culture associated with modernity, modernity itself is a vital force in its own right. Whether we see it as a holocaust, a maelstrom, or a juggernaut, we are called upon to recognize the dangers inherent in romanticizing it. Modernity in itself offers no escape from terror, inhumanity, and vio-lence done in the name of progress. Still, we need to avoid its demoniza-tion. Marshall Berman has suggested that the modernism that results from modernity is reflexive; it holds out hope for what could be.[78] Many of the separations inherent in modern life are opportunities for experi-ment and change—creative opportunities for self-development and ele-vated understanding.

The following chapter explores the concerns of leading theorists in their quest for understanding the relationship of modernity and aban-donment. Drawing upon many of the elements used here, such as capi-talism, modernity, romanticism, consumerism, and modernism, these theorists vividly illustrate modernity's power as a force of destruction and innovation.

Chapter 2

Abandonment and Social Theory

Romantic philosophy is said to have originated in the metaphysics of Immanuel Kant with his distinction between the unknowable noumenon (*Ding an sich*) and the more accessible phenomenon—understanding gained through the mind. Here the world is reflected in sense perception and imagination and is predicated on intimate subjective knowledge and feeling. Johann Fichte also reaffirmed this view, suggesting that reality is no more than an imaginary construction. Still, as it evolved romantic philosophy was significantly diverse and included ideas ranging from Schelling to Hegel. It was Schelling who most significantly connected this romanticism to the arts by deeply influencing the English poets, particularly the work of Coleridge. In Schelling's work, and that of some other romantics, the idealistic celebration of the individual and a strong rejection of the rationalism and empiricism associated with the Enlightenment carried forward into a new aestheticism. Here too was an elevation of nature to a central position in the quest for truth: one needed to start with nature to find oneself.

The ideas presented in this chapter depict intellectual landscapes of abandonment that resonate with separations generated by the historic, materialistic conditions of capitalism and modernity. They portend a type of cultural turn. These highly graphic intellectualizations present deep unsettling feelings and, at the very same time, serve as a psychological defense against them. Each theorist attempts to understand his or her surroundings—often putting their sentiments into some rational equation. Compositional methods of the landscape artist can be easily discerned in the construction of modern social thought.[1] In fact the dialectic of being part of nature and being alien to it, being at one with nature and being alone in it, can easily be seen in the work of theorists and in the great paintings of such artists as John Martin or Caspar David Friedrich. The focus on dread, the quest for some sort of transcendence are colorfully expressed in these perspectives.

Still, no integrative theory of abandonment is to be found in the works of those discussed here. Taken by themselves there is no clear, comprehensive insight into the modern predicament of abandonment. However, taken together the work of the following theorists provides the basis for understanding the intellectual focus on abandonment, separation, and loss in modern life, and how this concern became a part of modern social discourse. This chapter establishes thematic connections between the early modern notions of abandonment anxiety, as they were developed in philosophy, psychoanalysis, and social theory. It examines some of the essential theoretical elements that were responses to feelings of personal alienation and separation that had their source in the social environment. Although this survey is necessarily selective, the choice of theoretical elements is broad. These range from Hegel's ideas on estrangement to Kierkegaard's notion of dread. They include Marx's insights into the social and economic implications of alienation, Freud's transition from drive theory to what is now called object relations, and some of the central themes in the work of critical theorists, existentialists, and postmodernists. Individually these ideas represent unique interpretations of abandonment in modern life. Taken together, they help to construct what might be called an intellectual landscape of abandonment.

HEGEL: REASON AND SEPARATION

The writings of Georg F. W. Hegel provide one of the first modern philosophical explorations of attachment and separation. Although not a theorist of abandonment *per se*, Hegel develops key concepts, ideas, and insights into the association of abandonment and modernity and prepares the way for a fuller elaboration of abandonment theory. Hegel's *Phenomenology of Spirit* (1807) lays much of the groundwork for both Marxist speculation and psychoanalytic thought. By a thorough analysis of subject and object relations culminating in a theory of dialectics, Hegel formulates some of the key ingredients for the construction of modern social science theory of abandonment, attachment, and separation.[2] Hegel's philosophy is frequently characterized as an attempt to realize the synthesis between the rational and the spiritual. Yet, on a deeper level, it is an attempt to confront feelings of separation and isolation inherent in modern life.

For Hegel, as well as for other modernists, the schism between rational intellect and the sensual is the basis of the modern condition. One's separation from nature is the first stage of knowing. Building on the work of Enlightenment thinkers, Hegel accepts the view that individuals have turned against nature, within and without, in order to curb instinct, advance personal knowledge, and promote human progress. This requires an initial separation of cognition from feeling—reason from emotion. Until such a separation is achieved there can be no true personal freedom, which is based on the conquest of nature and the interconnection of people in a comprehensive web of universal rationality. For Hegel, the ultimate quest of each individual is "becoming"— achieving a state of oneness, united by universal *Rational Ideal* that is God. To do this end, one must first enter into a state of aloneness. This separation eventually leads to a state of conflict and finally synthesis. It is only through this ongoing dialectical process that one ultimately achieves reason and finds completeness. Thus, Hegel prepares the way for a psychological theory of attachment and separation. He structures this theory along normative developmental lines. Although he identifies a universal duality of mind and matter that is explicit in the work of Hume and Kant, he begins with a recognition of the importance of separation and individuation.

Inherent in this model is estrangement. It is the disunity of each from all that provides the basis of what Hegel refers to as "unhappy consciousness."[3] There is despair in the disunity associated with the struggle to separate from and conquer nature. But in order to evolve, it is necessary that humans do just this. Hegel, therefore, believes separation to be the cornerstone of progress. The alternative is a natural state of animalistic savagery, a state of undifferentiated oneness. Nevertheless, the road to reason, which is marked by constant isolation, results in an unconscious craving for wholeness—a return to oneness with the world. Yet, this totality of a sensual connection of all to all is a form of madness. There can be no retreat, only the drive for a new rational synthesis. Growth comes from giving up the security of the past—the familiar—and embarking on an adventure filled with fear, doubt, and despair. Thus, the unfettered rational ego stands at the center of this western model.

Also, at the core of Hegel's work is this idea that reason is the key to all knowledge and progress and the way to an authentic unity. Reason is both a divisive and connective force. For Hegel the first step in achieving any advanced awareness through reason requires detachment and a rejection of primitive connectiveness. In this way he promotes the notion of unity through disunity. This is both an ontological process as well as a prescription for social and personal enlightenment. It is Hegel's quest for spiritual unity through the vigorous application of reason and intellect that drives much of his work.

Hegel's theory is similar to the work of other German idealist philosophers, such as Immanuel Kant, who proposed that the world was constructed by thoughts and ideas and who was concerned with the possibility of absolute knowledge. For Hegel, this unity in knowledge was expressed in his concept of "geist." For Kant, it was his notion of "transcendental ego."[4] Still, Hegel's quest was significantly different from that of German romantics such as Schelling who insisted that we can only know nature by being part of it, and we can never know it by separating from it. For Hegel, the distinction of subject from object is primary to the initial stage of understanding. Therefore, personal alienation is key to enlightenment, order, and progress.

Hegel claims that all reality and history are creations of the mind. Yet, he infuses this notion with a radical theology. Unlike Kant's knowing ego, geist is a spiritual manifestation of knowledge. Also, where many other idealist philosophers viewed the world of things pluralistically and saw ideas as personal human constructs, Hegel subscribed to a monism—a belief that there exists only one ultimate thinking substance or unified force which is geist. For Hegel, God represents the whole, which is the only truth, and all thoughts and truths must come from God. This totalism is deeply grounded in both the philosophical tradition and late eighteenth century theological reasoning. Unlike Kant, who suggested that the order to the universe arises out of human construction in an attempt to understand it, Hegel posits the view that the objective world is inherently rational, and we can come to know it only through reason. Yet, he suggests that any propositions or theses developed by individual men and women are inherently incomplete and will turn out to be self-contradictory. It is in wholeness or synthesis that we find the divinity, which is the only truth. [5] Thus Hegel's phenomenology is a historical narrative of change—an evolutionary, developmental struggle from natural matter into spirit. Reason emerges from a dialectical pilgrimage beginning in primitive attachment, moving on to separation, and finally culminating in grand synthesis. Ironically, the only way one can discover this truth is through systematic, rational contradiction. Dialectical opposition is seen here as the key to truth, to grand synthesis and ultimately to God—the basis of rational unity. This dialectical process is both a mode of understanding and a history of the world. It is a process grounded in what he views as a rational and liberating dynamic of separation.

Although subject-object dualism had been an important element of classical Greek philosophy, separation takes on a new importance in the work of Hegel. Where the Greek world emphasized an organic synthesis, in Hegel's world of radical individualism this had to be discarded. Opposition to nature, not unity with it, makes us truly modern. Detachment, separation, and abandonment are important rationalistic tools. Enlightenment thinkers proposed that such tools could be used to allow us to come closer to knowing the world and ourselves. Thus, Hegel emphasizes the role of estrangement as essential to knowing. It is only through our estrangement from the world of objects surrounding us that we can achieve a higher level of understanding. It is this self-estrangement that brings about self-awareness through which we ultimately connect with God.[6] Through his work on personal estrangement, Hegel lays the cornerstone for modern existentialism, particularly influencing the work of Søren Kierkegaard.

For Hegel, all reality is simultaneously spiritual and rational. We are estranged from ourselves, from nature, and from our own spirituality by the very objects we have created. In this way our lives are characterized by "unhappy consciousness," anxiety, and despair reflecting our disconnectedness. By labeling the world through words, language becomes a prime instrument of this alienation. It provides for the basis for self-objectification and, therefore, self-estrangement. Paradoxically, language is essential to both the universality of conscience and to our self-awareness. It allows for the establishment of moral and social bonds, and separation of subject from object. Language becomes the means by which spirit finds essence and essence finds spirituality. All is separated and joined by language.

One of the most important concepts to emerge from *Phenomenology of Spirit* was Hegel's notion of objectification, and it is here where we can truly gain a sense of the importance of alienation and abandonment in his work. Objectification provides the basis for what is to later come in Marxism, psychoanalysis, critical theory, existentialism, and postmodernism relative to their particular focus on subject-object relations. It is Hegel's notion of objectification and the tension between subject and object that lays the groundwork for Marx's notion of alienation and the psychoanalytic concept of object relations. For Hegel, the dialectic of objectification is not just a subject-object tension, but a true separation or alienation of the object from the subject, and the subject from itself. It has to do with loss and related dread of disunity. Accordingly, it is only when something is externalized, alienated from the subject, that it can be understood. One must be individuated, stand independent from the primal, communal world of nature. Thus, one must create a self in opposition to an other.

Desire and destruction follow alienation. For Hegel, whether consciously or unconsciously, separation promotes a drive to protect the subject from otherness by attacking and destroying that which is alien to it; or the subject launches into a process of eliminating otherness by incorporating and integrating the external object into the self. However, it is through the process of destruction or nullification that one attempts to preserve the self. Yet, Hegel sees the desire to destroy this otherness as an obstacle to progress.

To be fully understood, in order to achieve mature reason by synthesis, the object must be incorporated by the subject—taken into it. While separation is essential to the development of explicit understanding, it must lead to synthesis. Objectification, therefore, is when the subject externalizes itself in a creative differentiation, establishing otherness, and reappropriates this externalization through what Hegel has called "sublation." In order to understand oneself, gain a self-awareness, one must begin with self-estrangement and an understanding that there is something that the subject, or self, is not. Self-awareness can only be gained by an awareness of the other and a recognition of an externalized world. It is through this recurring process of reincorporation of an increasingly complex external world of its own creation (created through language) that consciousness is expanded. Therefore, in his notion of objectification Hegel proposes that the ultimate understanding of our world and ourselves is achieved through self-alienation, connection with the other, and integration of the other into ourselves. The only avenue to true independence, therefore, is through a recognition of dependence on others. It is this tension between needing the other, incorporating it, and being independent of it that gives focus to much of Hegel's work. It is essential to his notion of wholeness. The dilemma of the tension between otherness and the subject is brought out in his most famous master-slave illustration.

In this example, Hegel begins by suggesting that desire provides the basis of all human action. Desire of the subject is a recognition by the subject of an internal lacking, an emptiness, an incompleteness, and a corresponding need to fulfill it. But it is perceived that this need can only be satisfied through what he terms "negation," the transformation or destruction of the desired object. Inherent in all desire is a recognition of the self and its separation from the object of desire. The true mark of becoming human, contends Hegel, is not to desire an object, but to desire the desire of another—to become an object of desire. The master-slave parable is predicated on this notion of desire, especially the desire for desire, or the desire for another's recognition. Hegel suggests that in the multiplicity of competing subjects there occurs a struggle of each against the other in a drive to exert one over the next—one's status as subject over the objectification of another. The outcome of this could be the rendering of one contestant as master and the other as slave.[7] And here is the dilemma. To satisfy the desires of the master, the slave must repress all personal instincts, and transcend his or her own ego. The slave submits to the master and must, therefore, find his or her self in the master. It is in this submission and the abandonment of the egoistic self that Hegel finds the essential elements of transcendence. Thus, once the slave gives the self over to the master in the complete servitude to the other's will, there is not only greater self-awareness but increased consciousness. Thus, desire is fulfilled through a process of self-negation.

The slave is forced to do the work for the master; and since labor is the transformation of nature, the slave in working for the master is enabled to change the objective world and ultimately regain a sense of self as a part of it. On the other hand, the master who is content with his mastery over the object and enjoyment of its second-hand production becomes dependent on the slave for labor, recognition, and identity. The slave, however, in doing the master's bidding develops an enhanced ego and becomes an actualized being while the master fails to fully develop. Thus, Hegel believes that the burden of establishing liberty in society rests with the oppressed. The locus of liberation is in work in the transformation of nature.

Hegel describes four stages of liberty through which the slave passes. The movement from a lower to a higher stage occurs when a slave negates what he or she formerly believed. These stages are stoicism, skepticism, the unhappy consciousness, and rational consciousness. Stoicism here implies a withdrawal into the self and away from the world where one might find some sort of inner liberty. Skepticism is a turning toward the world filled with doubt and includes a disbelief in the role forced upon the slave by the master, and a disbelief in the master's moral superiority. The unhappy consciousness is an internalization of the master-slave relationship—the recognition that within the self there is a slave-master duality. Finally, rational consciousness is a coming to terms with this duality of the self and others and, therefore, an ability to recognize the self in others. It is at this stage when the struggle stops and an absolute awareness of consciousness begins.

The master-slave tale has been interpreted in many ways, but essential to this parable is the notion of transcendence of self through labor and submission; thus, it strongly supports a Calvinistic ethic. Simultaneously, the idea that those who are oppressed are more likely to have a greater consciousness than those of the ruling class might also be seen as grounded in Hegel's philosophy. Hegel makes it a point to insist that the renunciation of one's own will, which constitutes the moment of true obedience, is the only path to "true knowledge." This obedience, by making oneself into the object of another, translates into freedom.[8] By being-for-another and seeing oneself in the otherness of the master, the slave gains self-recognition. Thus, there is strength in surrender. Hegel views the negation of difference as the essence of truth. Ultimately, there is no otherness, just oneness connected to reason. However, this emphasis on the renunciation of individuality and innate will ensures Hegel a place among the German Idealists, as well as some romantics and Protestant theologians. In Hegel's master-slave tale, self-negation connects one to the Spirit.

Nevertheless, Hegel was to set the tone for much modernist theory to follow. It is evident that his focus on dialectics, separation, objectification, and alienation not only found its way into the important writings of Marx, but also provided some basis for psychoanalytic thought, particularly theories of object relations. We can also see a significant influence on interactionist sociology, especially the work of Cooley and Mead. His dialectics, his focus on being and becoming, his coupling of alienation to knowledge likewise inspired the existential writings of theorists ranging from Heidegger to Sartre. Many of his thoughts have provided fertile ground for the development of critical, poststructural, and postmodern theory.

KIERKEGAARD: EXISTENTIAL *ANGST*

Although Hegel helped to lay much of the foundation for existentialism, it was Søren Kierkegaard who most clearly connected separation and alienation to feeling. Kierkegaard's work is deemed to be even more psychological than that of Hegel. In fact, although his work was heavily influenced by Hegel's, he was strongly opposed to what he viewed as Hegel's over-intellectualizations. Like Marx who was to find Hegel's ideological renderings too abstract, mechanical, and anti-materialistic, Kierkegaard was to find them equally devoid of affect.

Deeply grounded in religion himself, Kierkegaard takes issue with Hegel's theological speculations. He finds them lacking humanistic insight and far too rationalistic. But more significantly, he finds the detachment of Hegel from his work, from his own ideas, from his primal emotions, particularly regretful. Kierkegaard sees the individual as impassioned, attempting to find meaning in the subjective world of other individuals. The key to this quest for him is not the rational discovery of an ordered universality, a system intelligible to the contemplative observer, but a drive for existence or what Aristotle referred to as "being" through an intensity of feeling. Kierkegaard, therefore, defends the subjective over the so-called objective. In fact, in his work, he implies a new interpretation of alienation—the disappearance of the self into a dehumanized abstraction. Kierkegaard's focus on estrangement involves a disconnectedness from the self. He claims that the lost sense of self in modern society translates into a loss of existence—the loss of an authentic life. It is this disunity of self and thought associated with modernity that he identifies as a key to understanding the modern dilemma. In this respect he shares similar perspectives to many German idealists and romantics who had already identified this dissociation as source of the "modern malaise."

In 1844, the same year Marx produced his *Economic and Philosophic Manuscripts*, Kierkegaard published *The Concept of Dread*.[9] In this work he discusses modern anxiety or angst. Anxiety (or *angst*) is a psychological state emerging from the objectification of the earth and a human sense of separation. For Kierkegaard, angst encompasses a feeling of looming danger where the source of the threat is unknown, unclear. Kierkegaard discusses the relation of this feeling to the highly rationalistic, reified world that separates the individual from his nature or Being.

Kierkegaard connects this dread to a particular type of disconnectedness—a profound insecurity. He finds that this anxiety is most common to all who must confront a world of Becoming. Unlike the comfort of the feudal Catholic patriarchy, this new world involves decisions and the freedom to make them. One must confront the world alone and be responsible for one's own personal outcome. Making decisions is the basis of Becoming. Yet, each choice, says Kierkegaard, is a risk filled with uncertainty.[10] He makes much of what he sees as a separation from the initial comfort of undifferentiated oneness and the drive for an existent self. The development of this self, therefore, has major significance in his work and helps to lay the foundation for both psychoanalytic theory and existentialism. For Kierkegaard, and later for Heidegger, the existent self is only sensed from anguish experienced in relationship to this undifferentiation or nothingness from which all emerges and into which all collapses. It is Heidegger and the existentialists who later attempt to articulate this nothingness as the negative foundation of Being, itself.

In exploring the origins of anxiety in the development of infants, Kierkegaard finds that in early infancy, where there is little recognition on the part of the infant of separation from its world, there is little anxiety.[11] Unlike Hegel, he does not view this as a state of madness. Anxiety is a product of the child's gradual separation from the nurturing caregiver, or anticipation of this separation. As the infant is pushed further from its source of protection and love, it reluctantly explores the world. Eventually, in exploring its world the child brings itself to make conscious choices that significantly increase feelings of dread. Individuation is seen by Kierkegaard as the point of the greatest stress connected not only to aloneness but to the possibility of choice and self-will. It is the will to become oneself that is crucial in human development and the maturation of consciousness. It is what Kierkegaard refers to as the great leap into self-awareness that is at the core of modern anxiety.

Kierkegaard makes an important distinction between this resultant anxiety and the notion of fear. Where fear is represented by an external threat from which the individual turns, and perhaps runs, anxiety is internally generated—an inner conflict of potentialities to which the person expresses extreme ambivalence. One has anxiety because one is capable of self-creation. Anxiety is not possible without the recognition of potentialities. Without potential for self-directed change, there can be no anxiety. Angst, therefore, is inherently modern.

In the creation of one's separateness—in all creation for that matter—there is necessarily a corresponding destruction. Modernization and change is a process of creative destruction. For Kierkegaard, self-emergence is an inherently destructive/creative process for the individual. One's becoming requires that the person leaves behind a previous aspect of self, but it also requires the elimination of some of these attributes and previous ties. Should this leap into self-becoming and fuller self-awareness be denied, one must suffer guilt as a consequence.

The will to be oneself is seen by Kierkegaard as a strictly human vocation. But frequently people attempt to avoid self-becoming by engaging in activities that lead to personal estrangement, regression, and degeneration. People turn away from freedom, from a life coupled with creative potential and dread. They become "shut-up," insulated from the potentialities that surround them, desensitized, spiritually dead. Instead of accepting the dread associated with self-emergence, most people seek retreat into artificial security often into material possessions that stand in the way of this personal growth. In doing so they close down their sensual awareness of the world and themselves. They become fatalistic, insulated and small. Perhaps, they even turn to self-destruction. Kierkegaard asserts that the construction of a masochistic life can become an alternative to personal and emotional growth.

Kierkegaard sees guilt and anxiety as driving forces in modern life. To embrace change requires the destruction of the status quo and a rejection of that which one has clung to since childhood. This letting go produces intense feelings of dread and guilt. To develop, one must confront a world without a deep, ontological security. Any attempts to avoid dread by becoming shut-up are futile. One must be willing to acknowledge that a fulfilled life is one characterized by angst and uncertainty. For Kierkegaard, it is the aim of an existent individual to deal with this dread of freedom by embracing its potential. In order to gain self-awareness one must come to terms with the inherent dread of becoming by allowing anxiety to be the teacher. All creative genius is characterized by both guilt and dread. Such a philosophy of existence set into motion a modern discourse on abandonment and letting go.

The loss of Eden, which is a central allegorical narrative to which Kierkegaard returns again and again, and which provides a particular focus for his work, *The Concept of Dread*, is used to deepen our appreciation of his modernistic stance on becoming, individualism, and aloneness. Like Milton, the loss of Eden represents for Kierkegaard a new beginning predicated on abandonment that leads to angst, guilt, and eventually to self-awareness.

MARX: ALIENATION AND CAPITALISM

For Karl Marx, both Hegel and Kierkegaard were mired in reactionary thought. Their ideas seemed to be grounded in bourgeois mysticism and eighteenth-century intellectualism. Neither man appeared to understand, as did Marx, that at the core of human abandonment and alienation was capitalism—human exploitation in a brutal quest for wealth and power. Behind the feelings of estrangement and anxiety identified by bourgeois philosophers and poets lay raw and arbitrary power exercised in this system of accumulation.

As opposed to developing a philosophy of abandonment, as did Hegel, or a psychology of abandonment, as epitomized in the work of Kierkegaard, Marx looks at estrangement sociologically. He describes the intricate relationship between feeling and praxis and portrays the real life system from which these feelings evolve. Abandonment is created by the forces of capitalism directed against the workers.

Marx's work is both historical and expansive; however, there is an immediacy to it. While he dismisses German idealism and romanticism, he subscribes to a materialistic dialectic—an empirically based view of real world conflict. This is opposed to highly abstract Hegelian metaphysics. He believes in historical progress, and rejects what he views as the sentimentalism of Kierkegaard as well as the reification evident in Hegel. Influenced by Hegel, Marx is even more influenced by Feuerbach's reaction to Hegelian thought and repudiates the deification of reason as well as the sanctification of slave labor. In its place, he posits work as "essence"—that which gives meaning to human existence. Likewise, he rejects Hegel's notion of a mystical unfolding of the mind and proposes a historical theory of class struggle. For him, the dialectics of which Hegel spoke was a proxy for class struggle that was rooted in the real world and which seemed to determine all else. Marx dismisses the idea of estrangement as a spiritual or metaphysical concept, and proposes that it is real—the outcome of capitalistic exploitation through objectification and commodification.

In his *Economic and Philosophic Manuscripts of 1844*, written at the age of twenty-six, he takes a number of Hegelian concepts and makes them his own.[12] In the second section of the *Manuscripts*, the section dealing with estranged labor, Marx confronts Hegel's highly intellectualized notion of objectification and self-awareness. Instead of accepting the idea that the process is completely cognitive, Marx insists that self-understanding is achieved through labor. It is through the worker's transformation of nature with body and mind that the individual realizes the self. Thus, the self is produced in this process of work. Work helps us to form a distinctly human identity. That which one creates is an extension of the self. Therefore, the world is transformed physically—not merely intellectually. Workers understand their places in the world through this interaction with nature in the construction of culture. It is in this way that people realize their connection to nature and come to see themselves as human.

However, labor coerced under capitalism becomes estranged. Labor, itself, as well as its products are removed and alienated from the worker. Thus, the culture created by the worker does not belong to the worker; rather, it belongs to the owner of labor. Likewise, there is no recognition of the self in the objectified world the worker has produced. The world is not an authentic expression of the self. What is produced by labor stands in opposition to the worker since it represents an alien, exploitive power. That which is produced is merely a commodity—an objectification of labor, which is opposed to all that the worker is. What is consumed is not real in that it does not reflect the self. It is not true consciousness, but rather false consciousness—the consciousness of the owner-capitalist. Thus, the system as envisioned by Hegel breaks apart.

The market system works to separate both labor from the product and the worker from the self. It is the worker's dependence on the owners of production that forces labor into the position of a commodity. Thus, Marx views alienation and commodification as essential correlates of modern capitalism. Alienation is not simply a feeling of estrangement resulting from the separation of the individual from the

whole, but an important human process that took on social and economic significance during the industrial revolution. It is an actual separation of a part of the self from the worker. The feelings of estrangement,
which Hegel identified, were a direct consequence of the social and economic arrangements set into place under capitalism.

Like the slave in Hegel's parable, the worker is forced to take on the
consciousness of the master. Unlike Hegel's claim, Marx posits that the
experience of alienation is not a liberating one. It is a form of personal
disintegration resulting from social and economic oppression. Alienation
from nature and from the self is the result of an oppressive system of
social organization in which each individual becomes a tool of another.
Thus, the individual can never develop a coherent self as long as such
oppression continues to exist. As alienated commodities, workers are
separated from nature, their work, and themselves. Labor, just like the
culture it produces, is dehumanized. By taking on a false consciousness
it becomes difficult to make sense of one's oppressed position in the
world let alone recognize the source of one's feelings of estrangement. In
a world of objects, one can only view oneself as a thing, a commodity.

Thus Marx turns Hegel right-side-up, taking many of Hegel's
abstruse observations and grounding them in time and space. By connecting philosophy to the physical world and by denying his theological
assessments of feeling, Marx assumes a reality-based sociological posture.
For Marx, capitalism represents forces of dehumanization and estrangement. Not only does the new capitalistic order desanctify the world (as
Max Weber would later explain), but it converts it all into crude profit-
making matter. Under this system the individual is processed to become
an object in a world of other objects; commodified by the market and
forced to take its place alongside of other commodities.

Therefore, Marx sees a direct correlation between objectification and
alienation. Unlike Hegel, he does not view objectification as a means to
self-awareness through sublation or the taking-in of otherness; rather, he
understands it as a correlate of personal estrangement. Under capitalism
one's labor surrenders to powerful forces outside the self who appropriate the use of it for their own profit. There is an inherent surrender of
the self to alien forces. Therefore, the liberating potential of Hegel's
notion of objectification is viewed as romantic ideology. For Marx, capitalism, which nourishes master/slave relations, does not culminate in
self-awareness, but rather it opposes it.

In *Das Kapital* (1867) Marx develops the notion of "fetishism of
commodities." He begins by making use of Hegel's phenomenology and
particularly his emphasis on appearances. Aside from their use value,
commodities take on powerfully symbolic significance.[13] Imbued within

each commodity are what Marx calls "metaphysical subtleties and philo-sophic niceties." (This idea will be more fully developed by Georg Lukács, Thorstein Veblen, Herbert Marcuse, and postmodernist Jean Baudrillard.) Inherent in the commodity fetish is a symbolic value that conveys messages related to power relations and oppression. The com-modity takes on a power and life of its own. It becomes a means by which capitalism systematically and semiotically presents itself in a syn-thetic system of desires. Such commodity desire, which is both a func-tion and purpose of capitalism, requires a constant and renewable social reconstruction of desire. This becomes the basis for a disposable materi-alistic culture driven by personal alienation. It is from this condition that such wants emerge.

Marx's theory presents both an historical and psychological basis of modern culture. More than this, he provides a sociological model of abandonment predicated on involuntary alienation inherent in modern capitalism. For him, this abandonment involves the relinquishment of one's own nature—one's species being. It involves the coercive separation from one's essence. Alienation of labor produces stress and anxiety.[14]

Marx's theory of alienation as an outcome of capitalism provides a basis for understanding the dynamics of abandonment in modern soci-eties and dissociative feelings associated with it. While he does not sub-scribe to the theological problem of angst developed by Kierkegaard, he recognizes how individual autonomy under capitalism degenerates into atomization. The unhappy consciousness is not the price paid for reason, but the toll of capitalistic enterprise. For him the solution rests in a rearrangement of the means of production. The alienation generated by capitalism will be overcome only by a radical overhaul of society—one necessitating conflict. It is only through the resulting unity and commu-nity that reason and fairness can be served. To do this all workers need to assume responsibility for their own lives by attacking and nullifying the dehumanizing power of the bourgeoisie.

FREUD: FROM DRIVE THEORY TO OBJECT RELATIONS

Sigmund Freud's psychology was radical for its time, yet deeply influenced by European patriarchy. His thinking owes as much to modern philosophy and anthropology as it does to physical medicine. Freud's brilliance often involves his ability to comprehend how human biology and the interpersonal environment create the vicissitudes of mental life. There is little in Freud that connects to a utopian vision or celebrates the human potential or the human spirit. Progress for him is not measured, as Nietzsche had measured it, by one's ability to overcome obstacles with the power of the creative will. Freud's portrait of humanity is a Hobbesian one; he views the natural state of homo sapiens as vile and savage. Evil is innate to the human who is wolf-like in nature. For Freud, all civilization (to be read: instinct control) comes from patriarchal power in society. Yet, Freud's focus on innate aggression and the hidden power of sexual drives transformed social scientific thinking in the twentieth century. His explorations of the unconscious and his social construction of the "dark recesses" of the psyche forever changed the course of modern thought.

Freud's sociology of abandonment begins with a separation of the individual from society—an opposition of self and culture. Although he admits to not fully understanding it, he recognizes feelings of an oceanic connection of each to all, but rejects the religious implications of this.[15] He believes this sensation is rooted in human biology. Separation from one's mother through birth remains a primal force in each individual's life. The trauma of similar separations is repeated and experienced in many different ways. Freud posits that *Eros* is the ultimate quest to recapture this lost unity of oneness with mother. It is a libidinal desire for reconnection with nature. He asserts that human interconnectedness and, especially, the infant's dependence on a primary caregiver (most notably one's mother) are essentially physiological and related to species survival. In *Beyond the Pleasure Principle* (1920), he describes an eighteen-month-old child playing a game of self-amusement.[16] It is a game of *fort* (gone) and *da* (there). Freud observes the child throwing a cotton reel with a piece of string attached to it from his cot and uttering what Freud heard as "*fort*" (German for "gone"). Then pulling back on the string, which he hadn't released, he pulls the reel into his line of vision and cries "*da!*" or "there!" Freud suggests that this game prepared the child to experience his mother's absence and learn to develop a sense of what Piaget would later label object permanence. But beyond this Freud asserts that one's earliest understanding of separation was integrally connected to the development of language. Psychoanalyst Jacques Lacan would later expand on this idea by building upon Freud's most important observations.

Freud's focus on individuation was ground-breaking for the time in which he wrote and provided a core for much of his psychoanalytic theory. It is within this context that we gain insight into his contributions to theory of abandonment. Although not the first to emphasize abandonment, Freud gives it a central place in modern psychology. Separation anxiety (fear of being abandoned by one's mother) coupled with the oedipal fear of father's retribution become the essential mechanisms for male social control and the internalization of the parental superego. The anxiety associated with the loss of one's mother's love is related to one's biological survival.

As has already been noted, Kierkegaard laid much of the foundation for the psychoanalytic understanding of separation that would be further developed by Freud and his followers. He stressed the importance of early childhood separations from the caregiver and the creation of dread and guilt resulting from such a discontinuity. Unlike Kierkegaard, Freud's focus is on anxiety related to real biological dependancy needs rather than the dread of being unfettered to confront an existential abyss. He sees guilt as essentially oedipal in its origins and not necessarily connected to the destruction of traditional life, although he leaves room in his theory for this interpretation as well.

It should be recalled that Hegel had already established for psychology the concept of object relations as a means of understanding and assessing the dialectic of attachment and separation and, furthermore, assessing its psychological and social outcomes. Like Marx, Freud borrows many such concepts from anthropology and philosophy and translates them into immediate and practical concerns.[17] Object relations would eventually become an important component of psychoanalytic thought that could be distinguished from the more traditional concern with innate drive-related functions. For Freud the object was the target of all human drives and, therefore, the focus of all feelings. No drive could be expressed without the existence of an object as its target. Thus, Freud's theory of psychoanalysis was predicated on the relationship of each individual with objects (usually other individuals) in that person's life. Some of Freud's earliest efforts provide a modern social scientific framework that has helped to launch a more thorough exploration of object relations little of which is connected to orthodox drive-oriented suppositions.

While Freud, himself, did not fully develop this vein of psychoanalytic inquiry, he was among the first to draw attention to its importance in the emerging field of clinical psychology. His more formative ideas on object relations and their relationship to mental health and separation can be found in a 1917 paper entitled, "Mourning and Melancholia."[18] Here he links melancholy to a real life object loss. As already noted, melancholia was a malaise of disempowerment and disenchantment. Like hysteria , it became a catchall for a broad spectrum of convergence disorders and underlying dissociative feelings, but most particularly those having to do with desensitization and self-abuse. It had been vividly depicted by Goethe and the modern poets of romanticism. Although it was looked upon as essentially personal, it was broad in scope and could easily have been a response to rapid social and familial change brought on by capitalism and industrialization. It was related to personal estrangement and anomie, but was primarily a disorder of the bourgeoisie.[19]

Freud ignores much of the cultural history of melancholy and makes this disorder his own. Like hysteria, melancholy is taken from the realm of fashionable maladies of bourgeois sensibility—the focus of distressed young women, of poets, and artists into the scientific realm of psychiatric medicine and theoretical analysis. Underlying this disorder he sees an internal libidinal cathexis. In his 1917 article, he connects melancholy to grieving and loss. He distinguishes between a normal sorrow experienced as a result of the death of someone—a mourning that is worked through, and a mourning that doesn't go away. This is melancholy. Such a loss need not be the result of death but can stem from desertion, abandonment, and the like. For Freud all attachment to objects of desire is libidinal. When one loses an object of desire, the libido usually finds a external substitute. But in melancholy this is not the case. The libido is withdrawn back into the ego fusing the lost object to itself in an attempt to hold on to it. In melancholia there are harsh feelings toward the lost object that become internalized and turned against the self. The mourner develops negative feelings about the self that are actually displaced negative responses to the loss of the object—ambivalent feelings about the death, loss, or abandonment. Thus, to preserve a positive image of the lost other the mourner must identify with the other's ego, and direct negative feelings toward that internalization. Anger is turned against the self. It is in this essay that Freud showed how one's relationship with an object, here a loved one, changed the nature of one's psychic structure. Beyond this, Freud set into motion the construction of a whole range of theories that would be directed toward the psychology of abandonment and loss.

Over the years psychological theories of separation and abandonment have taken different forms, but most were built upon Freud's psychoanalytic model and were driven by object relations theory in psychology. Since much of it is constructed using real life examples of separation and loss and focuses on early childhood development, it has a particularly modern emphasis. Those who most contributed to this exploration have been classically trained British and European psychotherapists. It was not until the 1930s and later that many of these studies got underway. The work of Melanie Klein, Margaret Mahler, D. W. Winnicott, John Bowlby, Mary Ainsworth, Ronald Fairbairn, and others will be explored in the next chapter. Much of this work on separation and attachment helped to establish the importance of psychoanalysis in exploring modern abandonment concerns. But beyond this, it did little to explore the social and cultural dynamics that led to the conditions that would generate such feelings.

CRITICAL THEORY: ABANDONMENT AND THE DIALECTIC OF DOMINATION

The Frankfurt Institute for Social Research was founded by a German political scientist, Felix Weil, at the University of Frankfurt in 1922. As a collection of radical thinkers, its efforts were characterized by an all out attack on western positivism, the abuses of capitalism, and the failures of the Enlightenment. Beyond this, a prominent feature of the Institute was its fusing of radical Marxism and psychoanalytic thought.

Although Frankfurt intellectuals had their own particular research interests and agendas, they were all well versed in the concerns of modern western philosophy. A prime target of their collective criticism was the Enlightenment project, particularly the perversion of the Enlightenment ideal of reason and the separation of reason from nature. What connected these concerns to abandonment and related problems of interpersonal estrangement was a unique combination of psychoanalytic and Marxian analyses that examined the dissociating consequences of modern capitalism and the consumer culture it set loose. Capitalism and its totalizing forces of commodification were viewed as endangering the development of critical consciousness.

Frankfurt theory was a ruthless attack against the romance of modernity as well as those forces promoting domination, narcissism, sadomasochism, and control, which seemed to characterize much of modern life. It was especially an attack against the romance of traditionalism—the surrender of the self to a powerful leader. Because of an overriding concern with a loss of idealistic reason, and the crushing oppression of the human spirit inherent in the modern alienation, these theorists were frequently drawn to the analytic work of Marx, Freud, Weber, and Nietzsche to help in clarifying the social and psychological dimensions of social change. The connections the Frankfurt theorists made between domination, control, and feelings of abandonment were particularly significant. Although Erich Fromm and Herbert Marcuse are most renowned for their psychoanalytic and neo-Marxian approaches to this topic, Theodor Adorno and Max Horkheimer also made significant contributions to this line of thought. Having written more than twenty books in such areas as philosophy, aesthetics, sociology, psychology, and music, Theodor Adorno's most vehement attack was on the surrender of the individual to an inhuman, nonreflexive society. Like Max Weber, Adorno is disturbed by the disenchantment of the earth by a technocratic world view that was emerging. Both he and Max Horkheimer railed not only against Hitler and later Stalin, but also against modern capitalism and the bureaucratic state for its commodification of culture, society, and the individuals within it. Yet, unlike Horkheimer and Herbert Marcuse, Adorno rejects what he views as Hegel's romanticized notion of the whole. For him, there is no totality. His rejection of this wholism is combined with his rejection of grand, totalizing theory. Thus, he anticipates in his work some of the essential concerns espoused by leading existentialists as well as postmodern theorists. While he made extensive use of Marxism and psychoanalysis, he professed a disdain for all orthodoxy. Still, his work is heavily influenced by it.

Adorno proposed that the Oedipus complex plays a significant role in the development of the authoritarian personality. Borrowing from Freud, he suggests that the father's deflection of the son's libido from the mother prepares the child for submission to a super-patriarchal authority. This of course was a point that Fromm had reformulated and de-libidinalized in his most popular work *Escape from Freedom* (1944).[20] Furthermore, Adorno proposes that by postponing libidinal pleasure of the child and, eventually, confining that pleasure to the genitals, the rest of the child's body is purposely freed-up to become a complete instrument of labor exploitation. This notion came primarily from a reformulation of Wilhelm Reich's thesis contained in *The Mass Psychology of Fascism*, which seemingly had a very significant influence on the Frankfurt school.[21]

For Adorno, the breakdown of the patriarchal familial order and the subsequent emasculation of the father by powerful forces outside of the family, led young men to seek stronger authority figures in society—perhaps even in Hitler. Thus authoritarianism emerges from social changes that move the individual to want to be connected to an external domineering force in order to feel a sense of security in an insecure world—a world wherein traditional order was disintegrating. The fears of disconnectedness and abandonment seemed to rest at the core of this self-surrender to external controls. Adorno was to later suggest, in his postwar *The Authoritarian Personality* (1950) that cold and distant fathers were a significant factor in creating a sense of aloneness and insecurity in many German children.[22] The unresolved oedipal issues, which were converted into suppressed anger, would be played out in society in sadistic and masochistic practices. But the psychoanalytic interpretation of authoritarianism was most thoroughly developed by Erich Fromm who had taken considerable exception to Freud's biologism.

Fromm, a trained psychoanalyst who had worked closely with Freud's inner circle, articulated a particularly sociological perspective grounded in psychoanalytic and neo-Marxian theory. In rejecting the essence of Freud's "innate drives" thesis as the basis of human behavior, Fromm suggested that although the Oedipus complex did exist in the west and exerted substantial influence on parent-child interactions, it was not the source of most insecurities. Predicting more modern theorists, including such feminists as Jessica Benjamin, Nancy Chodorow, and Judith Butler, Fromm suggests that ego development is pre-oedipal, and issues of early caregiver–child connectedness lay the groundwork for autonomy, dependence, and powerful feelings of insecurity.

Fromm did not accept Freud's assertion that sex drives and innate destructive urges were the primary architects of personality. He found himself at odds with other critical theorists in this respect, particularly with Herbert Marcuse, who took a more orthodox psychoanalytic approach. Fromm insisted that people are cultural beings and primarily products of their social and emotional environments. He suggests that the root of abandonment anxiety rests in the ontological process of human individuation, not in biologically programmed drives. A staunch defender of reason, he suggests that one's psychic and social resistance to personal growth is to be found both in the repressive elements of one's primary ties and in one's culture. For him, such ties merely represent the values of society. They stand in the way of spontaneity, independence, and reason. Instead of fostering creativity, modern bureaucratic societies stifle it. In an individual's groping for maturity, there is the trade-off of freedom for security that prevented the individual's full development. One might cling tenaciously to one's primary caregiver for a sense of security until one adequately matured enough to seek a life of relative autonomy.

Taking his lead from Kierkegaard, Fromm posits the notion that freedom can mean feelings of isolation, insecurity, doubt, powerlessness, and dread. How one comes to terms with this freedom and these feelings fosters either a retreat from freedom into the knowing security of totalitarian patriarchy, or an advance into self-development and self-awareness. According to Fromm, much of history has been characterized by gradual personal advancement punctuated by episodic retreats. Like most critical theorists, he suggests that culture, not biology, is the primary architect of repressive socialization. Insecurities are not innate but inbred. He goes as far as to suggest that the individual in modern society has been psychologically and socially conditioned to fear otherness and to desire security above all else and, under capitalism, to see oneself as a unit of another's production—a means to an end. For Fromm the insecurities inherent in modern societies frequently contribute to the development of authoritarian personalities and eventually to the social development of police states. Destruction or control of otherness, not sublation, become the primary strategies for dealing with the new. Not only is there a lack of synthesis and a failure to recognize interdependencies, not only is there no internalization and personal growth, but also there is both suspicion and disdain for those who are different and, especially, those who are dependent. He proposed that culture of capitalism fosters this disdain and promotes a premature process of individuation and independence, which in turn leads to suspicion of otherness and a narcissistic craving for control. Strangers and immigrants are viewed as dangerous and are to be kept under strict surveillance.

Fromm is among the first to suggest that not just fascist Germany but most modern societies, particularly capitalistic ones, produce and support cultural narcissism and self-loathing. This position would be more fully developed by other social theorists including Richard Sennett and Christopher Lasch in the 1970s.[23] Early childhood socialization practices in societies characterized by heightened individualism and materialism appear to be guided by disdain for dependencies and interdependencies as well as an irrational fear of otherness. Furthermore, in his work Fromm sees a suppression of critical thinking and a substitution of media-generated thought that begins in early childhood. In modern societies success is measured not by achievement, but by manipulation. Early in life one gains an appreciation of the power of manipulation. Mass media become important instruments of control.[24]

Echoing Fromm and Adorno, Herbert Marcuse suggests that people are socialized by a totalizing capitalistic system prior to the development of the ego. Marcuse asserts that it becomes the basis for "one dimensionality"—signaling the collapse of reflection and discourse. The one dimensional society is driven by the need for sameness and order that is inherent in modern production and consumption.[25] Under market capitalism, the production of commodity needs shapes all individual values and ideals. The unhappy conscience, of which Hegel spoke—the doubt and despair associated with separation—give way to a "happy consciousness." The commodity economy creates a myth of orderliness and homogenization. There is an escape into what he terms "affirmative culture" which both helps to enslave and perpetuate the existing economic order. A world of beauty, happiness, and freedom is created that is entirely separate from work-a-day civilization. It is accessible to all with money. It is a "free spirit within an enslaved body." It is an escapist, anti-revolutionary world. It is a world of make-believe.

Insecurity in this world is addressed by attaching to consumables messages of happiness and security. Thus, consumer products help to construct an artificial reality and a nonthreatening culture of banality. Here people seek fulfillment by attaching themselves to consumer products that invariably alienate them further from one another. Authentic needs, such as self-actualizing ones, are repressed and artificial needs are created that can be satisfied only in the marketplace. These needs that are substitutes for authentic ones are imposed by the machinery of mass media advertising. Their satisfaction is often seen as compensation for alienated, unfulfilling work. Marcuse developed the notion of "repressive de-sublimation" to describe both the repression of libidinal desires and the substitution of nonthreatening false consumer needs that can only be satisfied in the marketplace.[26] Here those aspects of one's humanity that are denied in alienated work: eroticism, nature, self-empowerment, spontaneity, adventure, and the like are infused into various consumer products by advertisers. The consumer purchases not only a product but attempts to recapture a part of the self that has been repressed and denied. Since the fulfillment of one's true needs (the recapturing of these alienated aspects of life including love) are not available in the market, there is a perpetual quest to find those commodities that will make the self whole. In formulating this thesis Marcuse not only drew upon Hegel's notion of sublation, but on Marx's notion of commodity fetishism, combining the two. Still, several of his important insights, particularly his work on consciousness and commodification, can be traced to the work of Georg Lukács.[27]

For Marcuse the control of sexuality has much to do with the control of the forces of production under capitalism.[28] Unlike Adorno, Marcuse is drawn to the romance of wholism. Building on Freud's work, he views *Eros* as having enormous potential for human liberation. However, given the needs of mass market capitalism *Eros* is forced to give way to a combination of genital sex and commodity consumption, thus relegating sexual relations to mechanical, commodified activities. Since the full liberation of *Eros* involves an integrative, dynamic, sensual, and material existence as well as a drive toward self-actualization by breaking down the boundaries of otherness, it also poses a danger to market capitalism. Life and sex become counterfeit experiences wherein feeling is segregated from reason. Sensation eclipses love and one's need for human connectedness. For Marcuse, sex has a revolutionary potential. However, it has been co-opted by capitalistic enterprise. Sex's repression is aimed at the further exploitation of labor. Freud's reality principle, that which requires repression for the furtherance of civilization, is converted to a performance principle wherein the libido is made into an instrument of alienated labor.

Critical theorists such as Adorno, Horkheimer, Fromm, and Marcuse attempted to show that the individual was controlled and manipulated in modern societies by forces of individual and corporate greed. Individual estrangement, an inherent byproduct of modern bureaucratic capitalism, helped to foster a suspicion if not a distrust of otherness and a disdain for weakness while promoting one-dimensionality. Hyperrationality furthered the process of dehumanization. The consumer economy was predicated on a denial and a distortion of authentic human needs. Critical theory saw the individual as dominated and controlled by forces that promised security and happiness. The price paid for such a happy conscience was the denial of one's personal awareness, personal development, and connectedness to the natural world.

HEIDEGGER AND SARTRE: ABANDONMENT AND EXISTENTIALISM

Existentialism shares many of the same influences as critical social theory. While having its intellectual roots in the work of Kierkegaard and Nietzsche the modern existential movement can be traced not only to the *fin-de-siècle* Europe, but also to the unsettling aftermath of World War I and a shift away from the perception that the western world was on a positive, unstoppable trajectory of development and progress. The horrors of the First World War brought a new sense of pessimism emphasizing the fleeting and volatile nature of European civilization. A great suspicion arose relative to the value of science and technology and the roles they would play in the future. Oswald Spengler's *Decline of the West*, published in 1919, warned of hidden dangers inherent in modernization.

In some ways, especially in its emphasis on anxiety, despair, and detachment existentialism was a response to these events. On an intellectual level it was heavily indebted to the phenomenology of Edmund Husserl and his analysis of the subjective processes of consciousness and essences. At the root of Husserl's work is a drive to delineate the underlying structure of consciousness and the world it created by examining the information gathered by the senses. Phenomenology was a rejection of the old-world metaphysics of certainty and the shallow romance of positivist science. From this was to emerge an existentialism that focused on the problem of being rather than knowledge.

Martin Heidegger, a prized student of Husserl, published *Being and Time (Sein und Zeit)* in 1927. Heidegger's work helped to establish a foundation for this new philosophy of existence. While he later claimed not to have been an existentialist at all, he provided an existential agenda by concentrating on such questions as "what it is to be" and "how it is to be." In this sense he developed the essential elements of his ontology—his theory of Being. In *Being and Time*, he asserts that it is his project to go beyond traditional metaphysics and develop his focus on "Being as such." This is quite different, he asserts, than the totality of being, that is the concern of traditional metaphysics and which goes beyond the being of mankind. He is particularly concerned with the being of people yet views this as part of a vast Being. It is the traditional philosophical quest to find the last abstraction underlying all objects in the world. Traditional metaphysics leaves behind an existent world to find an ultimate truth, substance, or process. In its search it establishes a hierarchy of being and equates Being with the sum total of all being. For Heidegger the essence of this being can never be fully deduced—being as a whole is concealed. The only knowledge we can ever hope to achieve is the immediate being of people. While there are other forms of being: the being of things, the being of animals, the being of ways of thought, only humans truly exist. These other beings remain at our disposal. These are things seen, things created by our own Being. Thus, through our existence we bring things into being by making them visible, giving them essence, naming them.

Heidegger's search for the meaning of being takes seriously the phenomena of everyday experience, of the transiency of life, and attempts to discover the meaning of these experiences by relating them to Being. Thus the individual, apart from some system of platonic understanding, is the only path to knowledge and truth. Only through the individual can Being be discovered. While the individual is an object among other objects, he or she alone occupies a special place amongst them. Only the human individual can be concerned with making connections between all objects. Only he or she needs to be connected to the world by being-in-the world, and therefore asking the question "What does it mean to be?"

Dasein, which can be translated from the German to mean "being there," is used by Heidegger to represent existence of the person himself or herself who has the potential to know and understand, to ask questions relative to its own existence—its own being. Only *Dasein* has capacity to have a knowing existence, which Heidegger refers to as authenticity. He or she can exist like other beings, other objects, or can become authentic. Thus only the authentic essence or *Dasein* can experience Being. To be aware of being involves the whole person, body, mind, and spirit, not merely a Hegelian "pure consciousness." *Dasein* is likened to a closed, darkened window. Only through authentic existence can it be opened.

Heidegger's existential notion of abandonment centers on our being-thrown-into-the-world, into a complex and frightening world, without our consent. Each individual experiences anxiety and the dread of aloneness and nothingness. These feelings are associated with our abandonment and are not the result of some maladjustment. They are part of the basic human disposition, which grips the entire person making one aware of his or her estrangement from Being, making one feel threatened. However, it is out of this aloneness and abandonment that emerge liberating forces challenging the individual to make the world his or her own, to lead a life open to Being and authenticity. Thus the self must become central to the human experience. Taking care of the self, *Dasein Sorge*, is a sign that the individual recognizes his or her threatened existence, and recognizes the tension between venturing forth into the unknown and going back to a comfortable life of everdayness. This idea of rapprochement will later be taken up in theories of individual development in psychology. Because one is flung into this world each individual understands that its being is limited only by death. The movement toward death is eventually accepted as inevitable. This is what Heidegger refers to as "being-toward-death" or "the crucial fact of nothingness." However, anxiety is increased by this movement toward death as we are required to define ourselves through our decisions. While there is a fear of change, still the existentialist's worst sin is a failure to define oneself using free will. Poor choices or a failure to choose results in existential guilt. Time hovers over us. We are constantly moving from our futures to our pasts, from our hopes and dreams to our regrets, memories, and remorses. This is what Heidegger refers to as ecstasy of time.

Heidegger views humankind as in a crisis resulting from the "fall" or *verfall*. For him this fall represents alienation from the world, which has been promoted and intensified by technocratic objectification resulting from capitalistic industrialization. This moves us further away from the potential of *Dasein*. We are endangered of being submerged or absorbed by the things surrounding us—becoming a "no one" or *Das Man*. In becoming such we lose our path to authenticity, we measure ourselves only with reference to our peers. Our thoughts are confined, directed to and by others, we constantly crave new things or novelties, engage only in small talk. We have no genuine relationship to others.

Heidegger recognizes key modes of existence or *existentiala*, that he presents for consideration. While any significant presentation and analysis of these would be beyond the scope of this work, it is important to mention at least one at this point. While *Dasein Sorge* has already been mentioned in terms of self-care, it is important to connect it to the discussion of how death defines life. *Dasein Sorge* requires "being-in-the-world. It requires an acknowledgment of what Heidegger views as the artificial separation of subject and object proposed under positivism. Furthermore, it necessitates an understanding of the total interdependencies of the world. From this position of self-care one must be able to relate oneself to persons and things surrounding him or her, to see the self as an integrated part of the whole, to find connection with someone or something outside of the self. It means a caring for the self by directing one's own life through fulfilling one's physical and emotional needs. As with Kierkegaard, Heidegger believed the existence of a physical body preceded the existence of self. At some point in the development process one becomes aware of his or her own existence, thus for humans essence and existence do not appear simultaneously—existence precedes essence.

Despite some of these defining existential elements of his work, Heidegger refused the label of existentialist. Jean-Paul Sartre, on the other hand, welcomed this designation. He popularized the term and wrote extensively on the subject. His life was dedicated to the ideas expressed in this philosophy of existence. Though trained as a teacher of philosophy, his short stories, plays, and critical cultural essays won him even greater renown as a *littérateur*—particularly his award winning works such as *Nausea* (1938) and *No Exit* (1944). However, *Being and Nothingness (L'Etre et le Néant)*, published in 1943, was to bring him considerable fame as a philosopher. Yet it was only one of his several important philosophical works.

Sartre was very much influenced by both Husserl and Heidegger. He was in complete agreement with Heidegger's assertion that being is central to existence and that existence precedes essence. Thus, people must first exist and then create their own essences by throwing themselves into the world, suffering, struggling, and defining themselves therein. Humans are viewed as the only sentient beings on earth—forced to define who they are through living. Still, Sartre was significantly more radical in his thought and life than Heidegger and was an avowed humanist. He rejected the latter's belief in Being as the basis of all beings, finding this notion to be too deistic and mystical.

Sartre rejects the notion that the world harbors some hidden, comprehensive meaning apart from that given it by each person. His motif of abandonment suggests that there is no meaning or purpose; that life is absurd; and that we are abandoned in a world to look after ourselves completely. We are *outsiders* in a world of objects and due to our consciousness must struggle to give ourselves meaning. It is this sense of detachment, forlornness, separation, and abandonment that characterizes the condition of the modern individual according to Sartre. Acts of consciousness make individuals aware of their aloneness; yet each moment of consciousness creates meaning for both the self and the world. In a sea of nonthinking, nonreflexive objects—objects existing only in themselves (*en soi*)—only people can exist for themselves (*pour soi*), and form their own identities. This artistic, creative potential to *become* is the central value in Sartre's existentialism.

Thus the struggle in life is one between being and becoming—living as a thing and living as an existent. It is much more comfortable to be a thing—to be *en soi*. As such one is not forced to make something of life but instead may live it as an object among other objects. Sartre believes that inherent in this position is a resort to *mauvaise foi*, or bad faith. This is an attempt to escape the anguish of becoming by pretending that we are not free at all. To this end there are ready excuses. This is a life of inauthenticity, an estrangement from what one can be. However, there is a nothingness that haunts all conscious beings and an awareness of this can bring one to act. This nothingness is situated in the realization of our abandonment, our aloneness, our death. This nothingness is the essence of all Being; it is the only certainty. Out of it emerges all potential including *pour soi*.

In the world of Being we fight against our reactionary impulses to escape our personal freedom which is the source of our deepest anxiety. There is a real sense of aloneness in this struggle—a sense of abandonment or forlornness, which is always experienced in our solitary struggles for authenticity. "That is what abandonment implies," says Sartre, "is that we ourselves decide our being. And with this abandonment goes anxiety."[29] Authentic existence can only be achieved and realized in our absolute freedom—in our actions that bring meaning to our lives and give us a sense of authenticity. It is only through our actions, not our thoughts and dreams, that we enter into a personal transcendence—we transcend what we were, we surpass what was yesterday and enter into a perpetual becoming.

While there are real intellectual differences between Sartre and Heidegger the clearest difference might best be seen in the lives they led. Heidegger, who claimed not to have been an existentialist, found himself accepting a world created by Hitler and eagerly joined the Nazi Party, working to protect his position in the university while his Jewish colleagues and their families became exiles or were put to death in concentration camps. While other intellectuals fled Germany, he never disavowed the Third Reich, Nazism, nor his cooperation with authorities. Much of his later life was that of a relative recluse. His existentialism in many ways complemented the fascism that emphasized a type of grand totalism. Sartre, on the other hand, fought the Nazis and became a prisoner of war. Upon his release, he joined the French resistance, became a journalist, attached himself to liberation movements around the world in the 1960s, and dedicated his life to art and to social change. Sartre proudly admitted to his existentialism.

Existentialism must be viewed as a powerful intellectual and artistic force of the twentieth century because it resonated with modernity. It reflected a sense of abandonment and aloneness felt by those struggling to make sense of their world, those who rejected the notion that the world was ordered, determined and intelligible to the contemplative observer. It was a highly individualistic philosophy that could have only emerged in western, capitalistic societies.

POST-STRUCTURALISM AND POSTMODERNITY

One cannot discuss postmodernity without locating its roots in structuralism and post-structuralism of the 1960s. Structuralism is of course nothing new. But the structuralism of the 1960s or the so-called "linguistic turn" represented a retreat of sorts. Leading up to this theoretical turn was an era of social activism seemingly unprecedented in modern western history and then an increasing dissatisfaction with its outcomes on the part of a growing number of intellectuals. The year 1968 seems to have been a watershed in this regard.[30] It was marked both by an increase in violent protests and a splintering of radical politics into factions of interest. Many intellectuals became disheartened. Some perceived increasing limits to the power of social action; others feared the power such action unleashed in the masses. This dramatically altered the way many looked at the world.

Structuralism and later poststructuralism were both intellectual withdrawals from involvement in the social world. They were marked by a turning inward. The emphasis on internal structures—structures of the mind, the structure of language suggested a retreat from the existent world of Sartre. Most significantly structuralism looked at the power of language and de-emphasized the centrality of the activist as an instrument of change. According to Robert Hollinger: "Structuralism rejects the philosophy of the subject and the view of human agency and history that is central to critical theory and other modern versions of humanism."[31] To this end many intellectuals turned to nonhumanistic theory for inspiration. There was a significant appreciation of the work of Swiss linguistical theorist Ferdinand de Saussure (1857–1913) who proposed that language shaped all thought and, therefore, all action. Since language was structured by laws, one could work to discern these. By taking language apart and examining it as a system of signs and signifiers, one could better understand human action. Many others built upon this theory. Claude Levi-Strauss, the French anthropologist, used Saussure's ideas to illuminate the workings of systems of consciousness and thought. He applied Saussure's concepts to his study of tribal societies and myths. In fact he broadened Saussure's ideas and envisioned these so-called structures as something apart from the realm of logical consciousness—more connected to a primitive unconsciousness. These deep structures determined most human relationships. Levi-Strauss, along with a host of others ranging from Lacan to Althusser, prepared the way for a poststructuralism and later postmodernism.

Briefly, poststructuralism is today associated with the work of Jacques Derrida and Michel Foucault among others. Sociologist Charles Lemert traces the origins of poststructuralism to a paper given by Jacques Derrida in 1966.[32] Derrida embarked on a program of language, "deconstruction," in which he proposed that all language is unstable and that words have no definite meaning in themselves, thus rejecting this notion of internal laws and structures. His aim has been to debunk western logocentrism—a search for ultimate meaning and truth found in a universal system of words. Every word, he claims, is pregnant with its own opposition—the opposite of its normally recognized meaning. For him and many other poststructuralists language is not the unambiguous carrier of truth as it was once thought to be, but rather the generator of truth, and the harbinger of all distortion.[33] Yet, Derrida proposes that "there is nothing outside of the text," meaning that all we can ever know is in text, and that all a text can ever refer to is another text. Thus knowledge can only be contingent.

Foucault's project on the other hand was aimed at understanding the relationship between power and discourse. Foucault's work views knowledge as a mechanism of control and domination. His scholarly investigations range widely from topics dealing with the history of human sexuality to the development of mental hospitals and prisons. Foucault is particularly concerned with how knowledge is produced, and takes a special interest in the role of reason in the processes of modernization and domination. The work of both of these men frequently bleeds through the paper-thin boundary separating their ideas from postmodernism.

Innovative studies and critiques of this new global culture, whatever it might be called, have directed the recent work of a broad spectrum of cultural critics, architects, philosophers, historians, artists, and social scientists. That we live in a postmodern world as opposed to a modern one has been an issue of intense intellectual debate. The whole notion of postmodernity remains highly suspect in many intellectual circles, and is considered by some as nothing more than a faddish academic construct, but one that has held sway since the 1970s. In many respects, postmodern social theory continues to explore some of the Frankfurt school concerns, and maintains a relationship to elements of classical theory. In keeping with the critical tradition, postmodern thinkers make no pretense at establishing a comprehensive world-view. They reject both positivism and totalism and pursue a study of fragmented culture. In their social and cultural assessments the individual is frequently seen as characterized by a happy consciousness, segmentalized, atomized, and dominated by a growing, unseen impersonal power that is at once global and intimate. The dark pessimism of Adorno and other critical theorists is frequently transformed into a fatalistic new discourse wherein there is no center, no history, no humanism, no reason, no truth, no escape. For many postmodernists there is no substance, no ideology, no freedom. There is only the atomized, the superficial, the pastiche, the simulacra, the prison.

An array of intellectuals has gathered to form the vanguard of postmodern theory construction. The notables comprise a diverse group of social theorists profoundly influenced by poststructuralism, hermeneutics, and linguistic theory. While the methodologies of these theorists vary greatly, postmodern thought frequently builds upon a heritage of Hegel, Marx, Freud, and Nietzsche while rejecting many of the essential elements of each. It borrows generously from poststructuralism. Important thematic concerns focus on commodification, dehumanization, and social control. Culture is often viewed as fragmented, people seen as superficial, and the world is looked upon as a commodified global shopping mall. One has a choice of either finding joy in this by treating it lightly (which necessitates treating oneself lightly) and assuming a happy consciousness, or suffering a life of alienation, dehumanization, and angst. For Bauman anxiety and loss have contributed to the conceptualization of postmodernity by those intellectuals who have helped to construct the paradigm.[34] Still, abandonment remains a powerful symbol in postmodern discourse and serves to define it.[35]

Where modern theorists depicted the world in terms of binary relationships—left and right, freedom and totalitarianism, the civilized and savage—many postmodernists and poststructuralists see no distinctions. Their apolitical tone and disregard for the Enlightenment project is as unnerving to many conservative thinkers as it is to progressive humanists. Here the dualisms of the twentieth century are crushed, demystified by hermeneutics or subjective interpretive devices that have displaced more traditional forms of Cartesian empiricism, which itself is viewed as a primitive ideology. In a Hegelian sense, totalitarianism and freedom are viewed as two sides of the same coin, like mastery and bondage. In the postmodern world language has lost its power as a tool of reason and has become an instrument of control. Thus, it has become suspect. All history is "metanarrative"—text based upon text, recollection, and testimony. The importance of it is diminished in the postmodern world. It is eclipsed by the *pastiche*—stylized ideation of the past. Similarly, the importance of time and space is significantly diminished by technology as information flows transcontinentally in an instant and propinquity disappears into postmodern networks.[36] Linguistics occupies a central place in organizing knowledge in both postmodern and post-structural theory as these paradigms morph one into the other. Since all language is ideological, many of these new theorists contend that there can be no objectivity. Every word requires an examination of the context in which it is placed and the values that underlie it.

The intersections of knowledge, language, and power become central to postmodern theory. Those who control the organization and flow of language (including signs) control its meaning. With it they construct societies to their own liking. Language, instead of being a liberating force, can be seen as a tool of oppression. For Lacan and others it is a mechanism of personal alienation and dissociation.[37] Jean Baudrillard makes extensive use of this notion in his critique of consumer culture and the signs inherent in commodities. He draws not only from Marx, Veblen, and Marcuse, but also makes extensive use of semiology in developing his understanding of how commodities construct and dominate social and emotional life. Following up on Marcuse's notion of desublimation, Baudrillard views consumer capitalism as based on the human need to fill a void generated by an alienating and oppressive cultural and economic system.[38] Although radical to its roots, Baudrillard's theories, themselves, are often presented as pop-culture commodities in cartoonish commercialized paperbacks.

Disturbing to many on the left is the fact that a large number of postmodern theorists seem to retreat from the forces of control, or surrender to them without so much as a pretense of resistance. Acutely nihilistic, some postmodern theorists appear to display significant disdain for those on the left, for their programs of political or social action aimed at amelioration, and for their grand utopian visions and revolutionary spirit. They often appear to be content writing colorful academic descriptions of the postmodern *Titanic* as it sinks into a sea of dehumanization and banality. There appears to be too much consensus among these theorists that issues of social justice are completely subjective and, therefore, can never be addressed rationally and that revolutionary solutions are at best romantic illusions. Therefore, the very nature of postmodern analysis often appears to be a happy surrender to the forces of oppression. It is a finding of contentment and transcendence in slavery—an idea that was very much Hegel's and, ironically, the German romantics. Although it builds on the Marxian critique of capitalism, it does not see the slightest hope for a reversal of the conditions that seem to bring about dehumanizing inequalities. Thus postmodern theory serves, in some respects, as an example of the abandonment it describes.

However, there is within it a wealth of quiet radicalism. It is the potential of postmodern theory that appeals to many. While Fredric Jameson sees postmodernity as the highest stage of capitalism and, therefore, the generator of this new disquieting way of life, he also recognizes its liberating potential as an aesthetic—opening up new vistas or landscapes by attacking the established forms of bourgeois high modernism.[39] Douglas Kellner and Ben Agger have each noted the potential avenues of radical exploration of postmodern thought. Kellner sees postmodernity as possibly formulating a new critique of this late stage of capitalism, taking up the agenda of critical theory.[40] Ben Agger concurs: "Postmodernism offers Marxism and feminism an internal method of self-interrogation with which to examine fossilized assumptions about the nature of oppression and freedom."[41]

CONCLUSION

Each of these approaches helped to establish the importance of abandonment as a modern metaphor for a burgeoning intellectual and artistic elite. Separation, objectification, and commodification emerged as powerful components of modern and postmodern life that produced a strong sense of social isolation and loss. The landscape of abandonment is vividly depicted in these conceptualizations.

While these theorists and their respective speculations contribute to the overall imagery of abandonment in modern and postmodern intellectual life, their work also reflects strong Eurocentric proclivities and biases. The detachment and aloneness expressed in their work have a particular relationship to the western focus on individualism that was influenced by the Protestant Reformation, early modern capitalism, and the Enlightenment.[42] While most people in the world were still living in closely bound communal arrangements on "far away, exotic continents," relatively few lived in modern capitalistic cities—the centers of intellectual life, communications, and trade—places characterized by separation, rationality, commodification, and alienation. It must be recalled that as Hegel was writing, European cities were experiencing child abandonment of immense proportions.[43] The new economic arrangements were revolutionizing social relationships. Early modernity was exemplified by human transience, a great influx of the destitute into cities, and an increase in the spread of contagious diseases. The disparity between rich and poor, country and city became more obvious. Land divisions and peasant dispossession were not unrelated to that which was on the minds of poets, philosophers, and artists of the time. The ascendency of nation-states was ushered in on a wave of religious bloodbaths, witch-hunts, wars, and colonial atrocities, including genocide of indigenous peoples around the globe. Still, many sought understanding by turning inward to a world of abstraction and imagination.

For the most part bourgeois landscape artists of the eighteenth century, as well as the naturalist poets, directed vision away from the felled forests, polluted waterways, and smoke-blackened skies. Their work presented pristine and majestic nature-scapes, exalted mountain ranges reaching into the clouds, flowering open pastures and grand flowing rivers. Sometimes raw, at other times pastoral and refined, the landscape overpowered the individual. It was something still left to be conquered. This was in essence part of both Kant's and Burke's notion of the sublime. This aesthetic grew as a response to feelings of powerlessness and aloneness in the world. It combined the sense of being overpowered by something outside of the self, often something unseen, with an unfathomed feeling of freedom and yet remoteness. Sublimity was often a melancholy withdrawal, a detached perspective, and inner consternation while recognizing the potential for transcendence. Abandonment was captured in many of these intellectual landscapes.

The nineteenth and twentieth centuries produced great artistic responses to social upheavals and major wars. These were accompanied by a retreat from realism. The First and Second World Wars brought about a significant displacement, dislocation, and re-evaluation of those hopes for enlightened progress that guided Europe and those of European descent. Here the artistic works of the surrealists, particularly the surrealistic landscapes of Magritte, Ernst, Dali, and de Chirico reflected melancholy and dread associated with aloneness. The years between the wars produced new fears, new forms of estrangement that helped give rise to fascism. History spelled out the strains of alienation and separation, which were wedded to the process of modernization and the culture of postmodern capitalism.

The discovery of Auschwitz and Treblinka and the use of the atomic bomb to hasten the War's end turned away all hope of reason. The nation-state and its commercial interests had not only become the machinery of genocide but also the tool of colonization of both the farthermost reaches of the world and the innermost depths of the psyche.

Chapter 3

Psychology of Separation and Loss

The images of personal isolation and estrangement captured in the art and literature of the shadowy decades between the wars were neither intellectual fabrications nor flights of fancy. They were credible, impressionistic, renderings of modern life. While artists, writers, and social philosophers committed this imagery to canvas and paper, social scientists also constructed images of desolate human landscapes in their work. Psychologists particularly popularized the abandonment motif. Freud and those who followed him posited the notion that a malaise of anxiety, which was endemic to modern life, could be directly traced to the child's dread of abandonment.

This chapter critically explores the psychological renderings of separation and abandonment. Various interpretations of abandonment anxiety are presented and placed into a cultural context. In so doing, this chapter draws upon the lives of those whose work significantly influenced the establishment of an aesthetic of dread and alienation in modern life. It points to the connection between modern culture and the aloneness produced in individualistic societies, and the themes of separation and loss that emerge from modernity and capitalistic accumulation.

MELANCHOLY AND MODERNITY

Beginning in the sixteenth century, a rash of books on melancholy made their appearance in Europe.[1] By the seventeenth century, most

notably with the publication of Robert Burton's *Anatomy of Melancholy*
in 1621, the state of personal detachment was elevated to the position of
an aesthetic, finding its way into the hearts and minds of philosophers
and poets. Not solely a physical malady (characterized by an excess of
black bile), nor necessarily a psychological disorder (with frequent or
lengthy despondency), melancholy began to be defined as a sentiment
endemic to modernity. Inherent in Burton's description of the melancholy condition is a depressive withdrawal from society, a sense of abandonment, and an aloneness that stirs anxiety and sadness. Melancholia,
asserted Burton, was everywhere—from royal families to the court
poets, artists, and clowns. It was frequently connected to the creative
temperament. Thus melancholy was viewed not just as a depressive and
destructive force but a potential means of self-reflection and transcendence, an emotional separation or psychic break from the pressures of
daily existence.

Burton's book, brought to press eight times between 1621 and 1676
and re-released many times subsequently, became a staple in bourgeois
libraries and households throughout Europe. Translated into German
and other languages melancholy became an important feature of Kant's
notion of the sublime, Hegel's concept of alienation, and Kierkegaard's
idea of dread.[2] Beyond this, Engels refers to *Anatomy of Melancholy* as
filling him with "horror" and cites the work as "one of the most serious
psychological treaties of the eighteenth century."[3] It had definitely
influenced the work of Lord Byron, Samuel Johnson, and Charles
Lamb. In fact, the romanticism of Goethe and Schelling owed much to
Burton's work.

Literature and art of this period often reflected this quality of retreat
into a position of despondency. This was indeed present in the works of
the German romantics, particularly the work of landscape artists. In
1796 Johann Georg Zimmermann published *Solitude Considered* in
which he celebrated the romance of aloneness. Feelings of isolation, separation, and abandonment, he asserted, can be viewed as central to solitude, which can be considered in some ways regenerative; these
sensations can be sought in nature. Zimmerman urges the writer to "segregate himself off from people, to seek out the woods and forests, to
withdraw completely into himself."[4] Creative opportunities avail themselves by such detachment. He goes on: "A sort of sweet melancholy
overcomes us in the lap of rural tranquility when viewing all nature's
beauty . . . [*and*] solitude on occasion, but of course not always, transforms deep despondency into sweet melancholy."[5]

Sociologist Wolf Lepenies in *Melancholy and Society*, assesses how
the idea of melancholy became emblematic of modernity. In examining

its origin and development he attempts to understand its cultural meaning, historical manifestations, and sociological dynamics. He looks at its importance in defining modern life and early psychology. In his work, he cites Hans Hoff's classic study of the changing images of melancholy over the centuries and its common use in the area of mental health.[6] Lepenies posits the notion that the psychic withdrawal associated with melancholy was a response to changing social conditions. Certainly the rise of capitalism and the emergence of the modern family were part of this. While the clinical definition of melancholia emphasized a "retreat into an isolated ego," certain life circumstances sparked this sort of response. Among those factors considered by Hoff and Lepenies are breeches in mother–child relationships as well as other social structural changes. Yet, melancholy is seen more generally as an impaired coping with the world and represents a retreat from it.[7] Bourgeois melancholy, particularly, accompanied a retreat from communal life and a rise of individual solitude. Foucault, who views melancholy as a consequence of historic cultural forces points out that the modern world became less and less tolerant of melancholy, viewing it as something non-rational.[8] In fact, any overt expression of affect might be deemed to be a sign of insanity. Where emotional life was earlier an integrated aspect of one's public persona and a mode of human expression, in modern society it became something to be hidden away. "At the end of the eighteenth century," notes Foucault, "all forms of madness without delirium, but characterized by inertia, despair, by a sort of dull stupor, would be readily classified as melancholia."[9] Any sign of strong affect, including but not limited to that of a depressive state, needed to be carefully monitored and controlled. The asylum provided a place for confinement of the most expressive of these emotional states, the family was a place for less offensive ones.

Modern psychology sought the causes of emotional disturbances, melancholy, hysteria, and other pathologies in the interpersonal relations of the group and the hidden recesses of the unconscious. Seldom did it look to the broader social structure although this would have been a logical place to begin. Those who were political or too sociological in this sense were immediately censured by the profession for over-stepping their bounds. This was particularly true with psychoanalysis that had always worked to conceal its radical political roots.[10] Thus psychology made melancholy a personal malady despite the fact that it was based in culture, gender, and social class.

Melancholy was seen clinically as a retreat into the self—a type of self-absorption and emotional despair. Yet, this turning inward corresponded to the ebbing of a public expressiveness and the emergence of family as the primary arena for emotional expression and intimacy. Psychoanalysis, therefore, sought the causes of melancholy not in the world, but rather in the family. Lepenies points out that Freud's classic paper on mourning and melancholia attributed melancholy to an actual loss of an object (usually a familial loved one), ambivalence (a struggle between grief and hate primarily familial in nature), and regression of the libido to the ego, resulting in guilt ("the shadow of the object fell upon the ego" or introjection). He suggests that Freud attempted to move melancholy a step further from sociological analysis by assuming that it is constituted by an internal dilemma of the ego.[11]

The melancholic eventually became indistinguishable from the depressive. The latter was a more clinically organized version of the same and was defined by specific clinical criteria. Nevertheless, the state of melancholia remained emblematic of modern capitalistic societies.

FAMILIAL ISOLATION

While patterns of kinship and relatedness have existed throughout time, the nuclear family as we know it comes into existence only with the rise of market capitalism. This is to say the particular constellation or grouping of roles constituting the modern family is a pattern brought about by cultural and economic conditions of eighteenth-century Europe. Family, therefore, can be more accurately viewed as a social as opposed to a biological construction. Moreover, the dynamics of family life reflect and complement the order of other social arrangements that constitute society. Pre-capitalistic kinship arrangements tended to be more collectively organized units of production. Internal and external cooperation and coordination of efforts were essential to these extended groupings. Under capitalism, families were characterized by their individualization, monogamy, sexual control, patriarchy, competition, and class designations.

The bourgeois family represented a place separate and apart from that which was deemed to be public. What went on in family was private species existence. The role of women in this system became more narrowly constrained and domestic.

More than ever before, families came to represent a retreat from the world. They became the locus of investigation for that which was ailing society. In his pioneering study of modern families, Eli Zaretsky notes:

> Psychoanalysis arose at the point of capitalist development at which the family had ceased to be a unit of commodity production and was increas-

ingly being seen as a refuge from the economy and society. Its subject matter is the internal life of the family and personal relations abstracted from the mode of production. It comprehends the family as an autonomous institution subject to its own laws of functioning. On the basis of those laws, it attempts to construct a science of family and of personal identity. But psychoanalysis has no theory of how the family is itself socially determined—instead it explains the family in terms of itself. As a result, psychoanalysis cannot distinguish what is universal in the family . . . from what is specific to the family of a particular mode of production.[12]

One of the primary functions of modern families has been cultural reproduction, that is the reproduction of cultural patterns within the individual. Therefore, not only does the family reproduce a primary factor of production—namely labor, but it also promotes the ideology associated with that method. Engels reveals that the word family emerged from the Latin *famulus*, which meant domestic slave in Roman times while *familia* was the total number of slaves belonging to one man.[13] It did not imply a married couple and offspring. Thus, this modern monogamous, patriarchal grouping was one that best complemented the newly emerging market economy.

It has been proposed that the heightened focus on individuation, patriarchy, and sexual control in modern families helps to establish an intensity of anxiety. Freud understood family arrangements to be defined by incest taboos enforced by harsh sanctions. His focus on the Oedipus complex described an enormous disparity of power. *Totem and Taboo* dealt with a mythology that promoted male domination and sexual restrictions not in the service of *Eros*, but in the primitive quest for material fulfillment. Rebellion against the father could only result in overwhelming guilt and the introjection of a relentless superego accompanied by heightened anxiety.

The nuclear family that came into existence with the rise of industrial capitalism was viewed as an agent of stability in a tumultuous world. It was to serve as a means of withdrawal from society and is thus a place of isolation.[14] However, as Richard Sennett suggests, the family could in no way isolate itself from the world around it; it was a product of this world. This specific formulation of group life emerged out of the alienation of labor and the corresponding territorial division between work and home. Furthermore, family was nurtured by Calvinism and the Protestant Ethic. Engels tells us that it had its roots in the historic exploitation of women and the institution of private property.[15] Sennett proposes that this particular kinship structure of nineteenth-century Europe varied according to social class. Psychology was based on a particular bourgeois model of the nuclear family; one which American sociologist David

Riesman would refer to as "inner-directed"—wherein one's individualistic identity is governed by internalized standards. This is a world in which one's family is viewed as the source of one's life-long anxiety.

OBJECT RELATIONS

Freud proposed that anxiety is a reaction to the threat of object loss.[16] Far more than any other loss (even the young boy's fear of castration) one's loss of mother constitutes the greatest danger to the infant's well-being and survival. Freud insists that the infant's level of impressionability is profound since it is early childhood that paves the way for adult psychic life. Because the child experiences a prolonged period of dependency characterized by protection from all external danger, separation from the mother in any form presents itself as a problem. It is out of this anxiety that repression occurs. The true source of anxiety, therefore, is seen as located in mother–child relations.

The issues surrounding abandonment and separation anxiety hold a central place in the history of developmental psychology. Some of the most important studies that were undertaken by behavioral scientists such as René Spitz, Margaret Mahler, William Goldfarb, and others led to the conclusion that the earliest attachment and separation issues of children are related to a variety of emotional difficulties later on in life.[17] These difficulties are not solely due to a lack of physical contact with a parental figure, but also emanate from a failure to adequately relate with one's initial provider and a fear of separation or abandonment. Difficulties such as these can result in dysfunctional insecurity and a host of psychic terrors.

Various schools have emerged from Freud's earlier psychoanalytic framework. These have attempted to illuminate the central importance of childhood interpersonal dynamics and explain how these relationships with primary caregivers profoundly influence later life. These range from more orthodox Freudian interpretations of attachment and separation grounded in drive theory and oedipal relations to more empirically based behavioral explanations. Among the most significant of these approaches was the work of Melanie Klein and what has come to be known as the British object relations school. Added to this was the work of John Bowlby, Mary Ainsworth, and those separation theorists associated with the Tavistock Clinic in London from the early 1940s until the mid-1960s.

Klein's conceptual rendering of the human psyche appeared to be a reflection of the increasing human fragmentation and violence that characterized her world. It was in keeping with the growing anxiety associated with turn of the century modernity. It exemplified the primal bloodshed of World War I Europe and the post-war optimism of reconstructing a more peaceful, integrated world. Her concept of the psyche was a modernistic montage of id-like forces attempting to dominate and control the stable world. It was a clash of the civilized and the primitive, reflective of the imperialism of her time. Her prose were not that different from any of the other modern artistic renderings of a shattered, alienated reality. In many ways her work was dark and expressionistic.

Embedded in her theory was a recapitulation of her own experiences of terror and loss. As a young child she lost a sister to tuberculosis and a brother to suicide. Later, the death of her mother forced her to be hospitalized for depression. She saw herself as an abandoned, unloved child and displayed what some might now see as borderline tendencies: bouts of uncontrollable rage, sexual compensation for feelings of detachment and overriding sense of disconnection and rejection.

Klein can be credited with leading a revolution in the application of psychoanalytic method to better understanding children. Her work, which emphasized play, was often in conflict with that of Anna Freud whose focus was on education. Klein saw her efforts directed toward helping a child gain an integrative understanding of the world. She had several disagreements with the established psychoanalytic community and many aspects of her work to this day are still deemed quite controversial. While Klein subscribed to the essential elements of Freud's libidinal theory, she was particularly impressed by his work on aggression and supported his notion of a death instinct. From the 1930s on, her work emphasizes innate aggression in infants. However, the primary thrust of her effort was grounded in the relational aspects of child–parent interaction, not libidinal attachment.

In her work she asserts that the infant possesses an inborn awareness of his or her mother and is ruled by a set of internal fantasies including extremely aggressive ones directed against her. Klein rejects the idea that the superego develops at the oedipal stage. For her, it emerges much earlier. In this regard she de-emphasizes the early importance of the libido insisting that the infant's desire to control its mother's body is aggressive and not necessarily sexual. Nevertheless, it is the child's awareness of these destructive fantasies and impulses directed toward the mother that brings about the onset of anxiety in his or her own life.

Klein identifies two central positions in the child's emotional and maturational development. The first (under six months of age) is the paranoid/schizoid position characterized by the infant's fear, frustration, and rage directed against the mother. Here the child is torn between life and death instincts; it is confronted with its own needs and desires, which are sometimes fulfilled and other times are not. The world is both comforting and threatening. Both cognitively and as an unconscious defense the infant views the world as part-objects, thus the mother is a compilation of parts: breasts, hands, arms, legs, etc. In its imagination, the child classifies these as good and bad objects—some threatening and others pleasure-giving. Klein refers to this as splitting. The child cannot yet comprehend the idea that an object can be a mixture of good and bad. Fantasy plays an important part in the child's life at this stage, as he or she internalizes some of these objects making them a part of the self and draws upon other unconscious sadistic images that are phylloge-netic. It must consume these objects to destroy them. The child becomes full of fear that it will be destroyed in the process by these bad objects that constitute mother. The paranoid/schizoid position is full of confu-sion. Often the child's needs are unfulfilled and frustrated. This results in enormous degree of anger and aggression that must be projected out-ward onto the mother, or those parts representing her. The child wants to destroy the mother. But this anger is ultimately directed inward and against the self. This rage is so intense that the child eventually develops persecutory fears for its very own existence.

In the last half of the first year of life, the child enters into a depres-sive position. Earlier notions of omnipotence disappear. He or she is more able to integrate the fragmented and disjointed world both cogni-tively and emotionally. Mother is eventually made whole, both good and bad in the same person not just a collection of parts. Love is paramount here. At this stage the loss of the mother or even her absence is accompa-nied by enormous guilt and dread. The child sees its own hatred that was earlier directed toward her as responsible for her loss or disappearance. Thus, the pining for the lost love object is experienced in full force. It is only by an introjection of mother that the mourning child can come to terms with the world.

Klein's work provided a path for others to follow. Certainly, Freud would disavow much of what she had to say. His notion that the super-ego is the outcome of Oedipus complex resolution and the internaliza-tion of the father's authority was rejected by Klein as was his forceful emphasis on innate drives. She substitutes an emphasis on connection and the primacy of objects: "There is no instinctual urge, no anxiety sit-uation, no mental process which does not involve objects, external or internal; in other words, object-relations are at the centre of emotional life."[18] In focusing psychoanalysis on human interactions, she pro-foundly impacted the trajectory of modern psychoanalytic theory.

Those professionally drawn to Klein, or who followed her lead, distanced themselves even further from Freud. W. R. D. Fairbairn, who had been trained in philosophy and religion, saw the value in her overall approach. His work, like many of the interpersonal theorists such as Erich Fromm, Karen Horney, and Harry Stack Sullivan, moved even further away from the biological and instinctual explanations of earlier psychoanalysis. Like Klein, he dismissed the emphasis on drive theory and developed his own interrelational model.

Fairbairn proposes that the essential striving of each child is for human contact, not tension reduction. He views this as grounded in biological survival. Personality, he asserts, is the result of real interactions and not internal fantasies. It is the broken connection between child and caregiver that poses problems. Aggression directed toward the external object is not innate, but rather derived from the frustration of not having this connection. Thus, the frequently absent or distant mother causes the child to internalize mother as an object. This object acts as a substitute for the "natural object," specifically mother, in an attempt to self-comfort. Destructive fantasies are frequently signs of pathology as is splitting. Thus, he believes in an intact "unitary ego" of the child and contends that maternal deprivation is at the root of most psychopathologies. Object relations historians Jay Greenberg and Stephen Mitchell have pointed out that Fairbairn sees the child as having a "maturational sequence of needs for various kinds of relatedness."[19] Accordingly, children progress along progressive stages ranging from most attached to "mature dependence" through a process of gradual separation. Modernization and industrialization interfere with the mother–infant bond and the infant's dependency on its mother frequently becomes problematic. While other animals are connected with their mothers as long as is physically necessary, this is not the case where economic and social demands rupture the initial relationship.[20] Thus, Fairbairn's work might be viewed as providing support for attachment theory that would later be fully developed at Tavistock. It might also be recognized as the first sociological movement in object relations defined around strictly interpersonal and cultural concerns.

D. W. Winnicott, another contributor to the British object relations school, also stressed the importance of the earliest months of the infant's psychic life. Like Klein he sees introjection and projection as the child's primary means of dealing with earliest fears and frustrations. However, he rejects the notion of an aggressive instinct that was central to the work of both Freud and Klein. The role of mothering and the notion of the "good enough mother" are central to his work. He views the child's identity as vitally connected to his or her primary caregiver and tracks its growing separation from the immediate external world. For Winnicott, childhood is a continuous struggle for an individuated existence that allows for intimate relations with others.[21] He posits that separation can constitute a new mature form of union. Maturation is a negotiated path between dependence and independence that is fraught with dangers and hazards to the emergence of an authentic, healthy self. He suggests that maternal deprivation or impingement can lead a child to erect a "false-self" and to eventually become alienated from the truer inner self. But the "good enough mother" can prevent this.

Mother acts as a mirror, giving the infant detailed feedback in terms of a reflection. This is long before the child recognizes himself or herself in a physical mirror. Through this process the child gains a sense of self. The mother, in turn, learns much from the infant and becomes more capable of interpreting its nonverbal cues. The child's pattern of psychic development reflects a negotiation between an engendered sense of omnipotence and an extreme fear of its own vulnerability. Frequently, to this end, a child incorporates into its life transitional objects that are intermediaries between the imagined world and the real one. Such objects are representational of mother and frequently give the child a sense of security and control so that detachment can be less traumatic.

Winnicott had been a consultant to the British government during World War II and was responsible for an evacuation scheme that removed millions of children from cities and placed them in countryside hostels in an effort to keep them safe from aerial attacks. Based on his clinical findings he insisted that too soon a separation from mother severely damaged the psychic and social development of many of these young. He, therefore, sees a considerable portion of antisocial behaviors, hyperaggression, and delinquency as stemming from these early separation experiences.[22]

Object relations provides a method of explaining and conceptualizing early childhood experiences of separation and loss and resultant anxieties that could follow one into adulthood. For Klein and her followers, object relatedness displaces drives as the basis of all human associations. Klein, especially, maps the earliest stages of psychic development that Freud had only touched upon. While she never truly connected her findings to social structure, she and those who were to follow her understood narcissism and narcissistic culture, as retreats into fantasies of utter self-sufficiency, serving as defenses against expansive envy and rage that threatened to destroy the self and others. Pathological narcissism is seen by the object relations theorists as emerging from the difficulties encountered in the earliest stages of child–caregiver separation and individuation common to western cultures.

ABANDONMENT ANXIETY

John Bowlby's work on attachment, separation, and abandonment was in the tradition of object relations work, yet significantly removed from it. While he had worked for several years under the supervision of Melanie Klein at the London Child Guidance Clinic he rejected many of her underlying assumptions, including her support for classical notions of the libido theory and aggressive instincts in children. Bowlby's work was less expansive than that of Klein. His focus was on attachment, separation, and loss.[23] A considerable amount of his work centered on children who had been abandoned and institutionalized, those consigned to foster care systems, and children living at home who were separated from their parents on a temporary basis.

Bowlby asserts that all infants are born with an innate need and ability to develop a close physical attachment with whomever cares for them, not necessarily mother. This drive to achieve and maintain proximity helps to protect infants as they mature. It provides each child with a feeling of security, enabling it to explore the world. Although this attachment need is most obvious in young children, it is also evident whenever a person is vulnerable, frightened, or ill. According to Bowlby, attachment needs continue throughout the life cycle into old age. He views attachment as both instinctual and behavioral. Where behavioral theorists saw dependency as related to the infant's need for food and comfort, Bowlby rejects this notion of object/sensory dependency and instead advances a theory of attachment predicated on internal drives. His evidence for this position rests on those studies of Lorenz and Harlow, whose animal research showed attachment as a consequence of primary biological drives as opposed to secondary ones. Bowlby's theory of attachment provided the basis of his ideas on separation anxiety. For him, separation from a loved one not only threatens one's security by putting one's security needs at risk, but has a much deeper significance. If attachment is an innate requirement for survival, abandonment signals a threat to survival. Therefore, even temporary separations from primary caregivers or threats of separation might create strong feelings of anxiety. Bowlby identified this as separation anxiety. He notes:

> . . . just as animals of many species, including man, are disposed to respond with fear to sudden movement or a marked change in the level of sound or light because to do so has survival value, so are many species, including man, disposed to respond to separation from a potentially care giving figure and for the same reason. When separation anxiety is viewed in this light, as a basic human disposition, it is only a small step to understand why it is that threats to abandon a child, often used as a means to control, are so very terrifying. [24]

For Bowlby, separation anxiety emerges both in childhood and at various stages of adulthood. The aversion to physical separation and the fear of being deserted are innate. Such anxiety is part of a survival mechanism, which responds to the dangers associated with abandonment. Bowlby notes that the terror of sudden separation is especially great before the child gains a mature sense of self-awareness, and he expresses concern with parental practices of threatening the child with abandonment in order to assure obedience. While not denying similar stages of childhood development shared by children, Bowlby emphasizes the uniqueness of each infant's relationship with his or her primary caregiver, which emanates, in part, from phyllogenic preconditions. How the individual sees the environment and how one enters into relationships with others are derivatives of the perceived degree of security in the world established for her or him by the earliest caregiver (most often a parent). Certainly, this early attachment model established in childhood is likely to affect one's future relationships on an unconscious level.

In his own research, however, Bowlby found that children react to separation from their primary caregivers according to a predictable sequence in terms of feelings and associated behaviors: yearning and searching for the missing parent, sadness, increasing protest at his or her absence, growing anger directed against the parent, increased ambivalence on his or her return, and fear of renewed separation.

As the child begins to mature, the primary person with whom the child has developed an attachment must be readily accessible in order for the child to confidently explore his or her environment. Before age two, the child typically makes brief journeys away from his or her parent, as long as there is a feeling of trust that the parent will be there when the toddler returns. Should the parent be missing for a prolonged period of time, young children will typically seek out parent substitutes. Depending upon various factors and conditions at work in early attachment, some children will only need close proximity to the parent or substitute to feel secure, others may actually need to be physically held.

If the child develops normally, after the age of two or three these separations become more prolonged. However, should the child lose sight of the parent, exploration is usually forgotten and top priority is given to regaining the missing caregiver. This correlates with the child's developing object permanence—knowing something or someone can continue to exist when not immediately in view. Typically, older children will search for the parent while younger children will cry, perhaps attempting to signal for the parent.

As the child approaches school age, separation can be sustained for hours and later even days. During adolescence, separation can be endured for weeks or months; yet during such separation new attachment figures are liable to be sought. For Bowlby the human being is most comfortable when life is a series of these gradually extended separations.

Unlike Freud and Klein, Bowlby rejects the notion that separation anxiety is a result of a strictly cognitive process and related to the psycho-sexual patterns of development. Instead he sees individuals' personality development as intimately tied to their early attachments and separations. Bowlby also rejects theories proposed by some object relations theorists that specific phases of development were responsible for conditions of infant attachment. Rather, he proposes the idea that the central nervous system of each individual somehow develops unique pathways for modeling interpersonal attachment. He contends that certain ideal typical patterns of infant attachment, which carried with them particular behavioral outcomes, could be identified.

Bowlby's research was supported in part by groundbreaking studies conducted by Mary Salter Ainsworth. Ainsworth, who had done research on infant–mother attachment in Canada prior to the Second World War, joined Bowlby's research team at the Tavistock Clinic in 1950. She helped to devise several research instruments used by Bowlby and others to categorize infant–mother relational patterns. In 1954 she left Tavistock for Uganda where she conducted extensive field studies of early attachment. Her work confirmed much of Bowlby's initial findings relative to stages of attachment and revealed the importance of culture in conditioning the quality of early attachment relationships. Still, where Ainsworth's work left off and Bowlby's began is speculative in many instances.

Refining some of the initial attachment classifications developed by Ainsworth, Bowlby described three patterns that appeared to result from generalized modes of parental–child interaction. Accordingly, secure attachment, the healthiest form, occurs when the parent is accessible and responds to the infant's physical, cognitive, and emotional needs with understanding, affection and love. The child is provided with a sense of security that the parent will be able to meet his or her needs, and will be able to provide for its comfort and protection. Anxious attachment, another pattern, emerges when the parent is inconsistently accessible and responsive to the infant's needs. Therefore, the child becomes uncertain whether the parent will be comforting, protective, or helpful when needed. Because of this uncertainty, he or she is prone to separation anxiety, manifested by the tenancy to be possessive, to cling, and to be reluctant to independently investigate the unexplored world. This condition is frequently fostered by a parent who sometimes is available and sometimes is not. Also, separation from the parent often triggers this condition, as might the parent's threat to leave. Anxious avoidant attachment is the third pattern identified by Bowlby. Here there is no confidence that the parent will provide needed help when the infant seeks it. Frequently, the infant anticipates being ignored or rebuffed. Such a condition is often a product of a rejecting parent or even an abusing one. The outcome of such neglect or abuse is an attempt by the child to live a life without the love or support of others. Such parental unresponsiveness can result in an inability of the child to form deep relationships with others later on in life, or even abusive and violently aggressive behavior.

For Bowlby, the role of attachment in many respects complements Erik Erikson's notion of basic trust, which will be discussed in greater detail later. Briefly, Erikson asserted that the child's first social achievement is her or his willingness to let mother out of sight without undue anxiety or rage.[25] Bowlby views this as the most critical period as well. Both view trust as a healthy response to parental influences, which lay the groundwork for individual autonomy. Without significant attachment between the primary caregiver and the child, and without the sense of ontological security that results from this attachment, there is little chance that the child will be able to develop healthy trust. Neurotic, life-long anxiety is often the result.

Bowlby and Ainsworth were by no means alone in their emphasis on separation and attachment. Margaret Mahler, a psychoanalytically trained physician who migrated from Vienna to the United States, had been doing similar work. While her clinical experience was primarily with severely disturbed children, her theoretical focus was very much in the tradition of the object relations school and was considerably more psychoanalytic than that of Bowlby. In her work she saw the infant emerging from a sense of cognitive and emotional oneness with mother (symbiosis) to a point of healthy separation or individuation. It was the gradual process of separation and its various developmental stages that concerned her.

The separation-individuation process she described is comprised of a series of chronologically ordered phases and subphases leading to full maturation and healthy independence. Thus the infant emerges from what she refers to as "autistic" and "symbolic" phases in which there is no differentiation between self and otherness through "differentiation" and "practicing" phases wherein the child begins to differentiate his or her body image from that of mother and develops motor abilities to move away from her and actively explores the world. Not totally secure with separation, the child enters a rapprochement phase wherein he or she turns to mother for reassurances. The child needs to develop a positive internalized image of mother and her continued presence, object consistency, which can sustain it during times of separation, before she or he can gain a secure sense of self.

ABANDONMENT ANXIETY AND PATHOLOGY

While the attachment between infant and caregiver plays a significant role in the child's social and emotional development, Bowlby recognized that fear of abandonment serves the vital function of ensuring his or her conformity to social demands. In his works he posits that certain states of anxiety and depression, as well as more serious long-term emotional problems typically exhibited in some adults, can be linked to early childhood fears of separation. Feelings of anxiety, despair, and detachment displayed by children who were separated from their primary caregiver for long periods of time, or anxiously awaited such a separation, or lost a caregiver completely, were frequently converted into adult psychopathologies.

In his clinical work with adults, Bowlby found that many of their problems of dissociation and severe anxiety disorders could be attributed to the particular child-rearing practices that were engaged in by the patients' parents. For example, not responding to the child who cries for attention, ignoring the infant who needs to be comforted or held, expressing regret that the child was brought into the world, pretending to leave a child behind on the street, and threatening to send the child away from the immediate family could do damage to a child's overall sense of security. Such threats can generate intense feelings of anxiety, anger, and depression and even impair cognitive and social functioning. The consequences of these threats can easily be carried over into adulthood. Furthermore, Bowlby insists that frequent and regular threats of abandonment, which many of his adult psychiatric patients were subjected to as children, bore enormous consequences that could be equal to, or even more frightening than, the act of abandonment itself. Repression of such early abandonment threats seemed to be common in adults suffering from acute anxiety disorders. Since the idiosyncratic forms assumed by such threats often made them appear trifling, they frequently went unrecognized in later years by adults who struggled with their recurrent consequences.

In therapy sessions, Bowlby uncovered the importance of what others thought to be seemingly innocuous and insignificant threats of abandonment. Many adult patients failed to immediately recognize that they had been victims of such threats in early childhood; however, therapy helped them to uncover these experiences and their related consequences. For a number of Bowlby's patients, threats were used regularly by parents to control their behavior. For example, one patient's mother had concocted a story that a yellow van would pull up and take the child away if he did not do what he was told. Another patient's parent told her that if she misbehaved she would be sent to a school on a remote rock island surrounded by sharks. In a third case a mother told her son that she would send him away to a children's home where he would be forced to "eat margarine" (something he loathed to do at home).

In each of these cases, all the parent had to do was to use a code referring to the specific threat to control the behavior of the child: "Well, the yellow van will come," or "Then it will be the rock school for you," or in the last case simply the word "margarine" would suffice. Although seemingly amusing and harmless Bowlby insisted that children are highly vulnerable to such threats, and their impact can instill fear and mistrust that can last into adulthood and result in abnormal emotional development.[26] Threats to abandon, he asserts, are not merely personal techniques used to keep children in order. On a psychic level, they can be traumatizing.

ABANDONMENT AND SOCIAL CONTROL

Nightmares of abandonment loom large in the young child's mind. In his book *Landscapes of Fear*, Yi-Fu Tuan identifies abandonment as a central childhood fear, and notes its important role in the childhood process of socialization. Tuan cites the use of fairy tales as parental aids in controlling the child's behavior. The fairy tale reaches the child at a primitive level of awareness. They are frequently bridges between dreams and reality—existing in a twilight of both. Children often receive subtle threats and sometimes not so subtle ones through the use of such stories. Frequently in fairy tales children are deserted by their parents and forced to take care of their own needs while confronting overpowering difficulties. The night and the forest play important roles in the fairy tales. Abandonment of the child in the forest is common. For children, this threat is powerfully symbolic.

> The forest figures prominently in fairy tales. It is almost never a place for a stroll or games. It spells danger to the child, frightening by its strangeness—its polar contrast to the cozy world of the cottage. The forest also frightens by its vastness, its breadth and the size of its towering trees being beyond the scale of a child's experience. It is haunted by dangerous beasts. It is the place of abandonment—a dark, chaotic non-world in which one feels utterly lost.[27]

Stories of the brothers Grimm present us with evidence of how intimidation and threats of abandonment have been historically used against children. In *Hansel and Gretel*, for instance, the dialogue, overheard by the children is quite graphic. The father, a woodcutter who fears starvation due to his loss of work, speaks to his wife:

> *What is to become of us? How are we to feed our poor children when we have nothing for ourselves?*
>
> *I'll tell you what, husband, answered the woman. Tomorrow morning we will take the children out quite early into the thickest part of the forest. We will light a fire and give each of them a piece of bread. Then we will go to work and leave them alone. They won't be able to find their way back and we will be rid of them.* [28]

The children in this story must not only survive the terrors of abandonment, but they must struggle with their fear of being cast out, their feelings of being unloved and unwanted, and deal with the reality of having to be self-sufficient too early in their development, redeeming themselves by bringing home riches to their poverty-stricken parents. Only through such economic redemption is the child completely welcomed to return.

Sadism abounds in Grimm's fairy tales, and it usually proceeds from child abandonment. Children who lose their parents are treated to all sorts of physical and psychological abuse. They are traumatized, only to be rescued by divine or magical intervention. Sometimes they are saved by their own ingenuity. In some ways these tales support a popular psychoanalytic contention that abandonment disrupts the child's healthy individuation and fosters sadomasochistic coping strategies in later life.

Feelings of helplessness of the child as she or he confronts the powerful adult caregiver can have long term consequences. Franz Kafka's remembered childhood incident, which is described in a letter written to his father in November of 1919, is perhaps one of the finer illustrations we have of this. In this letter Kafka recalls an evening in his early youth when he was supposed to be sleeping, "whimpering" from his bed for water. "After several vigorous threats had failed to have any effect," he wrote to his father, "you took me out of bed, carried me onto the *pavlatche* (balcony), and left me there alone for a while in my nightshirt, outside the shut door." Kafka went on in the letter to say that this was typical of the treatment he received from his father, "typical of your methods of bringing up a child." Kafka noted:

> I dare say I was quite obedient afterwards at that period, but it did me inner harm. What was for me a matter of course, that senseless asking for water, and the extraordinary terror of being carried outside were two things that I, my nature being what it was, could never properly connect to each other. Even years afterwards I suffered from the tormenting fancy

that the huge man, my father, the ultimate authority, would come almost
for no reason at all and take me out of bed in the night and carry me out
onto the *pavlatche*, and that meant I was a mere nothing for him.[29]

Although Kafka's literary themes of alienation, detachment, anxiety,
estrangement, and helplessness might not be laid completely at the base
of this childhood experience, they can be seen as having been deeply
influenced by it. Kafka's expressionistic imagery and existential characterization make his work particularly modern and indicate the social
conditions surrounding him at the time.

ABANDONMENT AND PERSONALITY

The reflection of early childhood abandonment in personality formation was well documented in Adorno's ground-breaking study on the
authoritarian personality published shortly after World War II. In an
attempt to better understand Hitler's rise to power, Adorno conducted a
study of the habits of working-class families. The case study of Mack,
which appears as one of the clinical interviews conducted by R. Nevitt
Sanford (Adorno's colleague and a co-author), reveals that the long-term
absence of Mack's ill mother during his childhood and her eventual
death, left him with a cold and distant father whose "silence and distance" helped to foster a vast amount of insecurities and fears in the
young boy. There was little emotional attachment between him and his
father and he developed intense feelings of anxiety. Mack later became
incapable of developing healthy long-term relationships with anyone
and assumed the characteristics of an authoritarian personality. Wilhelm
Reich had earlier proposed that the modern German family severely
repressed sexuality in children and imposed a standard of autocratic sub-
missiveness on the part of boys. For him, capitalism emasculated men.
Adorno accepted most of this in his analysis. According to both men, it
was the nature of the nuclear family under capitalism that one could find
the roots of fascism in German society.

As noted in the previous chapter, authoritarian personality does not
necessarily mean an autocratic disposition. Actually, according to
Fromm, one could adjust to one's sense of insecurity by either attempting to rigidly control the outside world in order to feel more secure or
becoming inordinately submissive and compliant with those in authority. While Adorno and his associates thought that they would find the
former in post-war Germany, they found an excess of the latter.
According to Adorno, such a personality comes closest to what Fromm

referred to as the "sadomasochistic" character. Frequently, such an individual achieves his social adjustment by taking great pleasure in obedience and subordination. The individual's aggression, derived from the repressed oedipal desire to destroy the father, becomes a sadistic drive to inflict harm on others who are weaker and different from the self. While Adorno based this on drive theory, the idea was nonetheless complementary to Bowlby's later notion of anxious attachment and anxious avoidant attachment disturbances. Although the mechanism that converted such childhood insecurities and fears into neurotic disorders of masochism and sadism have been debated in psychoanalytic literature, especially the role of the libido, there can be little doubt that such detachment and fear of being distanced from one's caregiver can trigger an overwhelming number of anxieties resulting in personality disorder. Else Frenkel-Brunswik, who assessed a series of interviews for the study undertaken with Adorno, noted that the authoritarian personality's childhood showed that:

> . . . images of the parents seem to acquire for the child a forbidding or at least a distant quality. Family relationships are characterized by fearful subservience to the demands of the parents and by early suppression of impulses not acceptable to them. . . . [Parents were] apt to view the child's behavior in terms of their own instead of the child's needs . . .[30]

This was not too dissimilar to Kafka's relationship with his father. It seems that the young boy's call for attention or water could be interpreted in a number of negative ways by a parent who would simply like to get some sleep.

FAMILIAL LIFE AND BASIC TRUST

It is important to keep in mind that it wasn't until the end of the seventeenth and beginning of the eighteenth century that children were considered anything more than "incipient adults," and burdens to their parents.[31] Of course, there were some exceptions. Well into the eighteenth century, children of the well-to-do families were banished until they were grown. Sennett notes: "In both Paris and London, children from middle-middle and upper-middle classes were often handed directly from nurse to 'college,' an institution charged with the care of those from seven to eleven or twelve—'care' being usually interpreted as continual physical chastisement."[32] Poor children were frequently abandoned, sold into slavery, or murdered. It wasn't until well into the nineteenth century that organizations emerged to protect the rights of children and keep them safe from abuse.

The romance of the private family life hid much of this from public view. Death hovered over most urban working-class families particularly in the mid-nineteenth century. While life conditions improved for many, for more it worsened. The conditions under which people lived at those times deteriorated rapidly in the industrial cities. The early death of one's mother to tuberculosis, one's sister to typhoid, or one's brother to diphtheria were not uncommon events in cities where people were crowded together. Cholera and other epidemics were common until the middle of the nineteenth century. High birth rates were matched by higher death rates. The lack of sanitary conditions, the foul air, polluted drinking water, the flow of raw sewage in the streets, the poor and crowded conditions of housing were among the various contributors to poor health.

For many, the modern family appeared to be an escape from the outside world. But this was indeed a fiction. The family in many ways was a microcosm of that world, more of a satellite preparing children for life in it. It was often the scene of mistrust, disease, and harsh discipline. With the relocation of income-generating activity outside of the home, with the development of wage-laboring in factories, power over life and death was placed into the hands of a stranger, the owner of the means of production. Along with the cyclical booms and busts of market economies this arrangement generated waves of anxiety and dread. The market could wreck havoc on the family. It could tear the family apart physically, emotionally, and materially; it could force working-class parents to abandon their children. Children understood the powerlessness of their parents and greater powerlessness of themselves. Fear of abandonment became central to modern human social landscape. We know that relinquishment entered prominently into the psychic lives of eighteenth- and nineteenth-century writers, artists, and scientists. This had a profound impact on how modern culture was constructed. Charles Dickens, for example, had been abandoned by his father's removal to a debtors prison, and he was sent to the notorious blacking factory at age ten, and Emily Brontë, author of *Wuthering Heights* and other dark prose and poems, lost her mother to tuberculosis before she was four and her two older sisters before she was seven.[33] The list of those prominent in the arts and sciences who lost a parent at an early age is extensive and includes many of the leading romantics such as Coleridge, Wordsworth, and Mary Shelley.

Among the multitude of authors whose works reflected such an intensity of anxiety and melancholy were Charles Baudelaire of France and Edgar Allan Poe of the United States. Poe's style displayed an anxiety-driven surrealism. It was most certainly from Poe that Baudelaire took much of the inspiration for his *Les Fleurs du mal*, itself a collection of dark and beautiful poems. In fact Baudelaire spent much of his life translating Poe's poetry and short stories into French, and died in the middle of this project, considering his translations to be his major contribution to French culture. Patrick F. Quinn, in his classic study on this unique literary affinity between these men, found that Baudelaire's attraction to Poe most likely emerged from powerfully common childhood experiences.[34] Chief among these experiences were loss, rejection, and emotional abandonment. Poe lost his mother and Baudelaire his doting father in early childhood. At age three Poe sat at his mother's bedside and watched her die. His father had been an alcoholic who abandoned the family while Edgar was still an infant. Upon his mother's death he was left with no one. His siblings were sent off to live with other families and the Allans, who eventually took him in, welcomed him reluctantly. J. Gerald Kennedy, in his discussion of Poe's thematic focus on death, sees much of Poe's writing as having emerged from his early childhood trauma and deep-rooted fears of separation and loss of maternal love. Kennedy sees this as responsible not only for Poe's choice of subject matter, but for his desire to write.

> . . . Poe discovered the desire of writing in contemplation of a corpse. In an important sense . . . he remained fixated upon his dead mother, Elizabeth Poe, reenacting her loss endlessly in later compositions. . . . As we see, the threat of parental loss triggered imagery of personal destruction, which in turn compelled the urge to write.[35]

Later, in analyzing Poe's break with John Allan, his stepfather, Kennedy notes:

> Poe portrayed himself recurrently as an unloved abandoned child. . . . Allan's remoteness, his silence, and his suspension of care amounted to a symbolic death that repeated Poe's infantile separation from his parents. . . . this fixation on separation seems to manifest the insecurity of the existential self in the modern world.[36]

For Baudelaire, his father, who was extremely close to him, died when he was six. Although the young boy clung to his mother, upon her remarriage she became more distant at a time when he needed her affection the most. Her husband was cold and indifferent toward the boy as well. Baudelaire's later dandyism might well be interpreted as a reaction formation—a defense of his inner sense of great vulnerability. Both Poe and Baudelaire found themselves alone, left with uncaring, if not resentful fathers who sent them away to live at school at a very early age.

These early death experiences and prolonged periods of emotional isolation powerfully shaped the psyches of both men and colored their work. Death and decay occupied a central position in their lives and in their creations. Neither boy could adjust well to early loss and emotional rejection. Both were haunted by these feelings throughout their later years. For each, the world provided no safe haven. For both Poe and Baudelaire there was an abrupt end to childhood and an opening-up of a very dark abyss from which demons, never put to rest by a loving parent, would haunt them their entire lives.

The loneliness and alienation graphically expressed in the poetry of these two men helped to lay thematic and stylistic groundwork for generations of modern writers and storytellers to come. However, it would be quite wrong to conclude that their childhoods were the solitary wellsprings for such creativity and pessimism. Perhaps the popular appeal of the work of Poe, Baudelaire, and comparable artists whose creations expressed similar feelings of dread was that it resonated with the repressed inner sentiments of the many readers who struggled with their own ghosts and who were now exposed to an enormous wave of social and cultural change.

Other artists of this era reflected this same sense of melancholy, this withdrawal from life, and a compulsion toward death and the macabre. Edvard Munch's bleak renditions of death and distress reflected a childhood of intense consternation in a time of enormous social change. His melancholy landscapes such as *The Sick Child, The Storm, The Scream,* and *Despair* convey many of these same feelings of impending doom. Like Poe, Munch watched his mother die of tuberculous when he was only five years old. This death traumatized the sensitive boy, and the remembrances of his mother's loss haunted him his entire adult life. Couple this early childhood event with a father who grew cold and distant after his mother's death—a father who threatened his children with eternal damnation and never being able to see their mother in heaven when they died if they misbehaved at home. This was a man who, according to Munch, changed from a loving caregiver into an insane, sullen patriarch. Munch's artistic morbidity rivals that of Poe's most grotesque stories and are even suggestive of specific Poe narratives. In remarking on his own life, Munch sounds much like the brooding Roderick Usher.

> Two of mankind's most horrible enemies were granted to me as an inheritance. An inheritance of tuberculosis and mental illness. Sickness and insanity were the black angels that guarded my cradle. A mother who died young gave me a weakness for tuberculosis; an overly nervous father, so pietistically religious as to be almost insane, the descendent of an ancient

family, gave me the seeds of insanity. From the moment of my birth, the angles of anxiety, worry, and death stood at my side, followed me out when I played, followed me in the sun of springtime and in the glories of summer. They stood at my side in the evening when I closed my eyes, and intimidated me with death, hell and eternal damnation. And I would often wake up at night and stare wildly into the room: Am I in Hell?[37]

Munch's work was to underscore the loneliness associated with modernity and the fear connected to his own death. His artistic renderings of death, anxiety, and despair were reflective not only of his unconscious, but also of the life surrounding him. His unique renderings of disimpassioned sexuality and the relationship of sex to death, commodification, and decay articulated another mood of his day. Yet he was just one artist to express such themes at the *fin de siecle*. The overriding themes of loneliness, sullenness, and separation reverberated through art, literature, drama and invaded the social sciences.

Although it was not uncommon, an artist did not need to experience a radical and traumatic childhood separation from a parent to develop these sensibilities. One might be orphaned in a variety of ways: one could be rejected, beaten, ignored, or isolated as a child; one could experience aloneness in a lack of emotional connectedness essential to species survival. The sense of abandonment, which is referred to here, is a particular feeling of anxiety associated with the insecurities of modern familial life. As opposed to many nonfamilial kinship systems wherein the care of children is a communal function, for modern bourgeois families there is what Sennett refers to as a "tyranny of intimacy." Hidden away from the light of public view the family often saw itself as a safe-haven, a place that was secure from the heterogeneous world outside of it, often at odds with that world. The intensity of healthy and unhealthy attachment generated in families made separation from them emotionally arduous.

As previously noted, Erik Erikson was among the first modern psychologists to propose that basic trust rests at the base of healthy attachment and separation and, therefore, underlies a healthy society. He laid out what he thought to be critical psychosocial stages of development—stages one moves through from infancy into mature adulthood.[38] Erikson, who was born in Germany and studied child psychology with Anna Freud in Vienna, was an American psychotherapist who posited what he called "the eight stages of man." This was a humanistic and relational response to Freud's psychosexual stages of development. Each of Erikson's stages was represented by a crisis the person must pass through in order to grow into a healthy individual and connect with others in an unimpaired fashion. Erikson presents this movement through the life cycle as a dangerous narrative adventure in which there is a critical confrontation between the self and the challenges of one's social environment. At each stage the individual is encountered by the self it has achieved to that point and its limitations.

The most critical stage, as it relates to abandonment, is the very first: basic trust versus basic mistrust. For Erikson, this is the underpinning for everything else. Here the focus is on the infant's ability to let her or his mother out of sight without undue anxiety or rage. For Erikson, this requires the internalization of the mother and the development of a sense of security predicated on consistency, continuity, and sameness of experience. Accordingly, the child needs a sense that its world can be orderly and stable. Most interesting here is Erikson's assertion that basic trust is not predicated on a demonstration of love, but on the quality of the maternal relationship. "Mothers create a sense of trust in their children," he suggests "by that kind of administration which in its quality combines sensitive care of the baby's individual needs and a firm sense of personal trustworthiness within the trusted framework of their culture's lifestyle."[39] Accordingly, this forms the basis for the child's sense of identity—a sense of all-rightness. The caregiver provides the child with opportunities to develop a sense of self in a nonthreatening environment. But one must also learn social limitations and boundaries. The child learns to become a trusted person, so that the caregiver will not need to be on guard against her or him, or leave. The individual gains an integrated sense of the self only if his or her inner needs and expectations of the outer social world can be meaningfully integrated. Thus, children must come to understand the reasons for their frustrations and eventually make sense of the world. With basic trust they can confront the environment and learn from it. Erikson notes:

> But even under the most favorable circumstances, this stage seems to introduce into psychic life (and become prototypical for) a sense of inner division an universal nostalgia for a paradise forfeited. It is against this powerful combination of a sense of having been deprived, of having been divided, and of having been abandoned—that basic trust must maintain itself throughout life.[40]

The absence of basic trust translates into what R. D. Laing referred to as "ontological insecurity." Without this grounding in basic trust the individual is thrown into a world that appears overwhelming, in which one's weakened sense of autonomy and identity are challenged by forces outside of the self. A lack of basic trust condemns one to a world of anxiety and dread. Separation of the child from the caregiver without the inoculation of basic trust exposes the child to trauma and haunting feelings of abandonment and dread.

JACQUES LACAN

Abandonment and separation are essential to Jacques Lacan's post-structural model of individuation. According to Marcelle Marini: "Lacan's history is that of successive ruptures. For him, everything seems to center on these few words: to leave, to be left or abandoned, to be excommunicated, and in turn to anathematize."[41]

Firstly, Lacan posits that language is a powerful alienating force, separating us from the world while simultaneously giving people their only self-identity. Building on the work of Hegel, Freud and the phenomenologists—most notably Saussure and Husserl, he constructs a psychic landscape of human disconnection. Accordingly, all attachment and separation revolve around language. There can be no subject independent of language; no one can stand outside of it; people can exist only in and through their words. For Lacan, it is language that gives rise to the unconscious. He rejects the idea that the unconscious is in any way primordial or instinctual. He views it as structured in a way that is compatible with the development of language itself and, therefore, makes sense of the world through language formation that is governed by metaphor and metonymy, or linkages. It is the unconscious that is the source of authority.[42]

Part of Lacan's project, and of particular interest to the purposes here, is the desire to better understand separation and loss and feelings arising from interpersonal disconnection. Lacan's theory of individuation identifies a number of stages of loss. The first of these is birth and the infant's detachment from the womb. However, he makes clear that loss begins even prior to this moment. In fact, it starts in vivo with sexual differentiation and it does not actually become manifest until birth. Thus, the loss of androgyny is central to Lacan's work and will find an important place in his interpretation of Freud's Oedipus complex. Still another pre-oedipal loss is represented by what he terms the "territorialization" of the subject's body, which occurs prior to the acquisition of language. This second stage is characterized by the loss of generalized eroticism and erotic energy that is converted into drives—particularly into genital sexual drives. Eroticism is then placed into the service of the genital economy. The *Imaginary* constitutes for Lacan a third phase of separation and individuation. Here personal alienation from the whole and identity begin to take place. It is here, in what is referred to as "the mirror stage," where language is acquired.

Lacan uses the image of a small child before a mirror as a metaphor for both self-discovery and personal estrangement. Such imagery was of course common to German Idealist philosophy. It featured prominently in the work of Hegel and even made its way into the early interactionism of American sociology of the 1920s and 1930s such as the work of Charles Horton Cooley and George Herbert Mead. First, in looking into the mirror the child confuses its reflection with that of her or his adult companion. Next, the child acquires the notion of an image and now understands that the reflection is not a real person. Lastly, the reflection is understood to be her or his own image, which is different from other images. For Lacan, the child never acquires a stable self-image. The image is interpreted and often misinterpreted. One can only see oneself as one imagines others see her or him.

This idea of a coherent self is very much the construction of bourgeois individualism. Lacan rejects what he views as the utopian belief espoused by some relational and object relations theorists that a goal of psychoanalysis is personal integration. He proposes that there can be no stable ego because there is no fixed set of characteristics that can ever constitute the individual. Unlike Humpty Dumpty there is no "putting together again." In looking into the mirror the child sees the other staring back—a self that is separate and apart from the whole. This is the moment of one's personal atomization, one's sense of aloneness, asserts Lacan. One becomes defined by one's detachment from the world. The mirror reflection promotes ambivalence—an unconscious tension between attachment and disconnection—wholeness and autonomy.

Lacan suggests that the Oedipus complex plays a significant role in the process of separation. As a psychoanalyst trained in the Freudian tradition he needs to deal with its essential elements presented by Freud. This is discussed as part of what Lacan refers to as the symbolic order. He reintroduces the power of language here and views it as a means to express desire and as a method used in attempting to reconnect with all that was lost. For Lacan, like Hegel, the essence of being human is the desire to be desired. Thus, every child first desires to be desired by his or her mother—to reconnect to her and thus to the oneness of the universe. The Oedipus complex for him becomes symbolic of this craving. The child understands that mother lacks something, needs something to be whole. Unlike Freud, Lacan does not speak of this as penis envy, but instead refers to the lack of a phallus. It is the phallus that is representative of power and plentitude. The quest for wholeness is connected to this striving for power to make ourselves whole. One must believe that if he or she were the phallus or had the other's phallus she or he would be whole again. But of course this is not possible since wholeness, for Lacan, is illusionary. In Lacan's reinterpretation of Freud, the phallus itself becomes the metaphor for desire of a perfect union with another—a type of wholeness. In this sense children of either sex recognize their own lack and the lack of their mother and want to reunite with her and become whole by making themselves into phallic objects—objects of desire leading to reconnection. Thus, the desire for wholeness is not a drive for sexual release to which Freud refers, but it is a means of overcoming one's primal sense of abandonment and disconnection.

There is an ongoing dialectic in Lacan between becoming separated and becoming whole. Such tension produces an abandonment anxiety that is inherent in modern language. Thus when Lacan speaks of *le nom du père* or in-the-name-of-the-father, he is referring to the assignment of language and a name by the father. The castration anxiety of Freud is explained by Lacan as symbolic wherein the child is separated from mother and its desired oneness. By turning toward the father the child must negate its claims for reconnection and accept the word as Law.

Overall Lacan's contribution to our understanding of abandonment rests in his notion of absence or lack. At the moment we develop a sense of self we are abandoned to a world of others. We sense an alienation, a loss. We become objects among other objects. Although we may try to reconnect, we can never achieve a sense of wholeness again. This absence or lack is what drives us through life, especially in capitalistic society. It fills us with desire, making us into consumers—longing to fill some void with objects, but never achieving consummation.

THE FEMINIST PERSPECTIVE

Feminist theory has done much to illuminate the importance of abandonment anxiety in the socialization process. Feminist theoreticians have offered significant insights into the role of gender in the development of personal identity and the social construction of reality. The phallocentric nature of classical Freudian analysis has become the target of many of these thinkers. If there is a common theme running through feminist discourse it is how the caregiver–child relationship is distorted in the orthodox psychoanalytic narrative, and how this needs to be reformulated. Those theorists discussed here look beyond the familial in constructing their unique perspectives on abandonment.

Karen Horney was among the first women to directly attack Freud's inherent male biases and to construct a theoretical psychoanalytic model that was critical of some of the key psychoanalytic assumptions. Unlike Klein, she saw the more intricate connections between the social structure and intimate familial relations. She did not try to bend Freud's ideas to complement her own insights, but rather directly rejected many of them. She paid the price dearly by being excoriated by him and by later

losing her position in the New York Psychoanalytic Institute. Born in
Germany and schooled in Berlin, Horney migrated to the United States
in 1932. Her work is most closely associated with other neo-Freudians
who took a deeper cultural view of human relations. This group
included Erich Fromm, Frieda Fromm-7Reichmann, and, the American,
Harry Stack Sullivan.

Horney zeroed in on narcissism as a central problem in modern
societies and the underlying basis of neurosis originating in early childhood attachments and separations. She notes:

> As in all neurotic phenomena we find at the basis disturbances in the rela-
> tionships with others, disturbances acquired in childhood through the
> environmental influences. . . . The factor which contributes most funda-
> mentally to the development of narcissistic trends appears to be the child's
> alienations from others, provoked by grievances and fears. His positive
> emotional ties with others become thin; he loses the capacity to love.[43]

While narcissism was played out interpersonally, it was seen as conditioned by contemporary culture. "[T]he striving for prestige as a means
of overcoming fears and inner emptiness is culturally prescribed."[44]
Horney rejects the classical view that the striving to objectify and control others is primarily a result of anal or oral character structures associated with narcissism. While she does not dismiss these classifications, she
sees them as a result of deep-seated early childhood experiences marked
by feelings of helplessness, loss, and aloneness in a seemingly hostile
world. The traits associated with narcissism, she insists, emerge as a
defense. Again for Horney the social environment, particularly family,
fosters these tendencies of submission and control.

In modern families in which children are viewed merely as extensions and reflections of their parents, in families where there can be no
questioning of authority, in places where children seem to be loved not
for themselves but for imaginary qualities imposed upon them by parents there is an inability to develop a sense of self. Narcissism results
not from a fantasy of self, but from perfectionistic, masochistic, and
sadistic trends often emanating from similar sources. Again, these
emerge as coping strategies. Long before 1979 when Christopher Lasch
published *Culture of Narcissism*, Horney contended that modern capitalistic culture produces these narcissistic trends. In such societies:
"More often than not people are incapable of friendship and love; they
are egocentric, that is concerned with their security, health and recognition; they feel insecure and tend to overrate their personal significance; they lack judgement of their own value because they have
relegated it to others."[45]

While Freud sees these trends inherent in human biology, Horney, like Fromm, Sullivan, and other interpersonally oriented theorists, rejects this position. Instead she proposes that it is the culture that produces in children what she refers to as "base anxiety." She posits that capitalism produces fears and hostile tensions that alienate people from each other, limit individual separation, and promote a standardization of feelings, thoughts, and behaviors. Likewise, modern capitalistic culture produces a striving for prestige that becomes a means of coping with inner emptiness.[46] Narcissism and all of its discrete elements is a neurotic method of accommodation.

While Freud views female masochism and much of female neurosis as connected to penis envy, Horney rejects this concept as used and is particularly disdainful of the notion expressed within this argument that women are somehow sexually incomplete. For her the neurotic state of some women has less to do with desiring a penis than with their treatment within the patriarchal family. She insists, again, that one needs to look to the culture. Horney does ground-breaking work to show that masochism is not a female response, but a human response to oppression and a sense of powerlessness frequently emanating from feelings of abandonment.

By the late 1970s, women were beginning to react more forcefully to orthodox Freudian models of psychopathology and psychotherapy. Dorothy Dinnerstein's work, particularly *The Mermaid and the Minotaur*, shifted attention away from oedipal relations and focused on the processes of mothering.[47] Like Klein and Horney, Dinnerstein views pre-oedipal relations and the role of mother as central to personality development. Since mother is the primary caregiver who occupies an almost omnipotent position in the life of the child, it is this position that leads to her own social disempowerment.

According to Dinnerstein, at the stage the child is ready to break away from mother, he or she sees only the father as the individualized model—an alternative to motherly control and engulfment. The world of the father is viewed as a place of spontaneity, adventure, and freedom; one that is free from domestication. The consequences of such a division in power and freedom affect the socialization process condemning boys and girls, men and women, to rigid roles and feelings of ambivalence toward the place of woman in society. Mother is viewed as both comforting and unreliable, protecting yet malevolent.[48] She has far too great a power over the child's life, asserts Dinnerstein, in that she can give or withhold care, encourage or forbid individual autonomy. Thus women are the targets of blame and the object of vindictiveness. It is her assertion that responsibility of children must be shared between men and women.

This is the only way to address this significant problem. This idea was to become central in Nancy Chodorow's analysis of gender socialization.

Chodorow's work was also seminal and has been modified with time and significantly refined. While trained in psychoanalysis, Chodorow's central contribution has been that of a sociologist. Where Horney pushed psychoanalysis to consider culture, she still viewed aspects of femininity and heterosexuality as biologically innate. Dinnerstein's work was a bridge from a Freudian model to Chodorow's sociological take on feminism.

Chodorow's feminism is grounded in the contention that gender and sex roles are socially constructed and that gender and sexuality are cultural products.[49] Male and female personality development are viewed as culturally conditioned. Young girls, daughters, are cyclically conditioned to assume assigned feminine roles—especially that of mother.[50] They are trained to be nurturers and caregivers. In contrast, women produce boys, sons, whose nurturing capacities and needs have been systematically curtailed and repressed. Boys are trained to assume a less affective role in family, to deny or ignore their feelings, and to prepare themselves more fully for the extra-familial world of work. Girls are skilled in interpersonal relations and conditioned to be more emotionally accessible. This process is produced and reproduced in culture.

Chodorow asserts that in infancy both boys and girls are dependent on and intimately attached to their mothers. But boys are taught to distance themselves from mothers early on. They are even pushed away from mother at an earlier age than girls. They must learn to view mother as something alien to themselves, and to identify with their fathers. In this process boys sustain an emotional break—a loss to which they must never admit. Girls are not required to do this. They can remain attached to their mothers and are even encouraged to do so. The problems connected to these processes appear later on as the child matures. The separation anxiety of boys drives them. This has been well documented since Chodorow's initial observation.[51] Boys become men through separation, and leaving the comfort of a nurturing mother they develop a host of anxiety-related neuroses through which they function. Girls are conditioned to remain dependent and accordingly develop neurotic dependency needs and fears of abandonment. Women learn to tolerate dependency, men learn to fear and disdain it, yet unconsciously crave it.

While girls typically retain a strong emotional attachment to their mothers, their fathers have been conditioned to be emotionally and physically distant from their children as they mature. Girls learn to identify with their mothers and to use them as role models. However, both girls and boys learn that women are there to sacrifice, to care for others, and to mother. Because of this women come to be viewed as powerless in modern capitalistic societies wherein these traits are associated with weakness. While many more women enter into business today than ever before, still they tend to remain in less strategically significant positions within organizations; more become teachers, social workers, nurses, and helping professionals in the lowest paid strata of society. The culture often associates male images with power and female images with vulnerability. The feminization of poverty is both a reflection of this condition and a symbol of it.

Ongoing psychological issues in the lives of men often center around their inability to recognize and meet the emotional needs of others. They have fear of and longing for personal connection; they are more capable of objectifying people, especially women, and therefore can view the world as objects to be manipulated and controlled. Underlying male autonomy is frequently extreme emotional insecurity and an unconscious longing for dependency, which is a cultural taboo. Such a denial of dependency and the objectification of others can be easily put into the service of capital wherein people can be effectively used and discarded, with little sense of empathy.

Chodorow delves into the interconnections between object relations in family life and the cultural requirements that produce them. She sees in family a mechanism for the reproduction of a culture—one that dismisses the need for deep human connection in boys yet stresses the domesticity of girls. While this takes place on an intimate familial level, she views the entire process being shaped by phallocentric structural forces. The solutions lie in structural changes that provide space for greater role flexibility within the family.

Judith Butler's work supports Chodorow's but centers more specifically on what she refers to as "gender melancholy."[52] For her, these rigid identity formulations produced in modem individualistic societies, which await young boys and young girls, foster both a longing for and a simultaneous unconscious sense of resentment of otherness. In the light of harshly prescriptive gender assignment, the individual is left fragmented, unable to achieve an experience of completeness.

Jessica Benjamin also draws on many of Chodorow's insights, but moves the feminist psychoanalytic critique further along. Her work has been instrumental in illuminating important issues of separation and attachment as well as domination and submission inherent in the current processes of socialization. Under attack in her seminal work *Bonds of Love* is Freud's acceptance of the patriarchal family.[53] Much like Horney, Fromm, and other more sociologically oriented theorists, Benjamin focuses on the Hegelian dialectic of domination and submission, bondage and liberation in the construction of personal and social identity. While this is nothing new in itself it is driven by a reaction to the patriarchal biases inherent in orthodox psychoanalytic thought as well as more left-ist notions of Reich, Adorno, Marcuse, Lasch, and others that the undermining of familial patriarchy spells the rise of authoritarianism. "What is extraordinary about Freudian thought," she notes, " is that it occurs exclusively in a world of men. The struggle for power takes place between father and son. . . ."[54] When domination and submission are discussed, it is between males.

Benjamin's focus on domination is indebted to Simone de Beauvoir's notion that in modern societies woman serves as man's *other*, his opposite, "playing nature to his reason, immanence to his transcen-dence, primordial oneness to his individuated separateness, object to his subject."[55] Her contribution to the abandonment landscape is shaped by a combination of critical social thought, interrelational psychoanalysis, and object relations. Her locus of analysis is familial life in the west and the social conditioning patterns in forming the bonds of attachment, which significantly promote the dread of abandonment. The importance of recognition—the recognition of the self, of other, and of mutual inter-relatedness displaces the more orthodox phallocentric emphasis on oppositions characterized by submission and dominance. She speaks of the importance of mutuality and intersubjectivity—a term the meaning of which she borrows from critical social theorist Jürgen Habermas. For Benjamin the intersubjective view "maintains that the individual grows in and through the relationship to other subjects."[56] Thus, there are no objects, only subjects in this respect—each is an important self both dif-ferent from and similar to the other subject—capable of mutual under-standing and sharing common feelings and mental experiences.

Intersubjectivity is distinguished from the intrapsychic view wherein the self is a discrete unit with a complex internal structure—a view that underlies much object-relations discourse. Such a perspective sees the unconscious as the crucial target of exploitation. On the other hand, intersubjective theory looks at self–other relations in terms of interrelatedness. To this end Benjamin examines traditional theory of childhood attachment and separation promulgated by psychoanalysts. She particularly attacks Margaret Mahler's developmental theory of dif-ferentiation of the child as "unilinear"—going from oneness to complete separateness rather than understanding that there is never a real separa-tion, certainly not psychically. For her there is only an evolving balance between the two. The same would hold true in erotic relationships wherein there is mutual recognition without loss of the self. Just being attuned to the other gives one pleasure.

The intersubjective dynamic of infant–caregiver relations requires mutual recognition: the child's ability to recognize its caregiver as a person is an essential developmental goal of separation. Too frequently, asserts Benjamin, there has been an inadequate recognition of mother in her own right. She rejects the notion of self-psychologists that the recognition sought by the child from its mother is something the mother can only grant through virtue of her independent identity. Likewise she rejects Winnicott's position that it is the role of mother to mirror the child. Benjamin stresses the erotic union between caregiver and infant, mother and child. Arguing with the Hegelian notion of total dominance and submission, she suggests that this "struggle unto death" or complete surrender eliminates the possibility of authenticity. Such struggles can and do result in the realization that if we fully negate the other, that is if we assume complete control over the other and destroy his or her identity and will, then we have negated ourselves as well. At this point there will be no one to recognize us, no one there for us to desire.

Drawing upon Reagé's novel *The Story of O*, and the work of Georges Bataille, Benjamin critically disposes of the value of this Hegelian paradigm that is for the most part supported in classical psychoanalytic thought. For her, submission is viewed primarily as a quest for recognition of the other who is powerful enough to bestow it and not, as Freud suggests, as a desire for pain. The deepest fear of the submissive is abandonment which in Bataille's view can be equated with death of the self. Submission is one way of ensuring that one will not be abandoned immediately. Nevertheless, it is the fear of abandonment that drives the process, which often can include painful experiences. This is what drives O to Rene in *The Story of O*—a quest for connection. This is a desire for pleasure, not pain. Benjamin uses Bataille's notion of eroticism to further explain this.

> Individual existence for Bataille is a state of separation and isolation: we are islands, connected yet separated by a sea of death. Eroticism is the perilous crossing of that sea. It opens the way out of isolation by exposing us to 'death. . . . The denial of our individual lives . . .' the crossing of boundaries, is for Bataille the secret of all eroticism. . . .[57]

For Benjamin, it is the sadist who exists only through an ability to control the other and perhaps even inflict pain—to see the other as an object of manipulation, not as a part of the self. The sadist is also fearful of losing self, frightened by nonrecognition, driven by the fear of being abandoned and doubtful of his or her own existence if there is no one to control. Benjamin, drawing upon Chodorow, suggests that boys in western capitalistic societies are so conditioned. They are taught that their identity and independence can only be achieved by repudiating their most intimate connection, their connection with mother. They must see their mother as both different and separate, as submissive and weak. Girls, on the other hand, gain their identity only through the recognition of themselves in their mothers. Boys are therefore socialized to be nonsubmissive, nonempathetic, and controlling. They are easily frustrated when others do not yield to their wishes or demands. Girls, however, see themselves as objects of manipulation. Their identity is often derived from their self-sacrifice. They maintain their relationships with their mothers by being compliant, often sacrificing autonomy and later reenacting this erotic submission with male authorities.

Reaffirming Lacan, Benjamin makes the point that penis envy as proposed in Freud's oedipal theory needs to be reinterpreted as a desire for the phallus that represents power. The girl does not desire her father's penis, but envies his autonomy. The "lack" of which Lacan spoke represents this desire. Only when the girl can identify with her father, says Benjamin, can she gain a foundation for healthy development; only when the boy can identify with his mother and see himself in her can this be achieved for him. Until then, it is the dread of disconnectedness, a fear of abandonment that drives and perpetuates submission and dominance, much as it did in *The Story of O.*

COMMODIFICATION OF THE OBJECT

Jonathan and Sally Bloom-Feshbach posit that problems emerging from childhood separation are often believed to be compensated through attachment to inanimate objects which people frequently invest with enduring affect.[58] This accumulation of things frequently reflects a need for control, a need to fill a void. Daniel Buccino, who has explored the relationship between object relations theory and Marx's notion of fetish of commodities, is highly critical of neo-Freudian object relations theory. Like the Frankfurt school theorists, and like Benjamin, he concludes that it is not the object as a thing that creates desire, but the social relations attached to the object.[59] Fetishism for Buccino is the "reification of relations and the products of the mind." The imbuing of the object or commodity with meaning or value is what commodity fetishism attempts to explain in Marxian analysis. He proposes:

> Objects and products in exchange relations become more satisfying than they can ever be themselves. Indeed commodity fetishism has become our secular religion, manifesting itself in consumerism and, I submit, rationalizing itself in object relations theories.[60]

Buccino takes issue with object relations therapy as decidedly linked to servicing capitalism. He sees the word "object" as resonating with capitalistic fragmentation, depersonalization, and commodification. He notes that Marx promoted the idea that in modern capitalistic societies relationships are reduced to the status of commodity relations and exchanges. "Object relations theory," Buccino asserts, "is actually one of many methods supporting the status quo regarding human nature and the inevitability of mass production and consumption."[61] While people might be alienated in modern society, Buccino does not believe that the purpose of psychoanalysis is to insert them back into it. He warns that object relational approaches too frequently mirror the marketplace.

While Buccino might be correct in terms of object relations metaphors, he seems to de-emphasize the more radical dimensions of those theories that reject more orthodox notions. The effect of these newer approaches has been to open-up psychoanalysis to an array of competing paradigms for critically assessing capitalism, itself. The radical implications inherent in Klein, Kohut, Winnicott, and others have been identified by C. Fred Alford, who has drawn parallels between critical theory and theories of object relations.[62]

FROM NARCISSISM TO THE BORDERLINE

While object relations theory has given way to other, more useful psychoanalytic approaches, including self-psychology developed by Heinz Kohut in the 1970s and relational psychotherapy developed by Stephen Mitchell in the 1980s, it was extremely important in framing narcissism as a cultural malaise in post-World War II America. Christopher Lasch's work drew extensively on these theorists. Nevertheless, the narcissism he described reflected a particular stage of capitalistic development in the west. The sense of entitlement, the excessive exploitation of others, the lack of personal empathy, and the excessive need to control or to be controlled were human traits that complemented a fordist system of production. These were in fact qualities that might have been considered strengths in the capitalism of this era with its centralized locus of control.

However, the shift of theraputic concern from narcissism to what the DSM IV identifies as "borderline personality" is obvious. This near epidemic disorder is definitively more postfordist, and more postmodern. It represents the accelerated fragmentation and dispersal not only of the production process, but also of the self in relation to it. It reflects what Marion Toplin called a protracted fragmentation and enfeeblement of self-identity.[63]

Actually, the term "borderline" was developed by Adolph Stern in 1938 and was a label he used for patients he saw in his private practice who appeared to be resistant to treatment. The borderline occupied a space somewhere between the psychotic and neurotic. Often they were misdiagnosed as schizophrenic. All were highly narcissistic individuals with underdeveloped self-concepts and powerful feelings of inferiority, and insecurity. They seemed to display inordinate rule breaking and reality testing behaviors. The borderline personality has been characterized by very poor integration of the self.

Otto Kernberg views the borderline personality as exhibiting an array of intrapsychic problems associated with a typical constellation of symptoms, defenses, and patterns of disturbed object relations internalized in early childhood. In his treatment of borderline issues he draws extensively from the work of Melanie Klein. Klein's focus on splitting, the depressive position, and her emphasis on fragmentation and reintegration have deep significance here. Kernberg sees the borderline personality exhibiting primitive defenses that emerged in early childhood relations with the mother: denial, idealization, omnipotent control, projective identification, devaluation and splitting.[64]

The DSM IV identifies the borderline personality as driven impulsively by a frantic effort to avoid real or imagined abandonment. More than anything else, the anxiety of abandonment and the fear of loss is coupled with a chronic sense of emptiness and overwhelming anger leading to paranoia, dissociation, self-mutilation and suicidal ideation. In fact the fear of abandonment leads the borderline person to want to attach to or merge with others to avoid aloneness. Still, while this need for attachment is overwhelming, this individual is reluctant to connect for fear of being abandoned in the end. Such individuals tend to avoid those who might give them happiness and intimacy and seek out only superficial connections.

The world of the borderline is a reflection of the superficiality of the postmodern world. Like narcissism, it has become emblematic of the new era wherein there are few if any deep relationships and where primitive defenses have become strengths in dealing with an ephemeral, fragmented world. It is highly reflective of the postmodern, postfordist condition of disorganized capital, and flexible accumulation. The crisis in identity brought on by these forces meet to create an ephemeral individual with an overriding fear of disappearing into a world of objects.

CONCLUSION

Abandonment is central to the psychoanalytic landscape. There it is portrayed as producing intense feelings of anxiety associated with modern life. It is manifested in a variety of neuroses and psychopathologies that condition the processes of socialization. Psychologists suggest that if children were provided with a secure emotional base in childhood for their development, they would become more capable of exploring the new. Armed with a sense of personal security and confidence, an individual could more easily seek out challenges and be comfortable with change. Without being equipped in childhood with a sense of security, one is impeded in his or her ability to develop into a healthy self-directed human being. Without healthy attachment in childhood, and without trust, the prospect of forming healthy adult relationships is dimmed.

In modern societies, many children go without the support of caring adults for a significant part of the day. This phenomenon cuts across class lines. Since autonomy and self-reliance are emphasized in modern culture, the critical needs of children for physical connectedness and emotional intimacy too frequently go unrecognized or are ignored. There is an enormous degree of loneliness experienced by the elderly consigned to the assisted living industry. Unresolved feelings of loneliness and alienation contribute at several levels to social problems. Many compulsive and addictive behaviors have more than a casual link to abandonment anxiety. Compulsive consumerism, excessive TV viewing, computer gaming, spectator sports, drugs, and pornography become means of escaping these feelings of anxiety. It's easy to see how compulsivity has become a permanent aspect of modern culture.

In viewing the impact of childhood abandonment on adults, Colin Murray Parkes has emphasized the "search" that takes place in the lives of those who have suffered from early separation and the anxiety associated with it.[65] This anxiety is especially intense when we detach from a defined and known social world and enter into the unknown—our own private wilderness. Adolescence, old age, and other periods of personal crises are examples of these places in which we feel very much alone. The need to possess, to hold on to people or things, is often a sign of having been threatened with abandonment or having actually suffered it. Parkes's findings complement the work of Horney suggesting that narcissistic possessiveness and the need for control are major outcomes of dysfunctional bonding and child rearing. So is the state of disconnection and personal alienation. Without early bonds of love, without the comfort provided by a secure emotional base of trust, a venture into the unknown is lonely and ominous.

Finally, there can be little doubt that these modes of analysis are complementary to the evolution of modern market societies. The perceived fragmentation of the psyche parallels to the evolution of bureaucratic and capitalistic division of labor. The separation of affect from persona is in no way evolutionary or natural. It has obvious structural antecedents. As David Frisby notes:

> Modernity consists in a particular mode of experiencing the world, one that is reduced not merely to our inner responses to it but also to its incorporation in our inner life. The external world becomes part of our inner world. In turn, the substantive element of the exernal world is reduced to a ceaseless flux. The fleeting, fragmentary and contradictory movements of our external life are all incorporated into our inner life. Viewed in this manner, modernity presents a distinctive problem for its analysts . . . now it is possible to capture a fleeting, fragmentary and contradictory social reality that has been reduced to individual inner experience.[66]

In the coming chapters an effort will be made, using a variety of perspectives, to better understand these connections.

Chapter 4

Fragmentation and Abandonment
of Conscience

Psychological models of attachment and separation as well as object relations theories emphasized an acute sense of individuation. As cultural products, similar to other narrative works of art, these theoretical conceptualizations appeared to be consonant with the intensity of fragmentation associated with both early and late modernity.

Modern European philosophers, artists, and social scientists made it clear that the world in which they lived was breaking apart. Modernity and capitalism seemed to foster an array of ruptures and discontinuities that were manifest in the high culture of modernism. The fragmentation of the psyche and the significance of the primal unconscious, dramatically described in Freudian discourse, were unique products of modernist culture. They existed side by side within a European tableau of imperialism, sexism, conquest, war, and capitalism. Carl Schorske, in describing the city of Vienna at the end of the nineteenth century, frames this as follows:

> European high culture entered a whirl of infinite innovation, with each field proclaiming independence of the whole, each part in turn falling into parts. Into the ruthless centrifuge of change were drawn the very concepts by which cultural phenomena might be fixed in thought. Not only the producers of culture, but also its analysts and critics fell victim to the fragmentation.[1]

While this is not to say that segmentation and alienation were new concepts, they were given a special place in the narrative of modernity. By

121

the end of World War I, the processes of fragmentation seemed to be accelerating.

Through an examination of select discourse, this chapter explores personal fragmentation in the context of modern development. Particular attention is given here to the reification of consciousness that arose in response to the forces of modernity. It is the intent of this chapter to examine psychic fragmentation as essential to the culture of modernity, which reveals itself in the make-up of the modern consciousness and the reified conscience that emerges from it. While this is not intended as a survey of sociological phenomenology, it does suggest that phenomenology itself could have only emerged as it did in such a modern context.

MODERNISM AND FRAGMENTATION

Modernism is used here to mean an aesthetic expression of modernity. This does not mean it is exclusive to art, but rather it refers to something much broader—a type of understanding deeply centered in personal cognition and affect. It connects to such values as beauty and truth but reaches beyond them into the world of politics and social relations. It is above all a perspective or set of perspectives.

Modern art was never a uniform, comprehensive aesthetic expression; it has always been a movement made up of a constellation of other movements, often quite different from one another, often in opposition to each other. However, for modernism to exist there must be elements of commonality. Eugene Lunn identifies four such areas: first, aesthetic self-consciousness or self-reflectiveness; second, simultaneity, juxtaposition, or *montage*; third, paradox, ambiguity and uncertainty; and finally, dehumanization and the demise of the integrated individual, subject or personality.[2]

While one may wish to add or subtract elements, it is clear that Lunn sets out a very broad framework here. In art such components are often combined to portray the modern landscape. All have relevance to the foregoing presentation of social theory, which itself comes out of the same social forces: the waning of religion, political concentration of power, the Kantian revolution, positivism, science, the industrial revolution, bureaucracy, capitalism, and so on. For early modern artists, the world was revealing itself through a radical disruption of form and a fragmentation of substance. Writing in 1933, Herbert Read noted:

> There have been revolutions in the history of art before today. There is a
> revolution with every new generation, and periodically, every century or

so, we get a wider deeper change of sensibility which is recognized as a period—the Trecento, the Quattro Cento, the Baroque, the Rococo, the Romantic, the Impressionist and so on. But I do think we can already discern a difference in kind in the contemporary revolution; it is not so much a revolution, which implies a turning over, even a turning back, but rather a break-up, a devolution, some would say a dissolution. Its character is catastrophe.[3]

Malcolm Bradbury and James McFarlane claim that modernism is often characterized by a radical form of abstraction, an undermining of traditional form and language and a violation of expected continuities. They see it as both a reaction to and a reflection of a myriad of disruptive social forces. They go on to say: "[modern art] was free to catch the manifold—the atoms as they fell—and create a significant harmony, not in the universe but within itself."[4] Modernism represents for them and for many others a continual becoming, and an ongoing process of disintegration and re-integration, a project of experimentation. It confronts each individual as both a hope and a threat.

> . . . Modernism might mean not only a new mode of mannerism in the arts, but a certain magnificent disaster for them. In short, experimentalism does not simply suggest the presence of sophistication, difficulty and novelty in art, it also suggests bleakness, darkness, alienation and disintegration.[5]

It would be impossible for us to understand modernism by limiting ourselves to artists and their products. Modernism was equally expressed in social theory of the day. The aesthetic of modernism entered the lives of philosophers, sociologists, and scientists of all sorts who attempted to gain a sense of meaning from the fragmented world that they were confronting.

FRAGMENTATION OF LABOR

Adam Smith's focus on the fragmentation of work and the ever-increasing division of labor in *The Wealth of Nations*, spoke to the many ways in which commerce was transforming society, not just the marketplace. He posited that the processes of industrialization and commercialization were lowering the intelligence and reasoning capacity of workers. Capitalism encouraged specialization to the point of promoting stupidity.[6] Later, Marx would look at the same division of labor in relation to fragmentation and alienation of labor. And of course Emile Durkheim saw this specialization as weakening the collective conscience and transforming communities into society. Other *fin-de-siècle* sociologists, most particularly Tonnies and Simmel, made much of this breaking apart.

For Max Weber, the processes of spiraling bureaucratization, with its attending specialization, along with the ever-sweeping reign of rationalization was radically altering the character of modern society and those who were a part of it. His rendering of a gloomy landscape of social atomization and iron cages with heartless bureaucrats overseeing the dismantlement of a once enchanted world crystallized the sentiments of many. Yet it was Weber's acute cultural analysis, his detailed study of specific human conditions, social structures and processes, which set his work apart from the more totalizing analyses of Karl Marx. Inherent in Weber's work was a Kantian belief in the importance of maintaining a division between facts and values. While Weber lamented the loss of potential freedom that bureaucratic capitalism and western modernization implied, he maintained a strong personal reverence for authority. And while Marx called for revolution, Weber subscribed to what Kant termed moral imperatives, duty and loyalty. His overall tone was guarded pessimism, sometimes more overt despair and fatalism, revealing his own underlying depression that necessitated his hospitalization in 1897.

Weber saw rationalization and fragmentation arising in the west from specific cultural conditions and particularly accelerated by increasing bureaucratization and the application of expanding technical knowledge to the realm of work and, particularly, its institutional organization and administration. While he did not see these same conditions at work everywhere, he made it very clear that capitalism was responsible for much of its modern form:

> Though by no means alone, the capitalist system has undeniably played a major role in the development of bureaucracy. Indeed, without it capitalistic production could not continue and any rational type of socialism would have simply to take it over and increase its importance. Its development, largely under capitalistic auspices, has created an urgent need for stable, strict, intensive, and calculable administration. It is this need which is so fateful to any large-scale administration.[7]

While capitalism might take some of its bureaucratic structure from antiquity, the Church, the military, and elsewhere, it developed a uniquely rational structure. Bureaucratic capitalism became the most important instrument for organizing, managing, and controlling power.[8] Through increased specialization, rules and technocratic procedures, through impersonality and hierarchy of command, the modern bureaucracy became an instrument of human domination.

Such bureaucratization seemed to be associated with changes in perception and thought. It is important to note that Weber distinguishes between several types of rational thought, but the most relevant categories to this discussion are instrumental reasoning and ethical reasoning. The first type is a form of bounded rationality, a means-end type, confined to a particular framework governed by rules, regulations and understanding. Here what is rational in one setting might be irrational given another framework. The second type is concerned with values. Like Kant, Weber holds that values are *a priori* and speculative; only speculative reason lends itself to this sphere. Thus he arrives at a belief in the feasibility if not the necessity of dualistic analysis—separating one from the other. The working of modern bureaucratic systems is typically divorced from cultural values, which rest outside of organizational needs and might often be in conflict with them. This disturbing element was viewed as an inevitable condition of modernization, something that could not be rectified. Weber proposes that bureaucratic sensibilities would come to dominate the future making their way into most aspects of life.

The dark pessimism of Weber jumps from the pages of his narratives. There is an unstoppable finality to those systems that seems to condemn people to an ongoing process of dehumanization. Like in a Kafka novel, the unseen bureaucrat rules the day creating an irrational world with his rational rules void of moral reasoning. Weber's ideas, while deeply disturbing eventually make their way into more radical analyses, such as that of Lukács, which will be taken up later. But before doing this, it is important that some attention be given to the work of Georg Simmel in this regard since he is a bridge between the two.

MONEY AND SOCIAL DISINTEGRATION

Georg Simmel's work on fragmentation is best understood through his *Philosophy of Money*. The book is highly complex in that it is primarily a set of loosely connected theoretical observations of the modern conditions which have money exchange as their essential fulcrum. While the work focuses on the money economy with an emphasis on modern capitalism, it is a far-ranging work that often meanders—hovering between psychology and sociology but covering more ground than can be approached here. A fascinating history of the book, which was first published in German in 1900, is presented by David Frisby in his Introduction to the 1990 Second Edition.[9]

In this work Simmel uses money and exchange often metaphorically not only to discuss structural change in society, but also to develop his impressions of individual psychology relative to these. He begins by taking a Hegelian position that mental life begins as a state of undifferentiated oneness wherein the ego and its objects are not yet distinguished. He asserts that early consciousness is filled with impressions and perceptions (representations not yet objectified) since there is no conception of object and subject. It is only when one detaches from these impressions and objectifies them through developing an external sense of subject–object relations that she or he can see oneself as separate, as a subject. It is only through these object relationships that the individual can develop a personality. Thus, the self, or the "subject" can only become manifest through a sense of the object, specifically detachment from it. And it is through object relations that one experiences the world. Simmel's conceptualization of separation and attachment is similar in some respects to that of Melanie Klein's and other early object relations theorists. Yet, Simmel frames these relationships in terms of subject–object exchange, a type of relatedness that has as its basis a more macro-ordered structural foundation.

A sense of value and exchange emerges at the onset of subject–object relationships. It is proposed by Simmel that satisfaction is gained through object consumption or internalization, not through one's own production as Marx had posited. It is this dynamic of exchange and the process of consumption that develops a sense of self. Our earliest and most primal exchange entailed a loss of self by merging with the object and becoming one with it. However, it is only through subject–object exchange that relative value can be determined. Simmel asserts that it is only through the creation of distance between the subject and the object that consciousness can arise.[10]

Drawing upon Kant, Simmel also proposes that the value of an object is determined by one's distance from it. Thus, part of the Kantian aesthetic is that desire of objects can only exist if they are not immediately given to us for our personal pleasure. While Simmel believes in a primal natural equality of all things, he views value as subjectively determined by the degree of desire. Desire, therefore, is essential to the creation of consciousness:

> This tension which disrupts the naive-practical unity of subject and object and makes us conscious of each in relation to the other, is brought about originally through the mere fact of desire. In desiring what we do not yet own or enjoy, we place the content of our desire outside ourselves.[11]

In a Lacanian sense, this would represent a lack. Thus, reality presses upon our consciousness by the resistance of objects to our desire—through a perceived lack. Such objects are seen as independent of us and are recognized as real and part of an objective world. Increasingly, the subject becomes aware of the existence of other subjects and the possibility of other values, other subject–object relations.

Exchange becomes a means of expanding consciousness, opening the subjective internal perspective to a more external or objective one. It is a way through which subjective values become objectified. Through such objectification, one then comes to see oneself both as subject and as object and understands that there is an objective culture outside of oneself, values outside of one's own. Exchange is viewed by Simmel as a foundation for society and culture. Through it one moves to a higher level of abstraction wherein objects are not only attractive because of some essence one subjectively sees in them, but also for their value in the exchange process itself. In modern societies money comes to represent objective values and is used to express the value of one object in relation to another.

Early on, money, such as coins, had an intrinsic value of their own, but in modern society money expresses a more abstract condition of value. Simmel views credit and paper money dominating modern social conditions, as dramatically increasing the velocity of exchange, increasing the number and rate of interpersonal relationships, promoting trust among those who use it and, therefore, frequently creating an objectified form of solidarity. However, money also expands the power of central authorities that guarantee its worth; it increases depersonalized social relations and substitutes a money calculus for values. It was Simmel's observation that money extended itself into all spheres of interaction, penetrating even the most intimate social relations.

Simmel acknowledges that money helps to promote personal freedom in that it removes the subject from totalizing subjective culture. At the same time it promotes a type of personal evanescence and estrangement in that it detaches one from the solidarity of the subjective. It fosters rationalization of a particular type, and as such it is in best harmony with industrialization and technological advancements that it helps to produce. However, money also produces anomie, reification of human relationships, and personal alienation including fragmentation of the self.

It is the rapid expansion of objective culture during the nineteenth century and its dominance over the subjective that drives much of Simmel's analyses of the modern condition. He sees an "enigmatic relationship" developing between "social life and its products on one hand and the fragmentary life-contents of the individual on the other."[12] The objectified culture represents a material world that overwhelms the individual in terms of its inexhaustability. This world is comprised of the mental and physical works of a host of subjects who have helped to construct the culture throughout its life history. It is one that lies outside of subjective culture, but is related to it in that it emerges from the collectivity of subjective experiences. There is an existing asymmetry between the two. It is a type of rapprochement between them that is at the heart of Simmel's object relations. For the modern individual, however, the only knowledge that becomes "real" lies within the objective culture. Simmel notes: "Our practical existence, though inadequate and fragmentary, gains a certain significance and coherence, as it were, by taking in the realization of a totality."[13] It is from this condition that one often becomes alienated from the self.

Simmel's discussion goes easily from the micro-order to the macro-order, making intricate and often profound connections as he narrates his view of modernity. The construction of objective consciousness and its relation to the division of labor warrants close consideration for this presentation. It is here that his analysis closely parallels ideas of both Marx and Weber. Simmel views the worker's separation from the means of production through money as part of the division of labor. He proposes that money is the most impersonal of objects and at the same time the most personal in that it is a means to an end, too frequently becoming an end in itself. It hollows out the social and cultural significance of the world and through the division of labor, which it helps to support, depersonalizes, and further fragments the laborer and his or her relationships with others. Like Marx, Simmel focuses on reification. Where Marx attributes this to the division of labor, Simmel attributes it to money. It is money that helps to objectify the world including the worker. The laborer is made into an object to compete for value in the ebb and flow of currency. Hence, what Marx sees as emanating from capitalism (alienation, personal estrangement, and fragmentation) Simmel sees as the outcome of impersonal exchange associated with modern money economies. The division that takes place in the consciousness of the individual with one foot in subjective culture and the other in the objective world, is assessed in these terms. However, they would be much further developed by Simmel's student, Georg Lukács.

GEORG LUKÁCS AND THE REIFICATION
OF CONSCIOUSNESS

One of the more important intellectual products of twentieth century Marxism was Georg Lukács's *History and Class Consciousness*, published in 1922. Lukács, who was born into a bourgeois family in Budapest, was perhaps better known for his cultural criticisms and less for his speculative scholarship. His father was the Director of the

Hungary General Credit Bank. His mother, a descendant of a well known Talmudist, was well educated but emotionally removed from her son. Since there was growing anti-Semitism in Hungary at the time, the family distanced itself from Judaism. The young Lukács was enrolled in an Evangelical Gymnasium as a child and later attended the universities of Budapest, Berlin, and Heidelberg. He attended lectures given by Georg Simmel in Berlin and studied with Max Weber—both of whom he came to know personally. In fact, Weber took an interest in him.[14] Among those whom Lukács would call friend were Leo Popper and Ernst Bloch. In 1915 Lukács became a leader of what was referred to as a "Sunday Circle" in Budapest, which included such thinkers as Karl Mannheim, Michael Polanyi, René Spitz, Béla Bartók, and Béla Balázs, his closest friend. While he spent much of his time engaged in writing, he was also a political activist and leader of the Hungarian Communist Movement; he became an active participant in the Hungarian uprising of 1956.

Georg Lukács was among the first theorists to deal with Marx's more humanistic work on alienation and human commodification, well before the dormant *The Economic and Philosophic Manuscripts of 1844* were made available to the public. His biographer, Lee Congdon, contends that his personal feelings of isolation and estrangement in early childhood, particularly his distance from his mother, were central influences in his life-long attraction to human alienation as a problem central to modernity.[15] In *History and Class Consciousness*, Lukács amplified Marx's work on reification and class consciousness from *Das Kapital* bringing them into the twentieth century and connecting these ideas with theories of Weber and Simmel. This angered many orthodox Marxists of the day; and while there is much in this particular work that Lukács later regretted having written, there is more that makes this an important synthesis of modern social thought.

Perhaps a key essay, which attempts to shed light on the disintegrating effect of modern capitalism, was "Reification and the Consciousness of the Proletariat."[16] Lukács contends here that commodity production was the central, structural problem in capitalistic society and was responsible for the vaporizing nature of modernity. Taking Marx's notion of fetishism of commodities wherein commodities were given an independent life of their own separate from those who produced them, he looks at this phenomenon as part of a totalizing process of reification. Marx had proposed that capitalism produces a fetishism through a process of production wherein workers become alienated commodities (alienated labor) and as such they converge, alienated from one another, to produce other commodities. These commodities gain a life of their own, alienated both from those who produced them and from the substance from which they came, and eventually assume a set of social relations among themselves. Lukács raises the question: "how far is commodity exchange, together with its structural consequences able to influence the total outer and inner life of society?" Of course, here he includes both the macro-order as well as the psychic conditions emerging from it.

Lukács begins his answer by reformulating Marx's notion of commodities. He looks at exchange historically, first in the form of barter relations in tribal societies. He suggests that primitive barter societies have a tendency to decompose over time. This is because barter usually began not in the interior of a self-contained community but on the borders between the different communities involved in such transactions. "We note," says Lukács, "that the . . . disintegrating effect of a commodity exchange directed in upon itself shows the qualitative change engendered by the dominance of commodities."[17] When commodity exchange penetrates a society in all its aspects, when it becomes universal, it then remolds that society to its own image, reconstituting its structure. For Lukács, commodity exchange only reaches this intensity in modern capitalistic society. It is here where one's labor becomes reified, made into something objective and independent of the worker; it is something that controls the laborer and at the same time is an alien object having power over the worker. "Objectively a world of objects and relations springs into being (the world of commodities and their movement on the market)."[18]

The laws of the market confront people as invisible forces with their own powers over the workers. Subjectively, the worker's own activity is estranged and turns into a commodity subject to the nonhuman objectivity of market laws. Labor alienated from the worker takes on a life of its own. Thus, capitalistic commodity production makes labor into an abstraction that becomes incorporated into commodities.

Lukács claims that in this way modern capitalistic societies produce the objectification of labor, of things, of nature. The process of rationalization, the type of which Weber spoke, becomes accelerated to the point that qualitative human attributes of workers disappear and work becomes "progressively broken down into abstract, rational, specialized operations so that the worker loses contact with the finished product and his work is reduced to the mechanical repetition of a specialized set of actions."[19] Lukács continues:

> With the modern "psychological" analysis of the work processes (in Taylorism) this rational mechanization extends right into the worker's "soul": even his psychological attributes are separated from his total personality and placed in opposition to it so as to facilitate their integration into specialized rational systems and their reduction to statistically viable concepts.[20]

Lukács thus combines Marx's notion of commodification with Max Weber's emphasis on rationalization to present a landscape of worker alienation brought about by a rationally mechanized process of dehumanizing proportions.

Accordingly, he sees rationalization and specialization leading to a destruction of organic unity of the commodity as well as an undermining of its use value. ". . . this fragmentation of the object of production," notes Lukács, "necessarily entails the fragmentation of its subject."[21] People become mechanically integrated into the production system and must shed their idiosyncracies to conform to mechanistic production demands. And as labor becomes progressively standardized, rationalized, and mechanized, quality is eclipsed by quantity in terms of its importance to the production process, and time takes on a central value displacing the primacy of space. "The fate of the worker becomes the fate of society as a whole . . . ."[22]

Individuals become atomized by universal "natural laws," suggests Lukács, which have no universal basis and only exist in the system that was put into effect with their cooperation. The workers are forced to recognize their labor as their sole commodity of value that can be plugged into this system to promote their survival and well-being. They come to recognize that there can be no alternative. Thus people come to see one another as commodities and develop their relationships accordingly: "Just as the capitalist system continuously produces and reproduces itself economically . . . the structure of reification progressively sinks more deeply, more fatefully and more definitively into the consciousness of man."[23]

Again recapitulating Weber, Lukács suggests that human consciousness is shaped by this modern bureaucratic system. Capitalistic reification makes labor into a thing that the worker sells on the market; key mental faculties are also alienated one from the other and ". . . detached from the whole personality and placed in opposition to it, becoming a thing, a commodity."[24] The worker becomes more and more of a thing as he or she absorbs a bureaucratic consciousness and related impartiality and is totally subjected to this means-end rationalist system of domination. Lukács makes the point that it is only under modern capitalism that a unified structure of such consciousness embracing the whole society is brought into being. He proposes that such consciousness is forever bounded and fragmented.

With different commodities competing with one another there is an assumption that natural laws are at work producing order and efficiency. The whole idea of natural laws regulating capitalism is denounced by Lukács as emanating from the imaginations of economists. The rationalization associated with capitalism is filled with contradictory propositions.

In such a system administrative functions become artificially isolated from each other in order to put on a show of rationality, but there never is a rational whole. Specialization of labor destroys every image of wholeness, which in turn produces a sense of loss and a desire on the part of the worker to find commonality with some specialist of a like kind. Lukács launches into a discussion of the undermining influence of the division of labor on the sciences, including economics. It is his discussion in the section entitled "The Antinomies of Bourgeois Thought,"[25] however, that is most revealing and revolutionary. It is here where he attacks the rationality associated with capitalistic development for insinuating itself into all aspects of thought, including western philosophy and art. While this discussion is truly wide-ranging and much of it outside the scope of this chapter, it is important to at least touch upon the central thrust here, which is an attack against Kantian speculation, which he sees splintering reason.

Lukács rejects the Kantian notion of a nonintegrative rational system of processes and borrows the Hegelian notion that reason demands a unified, integrated system of thought. Like Marx, he attacks Hegel's quasi-religious notion of an Absolute Mind, but does accept dialectics as a process that could lead to true integration of cognition. It is the internal clash between a system of reification, one that engenders inner emptiness, with an inability of this system to adequately explain and conceptualize the world that eventually will lead to its own demise. For Lukács, the advance of reason rested in the proletariat who needed to assume a true consciousness. Workers were in the best position to create a world of reason rather than one of fragmented rationalization. He envisions a time when reason will be salvaged from those who distort its purpose and will be put to use for enhancing social progress.

CONSCIOUSNESS WITHOUT CONSCIENCE

For Lukács, Immanuel Kant had revolutionized thinking in the nineteenth century by corrupting reason and undermining the notion of coherent consciousness.[26] He was not alone in his criticism. In his rejection of the hope for integrated, holistic understanding, says Lukács, Kant ignores history and accepts the shattering and disorienting nature of capitalism and modern politics as universal and timeless. In proposing a distinction between a *post priori* truth based on personal experience and empirical evidence and an *a priori* truth that exists independent of experience, he constructs a false binary relationship while dismissing the usefulness of speculative metaphysics. In the place of conscience, Kant argues for virtue and duty guided by categorical imperatives that he suggests exist everywhere and emerge from *a priori* reasoning. For Lukács, Kant's ahistorical focus was a symptom of his time.

Nietzsche had also vehemently attacked the Kantian notion of categorical imperatives: as ". . . virtue that is prompted solely by a feeling of respect for the concept of 'virtue'." Nietzsche chides Kant's assertion that virtue and duty are good in themselves with impersonal and universal validity forming the basis of categorical imperatives.[27] In *Genealogy of Morals*, Nietzsche attacks the moral constraints of modern conscience, as relativistic and crude. It produces a *consciousness of guilt*, or what he terms "bad conscience." Moral codes connected to principles or standards of behavior which incur guilt upon their violation often prevent people from taking action that might be in their own interest and the interest of others. For Nietzsche it is this system of morality, of rules, of duties, that corrupts the classical notion of character and is the essence of civil decadence.

Other, less radical students of philosophy such as Alasdair MacIntyre, attack Kant's moral imperatives, and modern moral precepts in general, as signs of ethical disintegration.[28] Conscience, in a classical sense, was considerably more than personal or social moralisms. It was an ability to make ethical sense of the world and one's place in it. There was no clear separation between awareness of truth and awareness of virtue in antiquity. Both myth and truth were considered part of a common whole. Virtue had much to do with character, it had little to do with rules. While there are many reasons for the movement away from this concept of virtue over time, MacIntyre assails both modernity and capitalism for fragmenting the world and with it moral reasoning. The moral codes that exist in modern western societies are decontextualized fragments from another time; they are frequently contradictory and make little sense. The modern world for MacIntyre seems to have broken into pieces; according to his thesis, one shared by Marx and others, it was once whole.

MacIntyre claims that virtue historically had some teleological significance. But with the advent of capitalism and modernity it disappeared. Virtue united people with a vision for achieving their own *telos* while inspiring a sense of community, commitment, and trust. Some theorists view the undermining of virtue as a gradual historical process, but MacIntyre links it to the collapse of religion in the west and the creative–destructive forces of modernity.[29] He suggests that the appeal of Marxism in modern life is that it presents us with an alternative *telos* wherein the person is viewed as having essence that defines his or her true end. It is predicated on the postulate of a totally integrated human being. He draws parallels between religion and Marxism and conceives that the latter had become a means of dealing with the morally unsettling influences of capitalism. (Of course, MacIntyre sees Marxism as a symptom of the modernist problem, not a solution to it.)

While Lukács sees Marxian utopian communism as providing some answers to the problem of reification, he does not condemn modernity for the condition. Still he views modern production techniques as promoting the reification of consciousness and accelerating the fragmentation of the individual. While splits had certainly existed even in classical cultures, the fragmentation was never as far-ranging, never as profound. He is quite specific in his condemnation of rationalistic capitalism for problems of reification of conscience:

> . . . all this points to the fact that the division of labor which in the case of Taylorism invaded the psyche, here invades the realm of ethics. Far from weakening the reified structure of consciousness, this actually strengthens it.[30]

For Lukács and other critical theorists personal and social fragmentation produced by the capitalist division of labor afforded the individual an ultimate, one-dimensional freedom. By relinquishing the human obligations that had defined one's humanity, by objectifying most interpersonal associations, the individual could now retreat into the realm of the ephemeral—the insubstantial. No longer would there be a need to struggle with issues of right and wrong, good and bad. Since all values are relative, floating freely in the gravity of money and market, connected to a utility of ever-changing situation and circumstance, one could merely act according to the institutional demands or moral imperatives of those instrumental forces. In such a world conscience takes its place alongside of other commodities just as Marx predicted, and it becomes a calculus for maximizing personal benefit—the ultimate value.

THE REIFIED SELF: GOFFMAN AND THE
SOCIOLOGY OF MASKS

It is impossible to discuss the fragmentation and reification of the individual in modern life without at least mentioning the important work of Erving Goffman. Radically different from most of the other social theorists mentioned up until now, Goffman celebrates the fragmenting prowess of modern existence accepting personal disintegration as inevitable. As a symbolic interactionist influenced by the work of

George Herbert Mead and the phenomenology of Simmel, Goffman helped to breathe new life into a floundering sociological perspective.

Goffman did his doctoral work at the University of Chicago while Chicago school theory was very much in a state of disarray. There he came under the very strong influence of Herbert Blumer who eventually left his position in Chicago to take a post at the University of California at Berkeley. At Berkeley Blumer was able to offer him a teaching appointment where they worked together for six years before Goffman eventually moved on to the University of Pennsylvania. Blumer had been a student of Mead and Dewey both of whom emphasized the importance of role theory in the process of socialization. Blumer passed on to his pupil a belief in the significance of micro-order analysis, but Goffman would reject the symbolic interactionist label of his mentor as too confining. He was very much a maverick, devising his own tools and methods and avoiding or ignoring the political turmoil that surrounded him in the 1960s. His ideas eventually caught the attention of poststructuralist and postmodern social theorists who used elements of his work in their own.

A good bit of his more interesting output appears to have been influenced by Simmel's exchange theory. Goffman was introduced to this at Chicago where Simmel was read and appreciated. Simmel was among the very first sociologists to develop the notion of the fragmented self in his work. Many have been intrigued by this idea. While Goffman is frequently criticized by progressive theorists for his ahistoricism and nihilistic views, he is also criticized by traditionalists for proposing as he did the following:

> In analyzing the self then we are drawn from its possessor, from the person who will profit or lose by it, for he and his body merely provide the peg on which something of a collaborative manufacture will be hung for a time. And the means for producing and maintaining selves do not reside inside the peg; in fact these means are often bolted down in social establishments.[31]

While there is much fun here in his description, there is also a hidden apprehension of powerlessness and disconnectedness at the core of this work. What modernity has created for its actors are sets of proscribed roles, costumes, positions. Such roles must be played out according to already established rules. While this frees the individual from the tasks of casting an authentic self, it also negates the possibility of such a project. It is interesting that in his acknowledgment page of his most important work, *The Preservation of Self in Everyday Life*, Goffman gives the reader a *Who's Who* list of some of the most outstanding conservative social thinkers of his time: Edward Banfield, Edward Shils, and William

Lloyd Warner who influenced him. Blumer is not mentioned in the acknowledgments, nor is there a reference to him in the work.

Goffman dedicated most of his life to formulating innovative macro-micro sociological methods to better locate the essence of self within a social context. In fact much of his theory concerns the abstract reified nature of the individual in society. In *Presentation of Self in Everyday Life*, he frames the social world as though it was a theatrical set.[32] He draws upon theater metaphors: actor and audience, front and back stage behavior, setting and dramatic effect. He tries to understand such phenomena as "impression management," which is an attempt on the part of the actor to elicit a desired response from an audience.

Goffman's work offers an excellent example of social theory as modernism outlined earlier here by Lunn: it is self-reflective, has a strong element of montage or simultaneity, it stresses ambiguity and, finally, it emphasizes dehumanization and the demise of the integrated self. All of these elements make their way into such Goffmanesque constructs as face work, appearance, and manner. There is little comprehensiveness here, however. That which makes it radically different from most other interactionist theory is form. Goffman invents his own fragmentary, noncomprehensive style.

Philip Manning in his study of Goffman notes:

> The overall tenor of *The Presentation of Self* is of a world in which people, whether individually or in groups, pursue their own ends in a cynical disregard for others. On the rare occasions when the audience and the performer cooperate, both endeavor to return hastily to the shelter of their various masks and disguises and avoid disclosing their inner selves. The view here is of an individual as a set of performance masks hiding a manipulative and cynical self.[33]

The goal of the actor in the stage production of life is to produce some type of simulacrum of happiness, of fulfillment, of existence. It is to present oneself as the best possible masked object to another masked object or set of objects. Of course it is all artificial, all staged and run according to strict social rules. That this resonates with the culture of modern capitalistic societies is the most frightening aspect of this theory.

REIFICATION OF CONSCIENCE

Reification and the form it takes cannot be separated from those institutional processes that produce it, nor can those who put the system into place escape from the objectification, which tends to be totalizing.

Unlike Goffman who takes little notice of social class, Lukács understands that each class is affected differently, but affected nonetheless by capitalistic reification. Both reification and false consciousness, therefore, exists for the bourgeoisie as well as the proletariat.[34]

The exploitation of workers for profit does not necessarily mean that the capitalist is unconcerned with the growing social ills or the plight of the poor who surrounded the factory walls or even those who work within them; however, business is business. Through this system the need for maximizing profit can be split-off from other human concerns such as the community's welfare, truthfulness to the consumer, or political and social matters. It is reasonable and necessary that such a fragmentary division of values exists within a capitalistic framework. Early modern capitalism revealed an intense religiosity that was a common characteristic of the small factory owners, work house trustees, and orphanage administrators. Frequently, the most notorious of these were regular church-goers, philanthropists, even ministers. One could be evicted from one's home for failure to pay a month's rent or fired from one's job, but still understand that this is a result of the moral imperative of the dog-eat-dog world of capitalism. One needed to learn to be accepting of this. The splitting of conscience is a product of the fragmentation of consciousness characteristic of modern western societies.

The knightly spirit of courteousness, gallantry, duty and honor, frequently exaggerated in eighteenth-century narratives (and particularly inflated by Kant), often appears illusory in the modern age. But such expected patterns of medieval chivalry were important for supporting the existing system of power relations and community. That remnants of such a code that find their way into modern life frequently appear ludicrous. Nevertheless, a romantic affinity for such values has continued to exist over time mythologized as cultural artifacts in romantic novels, theater, cinema, even popular tabloids.

The modern age was characterized by a shock-of-the-new, a rapid transition from behavior based in tradition to calculated action aimed at maximizing one's personal position in the economic world of supply and demand. At this point in time the split in consciousness becomes conspicuous. For example, western tradition dictated that the captain and crew did not abandon their ship when it was in trouble. The laws of the sea supported this position as did many accounts of sea disasters. When the British ocean liner the *Titanic* struck an iceberg on the night of April 14, 1912 and sunk, 1,512 passengers and crew members lost their lives. Not only did the captain go down with his ship, but so did most of the crew and all of the senior officers but one. In an account of heroic crew action that supposedly helped to save lives of many on that

memorable evening, Lawrence Beesley described the role of the self-sac-
rificing engineers who provided the light needed by many to escape up
until their own demise:

> The light failed then only because the engineers were no longer there to
> produce light, not because the men who worked them were not standing
> by them to do their duty. To be down in the bowels of the ship, far away
> from the deck where at any rate there was a chance of a dive and a swim
> and a possible rescue; to know that when the ship went—as they knew it
> must soon—there would be no possible hope of climbing up in time to
> reach the sea; to know all these things and yet to keep the engines going
> that the decks might be lighted to the last moment, required sublime
> courage. But this courage is required of every engineer and it is not called
> by that name, it is called "duty." To stand by his engines to the last possi-
> ble moment is his duty.[35]

Such narratives can be used to illustrate the moral imperative of the
crewman putting his life last for a common good. Such was the tradition
of the sea. However, today one might question the accuracy of this
interpretative account even in terms of class relations of senior level crew
to the lower level boiler men. Did these men, "deep in the bowels" of the
ship, understand that they were sacrificing their own lives to provide
light for the escape of their privileged passengers? How many of them
even spoke English or understood exactly what was happening? Did
they *all* actually believe that stoking a furnace was more important than
saving their own lives? Was questioning an order something that never
entered their minds? One can only guess at what Nietzsche's position
would have been.

Romanticism represented a carry-over of such sentimentalism into
the modern era. The romance with medievalism, the infatuation with the
ruins of ancient castles, and the gloomy obsession with all forms of gothic
imagery and suicide was a response to the reification and massification
that was changing the face of the newly industrialized world. While some
romantics clung longingly to a mythologized past, others wrapped themselves in the only thing more powerful than the creative destructive forces
that were bringing about the tumult; they clung to nature.

But for the modernists, for those who took it upon themselves to
change the course of artistic expression, those who would pick up the
fragments and put them together anew, they would have little of this. Art
became a tool for understanding the chaos generated by modernity, a
means of waking people from their romantic slumber, a means of making
sense of a seemingly senseless world. The narrative of the modern writer
was reshaping language and perception to fit the times. In such art, reification itself became a theme. Alienation, exile, loneliness, uprootedness,

loss, and abandonment became common motifs. Some writers were able to genuinely reflect the feelings of the age. Joseph Conrad entered into this time and changed the course of people's understanding. He sensitized his readers to the radical changes taking place all around them, ripping open the seams of the social world to reveal its dying heart.

Born on December 3, 1857 near the Polish Ukrainian town of Berdichev, Conrad (Teodor Józef Konrad Korzeniowski) was an only child. His father, an aspiring writer as well as a translator of Shakespeare and Hugo into Polish, struggled to survive by managing property for the gentry. He was an outspoken radical who fought for Polish independence. His mother was from a middle class family of a more conservative outlook. In 1863, when Joseph was only five, his father was arrested and imprisoned for revolutionary plots against the government and exiled to northern Russia. At that time he and his mother went to live with him there. It was only three years thereafter that his mother died from the harsh living conditions. Conrad's father was eventually set free only to die of tuberculosis in 1869. Orphaned at eleven, Conrad was sent to live with and be educated by his uncle in Cracow. We are told that it was then that a melancholy set in, affecting the rest of his life and his work.[36]

Conrad's personal loss makes its way into his novels, which resonate with modernistic themes of human abandonment, anxiety, searching, and exile. Conrad's own life at sea as a young man reflected a type of personal searching. He drew from his own experiences to paint a portrait of modernistic change.

The clash between romanticism and modernism is central to Joseph Conrad's *Lord Jim*, published in 1900. The novel is important for many reasons, not the least of which is its brilliant illustration of the reification of conscience. It stands as a quintessential modern novel, deeply psychological and yet sociologically relevant on many levels.

The novel depicts a young captain who abandons 800 Moslem pilgrims on board his ship he believed to be headed for imminent disaster. Jim, the new captain, not only had to face a tribunal for his behavior, but he had to confront his own cowardice as defined by preindustrial morality. The story of *Lord Jim*, represents a very modern dilemma wherein the protagonist lives between two worlds—a modern one characterized by individualistic determinism and another based on romantic fiction and fragmented virtue. Model behavior for Jim was to stand by tradition, to stand by his ship and his crew rather than to desert. Originally, Jim had seen himself joining the Merchant Marine because of his own sense of dedication to duty. Conrad tells us that he was schooled in "light holiday literature" and envisioned himself as "an unflinching hero in a book."

Yet Jim also was a modern man who believed himself to be an autonomous actor in a world that was not, in reality, held together by blind loyalty and custom. The internal struggle for Jim, who was faced with a crew that obviously reflected modern, self-serving interests, typifies the dilemma of modern society. This is the tension between traditional values and pragmatic self-interest. Here is a situation in which self-survival seems to require the outright abandonment of others.

In a dark, violent storm—with no expectation that his ship could survive—he jumps into the night sea leaving aboard his disreputable crew and the helpless natives who were relegated to the *Patna's* hull. And at this moment, we are told by Conrad, Jim no longer felt in control of his actions. Some shadowy force was now overpowering him and he felt hopeless, lost at the bottom "of an everlasting deep hole." Defying tradition loosened Jim's moorings in the world in which he lived. The moment of defiance, which was a physical act to save his own life above all else, created an overpowering feeling of detachment and estrangement. It also established him as the reluctant inventor of his own reality. From this point on, the character is an outsider—marginalized.

The reader is apprised by Conrad of the inevitability of disillusionment and loss when clinging to romantic notions of the past, and advised of the important place of tradition in shaping one's modern identity. But the reader is also warned of the high price modernity demands. In abandoning his ship, Jim also abandons tradition (whether or not spun of dreams), which he believed had anchored his life. Like the *Patna* itself, Jim was lost in a storm. He would spend the rest of the novel seeking a resting place where he could feel secure and perhaps recapture that which was lost—his youthful quest for an authentic self. For Jim, only union with others could provide this requisite security—a sense of stability in an unstable world.

To escape his past disgrace, Jim took up a new life in a far-off province of Malay where he befriended the natives. Here he seemed content if not happy. In some ways he struggled to become one with the Malays, but his actions and poor judgment eventually led to tragedy— the death of the chief's son, his own best friend. Instead of running from the province and saving his own life, he confronted the tribal chief with the corpse and was killed by the chief for his negligence. This was expected since it was part of Malay law and custom. Jim's search for communal union, therefore, was to cost him his life. Nevertheless, we are convinced by the author that Jim's death was to give him a sense of satisfaction and perhaps fulfillment. In death he came closer to finding himself than ever before . . . or did he?

Jameson's analysis of *Lord Jim* as the exemplary modern novel suggests a strong affinity between this work and *Madame Bovary*. For

Jameson *Lord Jim* is bifurcated—the first half of the novel deals with significant existential concerns similar to those taken up by Flaubert, particularly issues of meaningless, emptiness, and detachment in the modern world and the drive to escape these through romantic imagination-adventures. The second half of the novel is the romantic psychological adventure—an epic tragedy on a par with Emma's suicide. Jameson contends that the existential despair captured in Conrad's impressionism is representative of a whole genre of modern writers who would follow; those who would emphasize loss and detachment. "The most interesting artists and thinkers of such a period," notes Jameson, "are those who cling to the experience of meaninglessness itself as to some ultimate reality, some ultimate bedrock of existence of which they do not wish to be cheated by illusions or 'philosophies of as-if.'"[37]

It was a very real sense of insecurity and loss triggered by abandonment that haunted Joseph Conrad's early life. As an expatriate, much of his life was characterized by cultural marginalization in that he lived his life between two very distinct cultures: the quasi-feudalistic culture of Poland in which he was raised that emphasized tradition, and the utilitarian culture of England in which he matured. However, his earliest personal experiences reflected relinquishment of many sorts.

The quest for an authentic self was certainly a major element of the modern novel. It was not Conrad's venture alone. The pilgrimage for self-identity in the face of societal massification and de-communalization frequently ended in tragedy. The individual was condemned throughout modernity to an existential limbo between the irrational demands of decaying community and a quest for personal identity. The radical transformation of society by the forces of rationalistic modernization obliterated what many had held as sacred. It shook the very foundations of human perception. Consciousness was itself transformed by the hegemonic moral imperatives and bureaucratic instrumentality that ran the machinery of collective life.

MARCUSE'S HAPPY CONSCIENCE

The existential sensibilities of Conrad take up residence in the work of Herbert Marcuse. Marcuse inspired a generation of counter-culture radicals in the 1960s to look upon bureaucratic capitalism and scientism as denial of intrinsic humanity. In his classic works that included *Eros and Civilization* (1955) and *One-Dimensional Man* (1964), he proposes that capitalism, scientism, and the bureaucratic institutions they nourish are displacing politics and ethics with a technocratic imperative demanding the sacrifice of human sensuality and basic humanity to the technocratic rationality of the

marketplace. Furthermore, he asserts that the drive toward human emancipation is being restricted and discouraged by a newly imposed rational
social order that demands conformity above all else.

Where Theodore Adorno had viewed society and consciousness as
totally controlled products of rationalistic capitalism, Marcuse proposes
that critical consciousness is in some ways possible. However, like
Adorno and Fromm, Marcuse believes technocratic and administrative
rationality to be undermining individual liberty by establishing and
maintaining a monopoly over reason and culture. The superego no
longer remains a product of interpersonal familial and communal
dynamics. Instead conscience is imposed by a set of extra-familial agents
and agencies in the form of conditioning processes. Marcuse speaks of
the automatization of the superego wherein society exercises strict control over individual consciousness through the process of cultural indoc-
trination.[38] It is through this process that senseless material culture and
an array of equally inane leisure activities divert the human capacity for
reason. The end product of such a socialization process is a weakened or
fractured self.

Furthermore, Marcuse suggests that facts and values are manufactured to serve particular hegemonic interests. Promoted by mass media
and legitimized because of the power and social class they represent,
they command conformity and leave little room for debate. All good is
defined by a rationalistic and materialistic ideology that attempts to
thwart unregulated dissent. Free choice or free speech are based on pre-
determined options. Anything outside of these options is considered to
be irrational or silly. There is no space allocated in the narrowly controlled venues of public discourse.

Marcuse notes that societal needs and satisfactions can be readily
converted into individual, materialistic ones. These he calls "false needs."
Such false needs as well as false consciousness undermine the drive for
individual liberation and authenticity. Mass subscription to these false
needs and the values underlying them lead to further market indoctrina-
tion and manipulation. Every consumable carries with it a covert message that advances the cause of the hegemonic ideology. Commercially
displayed products promote the interests and life-style of those in
power. Free choice for most is frequently nothing more than a choice
among brands. Working for and choosing between consumer goods
both divert and debase mass powers of critical judgment. One-dimensional thought and behavior, therefore, are introduced in the form of
consumables that make living easier. For Marcuse both critical consciousness and authenticity yield to the powerful command of mass cul-

ture and its products. One's capacity to think beyond the manufactured culture seems to be dimming.

> The products indoctrinate and manipulate, they promote a false consciousness which is immune against falsehood. And as these beneficial products become available to more individuals in more social classes the indoctrination they carry ceases to be publicity; it becomes a way of life.[39]

Such a way of living appears to obfuscate authentic thoughts and feelings. The creation of a synthetic culture, which displaces political passion with materialistic desires, helps to establish a happy passivity. New desires displace the old; and these are burned into the unconscious. "No matter how much such needs may have become the individual's own, reproduced and fortified by the conditions of his experience," notes Marcuse "no matter how he identifies himself with them and finds himself in them satisfaction, they continue to be what they were from the beginning—products of a society whose dominant interest demands repression."[40]

Marcuse asserts that any fragment of authentic critical consciousness is immediately co-opted into the mainstream of pluralistic consumer culture. Here the expression of any dangerous political thought is permitted as long as it can be packaged and sold in shopping mall bookstores and advertised on radio talk shows. This has the effect of both defusing its impact as a challenge to the dominant culture and, at the same time, creating a profit from the threat itself. A prerequisite for liberation from this system, he asserts, is a consciousness of servitude—an awareness of one's own manipulation. It requires a comprehension of the limits imposed on individual development. But the emergence of such a consciousness is constantly opposed by false needs for consumables and a corresponding happy consciousness.

For Marcuse, in industrially developed societies a happy conscience supplants a more critical one. Such societies welcome dissent and differences as long as such dissent is defined by the forces that control the mass production of culture. Just as "happy talk" television newscasts entertain the audience with a host of sensationalistic images and distractions rather than providing it with critical information, happy conscience demands the blunting of critical judgment. Radical ideas are rarely presented in major media; and when they are, they are depicted as humorous curiosities. Both media and language work to synthesize and neutralize disturbances. In modern, pluralistic societies there can be no contradictions. Nothing can ever be taken too seriously since all must acknowledge the arbitrary nature of values in the face of the technocratic imperative.[41]

By denying all but the happy conscience immediate feelings of security and complacency are generated. This temporary comfort legitimizes the system that has established it. Personal conscience, the internal consideration of human values, is no longer necessary. In fact it stands in the way of human technological progress and material felicity.

HABERMAS AND TECHNOCRATIC CONSCIOUSNESS

Like Marcuse, Jürgen Habermas saw a corruption of the Enlightenment wherein science and technology were elevated to the status of ideologies. As such they provided a false basis for the legitimation of social change. For him, a technocratic consciousness had arisen to displace a more critical moral consciousness. He notes: "Technocratic consciousness reflects not the sundering of an ethical situation but the repression of 'ethics' as such as a category of life."[42] Although less ideological than all previous ideologies, it nevertheless acts to advance dominant class interests over the interests of workers. It provides the definitional basis of structural conditions through which class relations operated, and it promotes the satisfaction of privatized needs based on purposive-rational action. Thus, it vanquishes ethics. Through this brand of consciousness, people become objectified and their way of life depoliticized. Everyone is encouraged to seek individual gratification.

In the world of technocratic consciousness the distinction between practical and technical now disappear. All good is determined by scientific and technical progress, which in turn legitimizes political power. Thus, overt, dominant class ideology is displaced and obscured by this new ontology. According to Habermas, sociocultural development is determined by the power of technical control over the conditions of existence and passive adaptation to this new set of power arrangements. Unlike Lukács, Fromm, or Marcuse, who focused on the dialectics of materialistic culture, Habermas emphasizes what Marx called the "revolutionary instruments of production" and the societal relations that these produce. For him, technology is leading us into an ethical darkness.

Habermas asserts that the destructive and creative forces unleashed by technology were symbolic of the control and the political power they helped to bring about. These forces become the basis for reordering society and reorganizing consciousness. Like the rest of nature, society appears to be subject to technological manipulation. All oppressive societies make some use of technology by espousing the benefits to be gained through this manipulation.

Habermas notes that ordinary language is being corrupted by the new scientism. Language is yielding to technocratic taxonomy as efforts are made to reorder society according to the needs of powerful elites. Psychotechnic manipulation wherein the individual's perception is altered according to the needs of these elites is just the beginning of behavioral control necessitated by this new order of technological consciousness. Knowledge has become increasingly dominated by the technocratic imperative that has commanded the modern communicative system. Habermas, therefore, argues for some sort of control of technology.

Habermas continues to see the potential for liberation based on an authentic application of reason to address the problems of society. It is the technocratic form of rationality and its elevation to a place of moral efficacy wherein the problem lies. For Habermas, modernity is not the issue, rather it is the corruption of rationality and modern consciousness by repressive social forces and the evolving cybernetic character of this new rationality. This seems to be his overriding concern. In this sense, Habermas remains a defender of the Enlightenment project while observing the decline of critical consciousness brought about by the forces of oppression.

He proposes that true awareness can only be achieved through what he calls "ideal speech." Such speech requires that all parties have equal access and opportunity to engage in discussion without inordinate domination by one party. In the ideal speech situation there is no ideological distortion and no restriction. It is only through such dialogue that critical and emancipatory forms of knowledge can be achieved. It is only through ideal speech that true moral awareness can arise.

Habermas' thoughts, therefore, are in some ways more comparable to Max Weber's position (and less compatible with the ideas of Adorno or Marcuse) regarding some of the benefits that can be derived from the process of rationalization. Although many tend to see the negative consequences of a rationality that excludes all else, Habermas is more optimistic in his prognosis. He believes in the possibility of a consensus community built upon emancipatory knowledge—knowledge predicated on reciprocal understanding. Despite the fragmentation of modern existence, he contends that it is still feasible to have a unified world view. Habermas, therefore, defends modernity from those postmodernists who view the world as unalterably fragmented; and he attempts to promote the primacy of modern reason. At the same time, he remains highly critical of the consequences of modern capitalism. His insistence on the feasibility of a unified world order predicated upon an ethical rationality has made him the target of both postmodern critics as well as many on the left. Nevertheless, he has continued to maintain the belief that enlightened rationality offers the best opportunities for individual freedom and social progress.

TECHNOLOGICAL DEHUMANIZATION

According to Martin Heidegger technology constitutes a new type of cultural system that restructured the social world as an object of control.[43] For him as well as the critical theorists technology transforms the world in which we live, dehumanizing much of it. Our technology alters our existence through a process he referred to as "enframing." It deeply infiltrates human social existence giving it a framework. Whereas the medieval world had a religious frame, the modern world has a technological one. Our technology alters our perceptions of the world just as religion once did. The technology of modern life, characterized by technical thought, undermines nontechnical reason and values. It not only washes over us, but it processes us. It becomes embedded in us. Machines invade human existence more intimately than other humans can and radically change people in the process. In describing capitalist technology, Andrew Feenberg notes that it is based on the reified decontextualization of that which it controls. Accordingly, since technology is a set of techniques these can be abstracted from any particular context and reinserted into another.[44] It is his assertion that this decontextualization predetermines technology to serve capitalist power. But it may serve other power as well.

The incursion of the technological into our social relations assumed dramatic imagery not only in the work of critical social theorists but also in the works of modernists such as Karel Čapek, Marcel Duchamp, Franz Kafka, and others. Kafka, whose writings underscored the modernistic process of dehumanization associated with shadowy bureaucratic order, also saw the dark side of technological efficiency. In *The Penal Colony*, he displays the scientific wonders of The Harrow—a technologically elegant instrument of gruesome mechanical torture and death. Its operator views the device as both efficient and pristine—a groundbreaking innovation by which to punish those who might shirk their duty, no matter how inconsequential that duty might be. Kafka succeeds brilliantly in conveying the impersonality and primitive brutality of technological progress serving the interests of a bureaucratic civilization.

While World War I saw the efficient application of industrial technology to the production of exemplary carnage, it was not until the second world war that the horrors of science more abhorrently revealed themselves. And this was not only on the battleground. "The technical-administrative success of the Holocaust," posits Zygmunt Bauman, "was due in part to the skillful utilization of 'moral sleeping pills' made available by modern bureaucracy and modern technology."[45] For Bauman the seeming invisibility of causal connections, the decontextualization of human behavior in a complex bureaucratic system, and the distancing of morally contemptible outcomes of this behavior from the actor, were important elements of this system.

In discussing technological consciousness, Peter Berger, Brigitte Berger, and Hansfried Kellner identify the organizational structure of knowledge deeply sedimented in the modern consciousness.[46] A central characteristic of this, patterning itself on the technocratic organization of work, is the presumption that while one has only limited access and understanding of the comprehensive process of production, the total system is nonetheless reasonable and rational. It is taken for granted that there is a specialized system of interworking components, each with its own unique function, and that there is a hierarchy of experts in place overseeing and directing outcomes. An important element of cognitive style here is what they call "componentiality." Here components are self-contained but part of an unseen bigger picture. Reality itself is interpreted as a system of components rationally ordered in some particular way "apprehended and manipulated as atomistic units."[47] The real power is sequestered, very much like the embodiment of the New Commandant who never appears in *The Penal Colony*, or Klamm who is always absent from *The Castle* or the unseen legal authorities in *The Trial*.

A second important characteristic of modern consciousness that emerges from this interdependence of components and sequencing is the separability of means and ends. Since reality is interpreted as a set of components that can be assembled in different ways to produce different outcomes, there is no particular relationship between a specific component of the sequenced activity and the ultimate outcome of the sum of these.[48] For instance, the computer component one creates can be assembled into an automobile or into a nuclear submarine. Again, this is the decontextualization of which Feenberg speaks. That is, technological consciousness is a compartmentalized consciousness that mimics a machine.

Finally, another important outcome of the technocratic organization of work is anonymous social relations. This is not to say that workers in technological society have few personal relationships in the workplace; rather it means that one must ultimately view oneself and one's co-workers as anonymous functionaries. This is dictated by the logic of modern methods of production. One must develop a double consciousness. That is, one needs to see the self as both an anonymous functionary and as a complete human being with unique feelings, perceptions, and intelligence. The worker self often becomes "less real" than the private self.[49] When society is organized in such a way wherein one's personal security and survival are tied to the performance of one's technocratic role enormous stress is exerted on the individual to function according to organizational prescriptions. One finds it personally beneficial to segregate and compartmentalize one's consciousness. Such splitting is commonly associated with borderline personalities.

In his book *The Nazi Doctors*, Robert Jay Lifton looked closely at German doctors in Nazi death camps and determined that individuals who seemed humane in many instances were able to commit atrocities by processes he referred to as "numbing" and "doubling." To Lifton, this meant turning off one's humanity under certain conditions of anxiety and protecting one's ego by finding rationalistic legitimation for such barbaric deeds.[50] According to Lifton, this form of ego dissociation, this compartmentalization, provided the basis of most Nazi behavior. In his book Lifton identifies two distinct selves that emerge under such conditions, an organizational one and a personal one. For Lifton, the organizational one, or the "Auschwitz self," was rational and impersonal. The personal self allowed the individual to retain aspects of his humanity and remain a good father, husband, or lover. Yet, the Auschwitz self permitted inhuman behavior. In order to avoid overpowering feelings of guilt associated with such actions, conscience was transferred from the personal self to the organizational self.

The disavowal of the organizational self becomes a method of coping with the horrors committed in the name of the impersonal bureaucracy—in this case Auschwitz. At his trial, Eichmann defended his participation in genocide by claiming that he was only a soldier obeying orders and would have risked his career if he refused the commands of his superiors. Besides this, he claimed, a more dutiful comrade would have taken his place. But as Bauman suggests, this cognitive style associated with Nazism is not an anomaly; rather it is a common condition of technocratic modernity. Given that modernity fosters a condition of perpetual anxiety in a driving need to satisfy organizational demands, and in capitalistic societies is oriented toward competitive contest of profit maximization, it is not surprising that doubling of a kind has its place in the routine of organizational protocol. With such an explanation we gain some understanding of the mind that can sell toxic pesticides to developing nations, poison pristine rivers with industrial waste, or knowingly design automobiles that are dangerous. We might even understand how the tobacco company executives find ways to avoid feelings of self-contempt and personal guilt.

Stanley Milgram's classic study on obedience to authority conducted at Yale in the early 1960s illustrated how far people would go in denying their own inner judgment and substituting for them orders from figures in authority. Milgram concluded that individuals drove themselves to abandon autonomy and enter into an "agentic state." By this he meant the person became an agent for carrying out another's commands.[51]

If there is loyalty, if there is responsibility, it has become a measure of obedience to the demands or requirements of a superior rather than an element of personal conscience. For Milgram, loyalty refers not to the person's own qualities, but to the adequacy with which a subordinate fulfills his or her technocratically defined role. For one to feel responsible for an action, there must be a sense that the action has flowed from one's self. However, in bureaucracies where individuals see themselves as instruments in the service of impersonal organizational goals or powerful others it is reasonable to see oneself as a form of automata. "Inside the bureaucratic system of authority," notes Zygmunt Bauman, "language of morality acquires a new vocabulary. It is filled with concepts like loyalty, duty, discipline—all pointing to superiors as the supreme object of moral concern and, simultaneously, the top moral authority."[52] This externalization of conscience was part of Wilhelm Reich's critique of pre-World War II German society wherein he exposed underlying elements of this psychic insecurity emanating from patriarchal authoritarianism that led to the rise of fascism. The Frankfurt theorists also saw the authoritarian personality as a consequence of an authoritarian culture.

In *Escape from Freedom*, Erich Fromm describes an abrupt shift in European traditional society in the sixteenth century from a prolonged state of perceived feudal security—a pastoral dreamlike condition of semiconsciousness wherein each was assigned a specific place in the world ruled over by the Church—to radical and constant upheavals brought about by capitalism, the Enlightenment, and the Protestant Reformation. Fromm viewed such forces as catapulting people into a boundless freedom that wrecked traditional order and provided little guarantee for human stability and consistency. In this work he draws a comparison of this to an abrupt separation of an infant from his or her caregiver. Modernity is perceived as a perpetual state of personal abandonment and insecurity, and at the same time a cornucopia of opportunities—of freedom and its potentialities. However, once the primary bonds that give a sense of security are severed, once the individual faces the world outside of the self as an autonomous entity, he or she must confront the alienation and dread associated with modern life. Then two courses are open to overcome the feelings of aloneness and powerlessness. One course is to progress to positive freedom; here ultimately a person can relate spontaneously to the world in love and in work, in a genuine expression of one's emotional, sensuous, and intellectual capacities, and become whole by uniting with others and with nature without giving up independence and integrity of his or her individual self. The other course is to fall back, to give up one's freedom, and to try to overcome the aloneness by eliminating the gap that has arisen between the individual self and the alienated world.[53] To Fromm this course of escape is frequently characterized by narcissism, compulsiveness, lack of spontaneity, and by either complete surrender of individuality and integrity of the self to someone else, or by the purposeful destruction or control of others who seem to represent a threat. Both resolute passivity and authoritarian control are likely outcomes of a type of separation anxiety that plays itself out in games of submission and dominance. Masochism and sadism become common means of adjusting to the conditions of anomie and alienation that characterized modernity. Fromm recognized how both were often methods used for coping with feelings of inferiority, anxiety, powerlessness, and loss. As Lynn Chancer points out, they have now become ingrained in everyday life.[54]

It was Fromm's contention that modernity, frequently characterized by a conscious fear of aloneness and powerlessness, compelled many to seek refuge and security by blunting one's own capacity for critical thought and constructing a consciousness in line with the demands of a superficial technocratic culture. Anyone who gives up the self and becomes an automaton need not feel alone or anxious as millions share the same state. This idea was later expanded upon by C. Wright Mills in his concept of the cheerful robot:

> We know of course that man can be turned into a robot, by chemical and psychiatric means, by steady coercion and by controlled environment; but also by random pressures and unexplained sequences of circumstance. But can he be made to become a cheerful and willing robot? Can he be happy in this condition and what are the qualities and meanings of such happiness?[55]

Karel Čapek's play *R.U.R.* (Rossum's Universal Robots), an expressionistic work produced in Prague in 1921, conveyed an apprehensiveness associated with the proliferation of pristine capitalistic technology after the gore and bloodshed of World War I. Here is a factory where robots are produced as slaves, made to perform the work of people. These robots were among the first cyborgs—part machine, part human. That which distinguished them from people was that they had no souls, no feelings. "They remember everything and think nothing. They'd make fine college professors."

Čapek and his brother Josef were Czech anti-fascists. They collaborated on the stage production in Prague. Josef, an early cubist and expressionist, designed the set of towering factories built by robots who swung on cranes across the stage, looming large against an emblazoned sky. The play itself was about both the mechanization of labor—the turning of people into slave-machines, and the ethical issues of what it means to be a feeling, thinking human being. The robots are liberated at the end of the play, and revolt against their makers.

Ashley Montagu and Floyd Matson synthesized much of the artistic and social science research on this theme of technology and dehumanization in the early 1980s. To them, it was evident that those in modern societies were entering an era void of human feeling—certainly an era void of its expression. In discussing this theme they write:

> What concerns us here is the pathology of mechanization, and specifically the emergence of a new type of social character which appears to be not so much deviant as *mutant*—an organic combination of man and machine. It is this freak product of cultural evolution to which Lewis Yablonsky has given the apt name of "robopath." The creatures of a society which worship mechanical efficiency, regularity and predictability, robopaths are individuals "whose pathology entails robotlike behavior and existence . . . they are people who simulate machines."[56]

Sometimes, however, this notion of technological dehumanization has conservative if not reactionary overtones. Postmodern feminists such as Donna Haraway reject much of this as fear as an expression of male apprehensions of patriarchal disempowerment—a dethronement of a Cartesian world view constructed of binary oppositions such as man/machine or man/animal. Haraway sees the liberating potential of technology for the individual. For her we are already cyborgs and while there can be drawbacks there are also advantages to the technological transformation of our societies and ourselves. She celebrates the confusion of boundaries between people and machines, between fact and fantasy, between north and south, between men and women.[57]

It is Haraway's contention that a human-technological synthesis can destroy repressive dualisms that tend to categorize and confine. It can liberate culture and expand human perceptions and connectedness. The transformative powers of human-technological relations for personal and social enhancement through the creation of new social forms is incalculable.

Thus Haraway views feminist epistemology as bridging the void that had been an essential element of Enlightenment thought. She focuses chiefly on positive outcomes. But while Haraway does recognize the ominous roots of the new scientism, she does not subscribe to the deterministic notion of the inevitability of dehumanization.

Many other feminists reject the romantic modernist orientations of Marx as well as phallocentric biases inherent in Freud and the critical theorists. Some, such as Jane Flax, view gendering as the essential problem here—an artificial dualism upon which the whole of modernist scientism rests.[58] Flax has proposed that for most males the self is stuck in a defensive infantile need to control and dominate others in order to retain individual identity. She argues for a degendered science, one without stale dualities, one void of rationalistic suppositions, as a possible means of addressing the so-called processes of dehumanization. Only through such a new perspective can people ever hope to enhance the world in which they live. Women and men need to work together to revolutionize the culture.

Zygmunt Bauman appears to agree with the notion that this so-called dehumanization is a consequence of the processes of modernization and the application of Enlightenment thought. It is part of the agenda of the civilizing process begun in the sixteenth century. His postmodernism, like that of the feminists, is a rejection of modernity and its inherent structural corruptibility. It is more in line with the work of Nietzsche who saw in the structure of modern consciousness signs of oppression of previous generations and vested interests. Bauman acknowledges that a new order, a more inclusive one, is necessary to build a more humanistic world.

To this end Bauman sets out to construct a sociological theory of values by first rejecting the moral industry associated with modernity. Morality has been perceived as a social product causally explained by reference to its mechanisms of production and operation. "The factory system has served as one of the most potent metaphors out of which the theoretical model of modern society is woven," he asserts, "and the vision of the social production of morality offers a most prominent example of its influence."[59] Such a theory concedes that every society with the power to impose sanctions for violation of norms does so in an effort to promote order and stability.

> This theory of morality concedes the right of society . . . to impose its own substantive version of moral behavior; and concurs with the practice in which social authority claims the monopoly of moral judgement. It tacitly accepts the theoretical illegitimacy of all judgements that are not grounded in the exercise of such monopoly; so that for all practical intents and purposes moral behavior becomes synonymous with social conformity and obedience to the norms observed by the majority.[60]

It is Bauman's position that bureaucratic societies demand a monopoly over values based on the supposition that if we do not have such conformity we have a law of the jungle where the true vile natures of people emerge. The belief that morality arises from some functional operation of society and is maintained through its social institutions and that it is essentially humanizing is viewed as misguided. "What is therefore presented and conceived of as savagery to be tamed and suppressed," posits Bauman, "may prove on a close scrutiny to be the self same moral drive that the civilizing process sets out to neutralize, and then to replace with the controlling pressures emanating from the new structure of domination."[61] The suppositions that morality is born out of social operations and that immoral misconduct may be primarily explained as a malfunctioning of natural social controls, and is never a product of society itself, need to be critically reexamined in light of the evidence from the Holocaust. Bauman argues:

> On many occasions moral behavior means taking a stance dubbed and decreed anti-social or subversive by the powers that be and by public opinion (whether outspoken or merely maintained in majority action or non-action). Promotion of moral behavior in such cases means resistance to societal authority and action aimed at weakening its grip. Moral duty has to count on its pristine source: the essential human responsibility for the Other.[62]

Bauman speaks much of the importance of intersubjectivity. He condemns modernity for having moved to abolish individual ethical responsibility other than that "measured by the criteria of instrumental rationality and practical achievement." He views such responsibility as having been shifted to impersonal bureaucratic levels; but he believes that the challenges of postmodernity's emphasis on the acceptance of cultural diversity and relativism can be a means through which individuals can take back responsibility for moral choice.[63]

TRANSFORMATION AND ABANDONMENT
OF VIRTUE

The normative tradition of moral goodness in western thought can be traced to the classical concept of virtue. In antiquity, virtue had been conceptualized as standards of character—traits of personhood to which one aspired or with which one could be identified. These were typically traits of the gods. Exemplary virtues included courage, justice, prudence, fortitude, temperance, truthfulness, and liberality. Historically, the conceptualization of virtue had its roots in Greek civilization and was conveyed through the works of Homer and Sophocles. Later, virtue appeared in the teachings of Plato and

Aristotle. Aristotle, particularly in *Nichomachean Ethics (Book II)*, had argued that moral virtues were desire-regulating character traits. Such traits could be virtuous only if their characteristic behavior could be seen as achieving *telos* for both the individual and the *polis*. Inherent in Aristotle's argument was the view that virtues constitute a humanistic balance. There is no application of rules here. He distinguished between doing what is good for the individual and doing what is good for the character of the individual. One is required to be reflective, therefore, in order to discern the difference and to act in the right way. It is important to understand that not all virtues are accessible to all people. Each rank had its own. Of course we are dealing with a state in which only Greek male citizens with property could aspire to the highest virtuosity. Still, there is a definite acknowledgment here that the interest of the community is the interest of the individual, and that situations may call for each person to put his or her own immediate gratification second to the interests of the *polis*. This is not sacrifice, but virtuosity—a means through which one develops character and achieves a life of dignity.

Thomas Aquinas was to reintroduce Aristotle into medieval religious and secular life. Added to the classical list of virtues such as justice, prudence, and temperance were faith, hope, and charity. Most of the so-called cardinal virtues would have been totally rejected by the Greeks. Virtues, such as humility, taken from the New Testament by medieval ethicists probably would have been viewed by Aristotle as vices. Aquinas explicitly connects conscience and virtue. He defines conscience in his *Summa theologica*, as the application of knowledge to activity. For him knowledge emerges from what was then referred to as "synderesis," a natural disposition of the human mind through which one can understand without inquiry the basic principles of good conduct. Synderesis lays the groundwork for virtue and includes a general notion of doing good and avoiding evil. However, one must add to these secondary principles from experience and instruction through the virtues. As an example in this regard Aquinas emphasizes prudence. Prudence is important because it dictates the application of personal perception to circumstance. In this way Aquinas connects virtue to conscience. While people innately know what they must do, it is virtue—specifically the virtue of prudence—that curtails their runaway passions. Aquinas develops a hierarchy of virtues and insists that it is through action that one becomes virtuous. Action is seen as a way of gaining knowledge.

Alasdair MacIntyre talks about the decline of virtue in terms of the "fragmentation of narrative and practice" wherein the modern market forces a separation between consumption and production, life and art, self and community: "to think of a human life as narrative unity is to think in a way alien to the dominant individualist and bureaucratic modes of modern culture."[64] As soon as the forces of capitalist production moved work outside the household and placed it into the service of the impersonal market, as soon as meaning was drained from work and the laborer became an extension of the machine, virtue declined. Separating personal meaning from practice one necessarily eliminates the significance of virtue as an essential life process.[65] For most, labor becomes a means to an end and a passport to the world of consumerism. What one produces has meaning in terms of the money it produces for workers and what they need or want as consumers. With this segmentalization of life, how can one have a comprehensive view of the world, or see oneself as an empowered actor?

According to J. B. Schneewind, beginning in the seventeenth century, discussions of natural law eclipsed the importance of virtue theory that was neglected until it was essentially abandoned as a focus of serious concern.[66] Hugo Grotius, the Dutch philosopher, advanced the notion that morality was ensuring that one's actions conformed to moral laws that were fixed in nature. These natural moral laws can be rationally perceived by all. Kant's focus on universal morality, categorical imperatives predicated on practical reason and natural law, obligation, and duty gradually replaced the classical concern of virtue. This line of thought stressed the importance of obedience to societal notions of good conduct.

While the processes of modernization and capitalism helped to further challenge the integrity and usefulness of virtue, they would not completely destroy it. Virtue had a slow and agonizing death. Adam Smith was to promote the notion of virtue as a necessary basis for free market capitalism. Only virtue could impede the unbounded passions of greed and avarice inherent in capitalism, itself.[67] Thus virtue (specifically civic virtue) became a modern liberal creed, a secularized theology of reactionary consciousness that was necessary for the healthy development of a benevolent capitalistic society.

The quest for reclaiming a form of virtuosity that existed in a kinder, gentler, and more noble time verges on Quixotic. Virtue frequently stands as an ideological trap designed to maintain unequal power relations just as it always has. Today the word "virtue" has come to represent an empty vessel for hosting an array of liberal moralisms. Civic virtue might be viewed as particularly corrosive in that it often endeavors to bolster allegiance to a corrupt system of human exploitation by promoting obedience and acceptance of civil order predicated on a debased system of inequality.

It was Louis Althusser who suggested that the ideology supporting an oppressive system of values could only be imposed through a false consciousness. Using Marx, Freud, and Lacan he suggests that the oppressive ideology of the state apparatus that ensures one's conformity to this system is predicated on a subjective craving to be recognized as a subject and a fear of not being recognized at all—a fear of being isolated and alone. While democracy gives the illusion that society is participatory, the true governing structures of inequality are deposited deeply within the unconscious by powerful conditioning forces of society that help us to veil and to rationalize our own alienated existences. Thus, for Althusser we take on oppression believing it to be freedom.[68]

CAPITALISM AND SCHIZOID PERSONALITY

The accelerating process of social and personal fragmentation, according to Gilles Deleuze and Félix Guattari, are essential consequences of what they refer to as "capitalistic deterritorialization." For them, capitalism is a destabilizing institution that fragments and undermines all power outside of itself, reducing individuals to hollowed-out desiring machines.

According to them, through this process of fragmentation and the reterritorialization of all social life, all that is human is in a state of flux. Put simply, capitalism is seen as a schizophrenic system, which simultaneously creates desiring machines and imposes repression of desire. Part of what it does best is to produce schizophrenics.[69] While many question the seriousness of the somewhat outlandish claims of Deleuze and Guattari, they nonetheless have struck a chord that resonates with many. They certainly capture, in a very abstruse way, the reification and fragmentation that is closely associated with western capitalism and the drama of modernity.

The search for reconnection has been a major project of the modernity. Whether it be efforts to mend the shattered psyche and pick up the pieces of broken social lives, or to envision new ways to protect the territorial community from total disintegration, it is an ongoing struggle for reintegration.

Chapter 5

Abandonment of Community

The separation from place and, more specifically, the estrangement from home and all that it implies can be a powerful source of human anxiety and can take many dramatic forms. It is the banishment of Ovid from Rome as recounted in his *Trisita*, or the exile of Dante Alighieri from Florence as depicted in a painting by Frederick Leighton; it is the escape of Leon Trotsky to Mexico portrayed in a fresco of Diego Rivera; or it is the story of migrant farmers leaving the dust bowl in the 1930s captured in John Steinbeck's novel, *The Grapes of Wrath*. Loss of home is the flight of Palestinian refugees from the ancient holy land or the expulsion of tribal people from the Bolivian rain forest by encroaching development. Separation from place is the story of modern capitalism—the powers of creative destruction leveling communities to build highways, razing tenements to erect skyscrapers. Community loss is the wholesale emptying of industrial towns as the factories and jobs are moved elsewhere. It is the eviction of the indigent from their homes. It's blockbusting, redlining, and the Disneyfication of cities.

This chapter seeks to unravel the meaning of community as well as the reasons for its abandonment. Just like poets and artists, sociologists produce variations on the theme of community and its loss. Some have spent considerable effort in simply defining the term. For instance, in 1955 sociologist George Hillery, Jr. found at least ninety-four distinct definitions of community.[1] But in this new millennium we continue to find little agreement on its meaning. Each social scientist approaches the concept quite differently. The same holds true for how they view its abandonment. In one such motif of communal loss sociologists try to

157

capture the degeneration of human associations in familial and social life; in another they explore what they view as vanishing pastoral communities—the displacement of the peaceful and naturalistic countryside by the dangerous and impersonal metropolis. In American sociology, many renderings focus on the lonely city dweller such as the hobo, the taxi dancer, the jack roller, the crack addict, and the like. On the other hand, sociologists often provided colorful, often highly romanticized, visions of neighborhood life.

This chapter looks at many of the assumptions surrounding the loss of community as a modernistic theme in the social sciences. In examining some of these it is hoped that the powerful relationship between the community and modernity can be better illuminated.

EXILE FROM THE GARDEN

If urban dwellers share something in common, it is frequently the sense of communal estrangement coupled with a separation from nature. Many who live in the city are refugees, migrants or exiles—people from elsewhere. Exile and loss are often components of the urban tableaux.

"The eidetic structure of exile," writes Robert Edwards, "is uprooting from native soil and translation from the center to the periphery; from an organized space invested with meaning to a boundary where conditions of experience are problematic."[2] This separation from place and, more specifically, the separation from home and all that it implies, is a vital aspect of exile and an important form of abandonment. "Under various guises," notes Edwards, "exile means separation, banishment, withdrawal, extrication, displacement; its emotional expression is loss, usually manifested by sorrow, though sometimes nostalgia."[3] While the central distinguishing feature of exile is its relevance to place, the personal break is also a severing from social continuity and collective history. Often to be cast-out is to be transferred from a position of the sacred and the immutable to a place of the transient and the profane.[4] Exile easily becomes a metaphor for conditions of alienation and loneliness.

Scholar Paul Tabori has indicated that *exul* came to mean a wanderer, a pilgrim, or an outlaw in the Middle Ages.[5] It meant to be outside the jurisdiction of domestic and religious law, to be without a sense of belonging, without protection. To be exiled was to lose one's home, to be denied direct access to one's culture. Thus, exile assumes important metaphoric significance often representing the modern condition. Tabori traces an early example of this metaphor to the biblical expulsion of

Adam and Eve from Eden. This loss of Paradise frequently stood as a metaphor for the loss of the pastoral community.

The loss of the Garden would remain deeply embedded within the cultural unconscious creating a dreamlike void, an emptiness that would have to be filled. And of course Milton's work resonated with an era of colonial exploration where ship after ship left the relative security of European ports to venture into uncharted dark waters, stormy seas to feral lands, deep into wild tropical forests or desolate frigid landscapes. Jeffrey Sammons noted that the need to find a natural connectedness or the "hunger for wholeness" not only fed the engine of colonialism but easily found its way into early sociological studies.[6]

The commodification of land, the leveling of forests, and the parceling of territory for sale appeared concurrently alongside the decline of the feudal estate. The wilderness and mystery of what was referred to as the dark ages began to disappear. In its place rationalization began to disenchant and illuminate. Fearing the complete abandonment of nature and the rise of mechanistic scientism, late eighteenth-century poets and artists strongly reacted to this trend.

Nature and solitude became emblematic of burgeoning modernity. The work of Caspar David Friedrich (1774–1840), especially, promotes a feeling of exile and human estrangement from wilderness. Many of his human figures stand in isolation before a restless untamed seascape or alone in the middle of a naturalistic convulsion. His landscapes take on an almost supernatural countenance—a sort of surrealistic quality. An immediate feeling of anxiety emanates from much of his work. In one of his more significant paintings, *The Monk at the Edge of the Sea* (1809), the canvas is divided into three unequal parts; the whitish earth, the virtually black sea, and an empty sky, which ranges in color from hues of green to white. A tiny brown silhouette of a monk stands to the left revealing the immensity of nature and the insignificance of humanity.[7]

For centuries artists, writers, and utopian theorists would attempt to recapture the garden in words and in paint. Many would come to invent remote and hidden worlds—serene *Shangri-Las*—naturalistic places to escape the vulgarities of civilization. The iconography of the lost garden, for instance, can be found in a substantial number of important and some inconsequential works particularly from medieval times to the present. The theme or genre of this work has been described by scholars as "the lost domain."

> The lost domain is a beautiful, visionary land, visited or witnessed for a brief time by a fictional character and then lost to him. The original

admission to the lost domain was frequently by tearing a very thin veil between our world and the new reality. It may have been as close as a dream away, through a special door in a stone wall, down a rabbit hole, a walk of a few blocks to a castle looming only a short distance away, a pony-cart ride to a garden party at a nearby estate. But the tragedy for the fictional character is that for one reason or another, he can never return. In instances he can never find the entrance again, or having found it, has not the time to enter or is barred from entry. In some cases he launches a full-scale search—even an epic journey—but finds himself unable to rediscover the land. In fact, his journey often carries him further away from the lost domain than when he began.[8]

Return to the lost domain usually is only achieved through a super-natural intersession and then only in death. Here one experiences ". . . a knife-sharp bitter sweet yearning, containing all the urgency of sexuality but at the same time often wholly divorced from the sensation of physical desire."[9] To return here is a sense of fulfillment of all hearts' yearnings.

The lost domain is often associated with a dream to which the dreamer desires to return and which provokes enormous post-dream longing. Here is a place typically colored with radiant flowers and birds. Always a garden, this place is frequently spotted with gentle lions, tigers, wild horses, and the like. Although elements might vary, frequently there is a woman in this dream, spiritually remote but often dependent of the dreamer's good will. This is a dream of sweetness and loss.

In his analysis of early American pastoralism, Leo Marx discusses the origin of the nostalgic feeling that was often attached to the unspoiled landscape. In his examination of the work of Freud and José Ortega y Gasset, Marx endeavors to understand the romance with the pastoral:

> Evidently it is generated by an urge to withdraw from civilization's grow-ing power and complexity. What is attractive in pastoralism is the felicity represented by an image of a natural landscape, a terrain either unspoiled, or if cultivated, rural. Movement toward such a symbolic landscape also may be understood as movement away from an "artificial" world, a world identified with "art," using this word in its broadest sense to mean the dis-ciplined habits of mind or arts developed by organized communities. In other words, this impulse gives rise to symbolic motion away from the centers of civilization toward their opposite, nature, away from sophistica-tion toward simplicity, or, to introduce the cardinal metaphor of the liter-ary mode, away from the city toward the country.[10]

In pre-industrial America, the romance with the pastoral was no better represented than in the work of artists associated with the Hudson River School. Chief amongst the founders of this movement was Thomas Cole. Cole's masterful *Expulsion from the Garden of Eden*

(1827) displayed the light and dark side of nature with a bright pastoral Eden funneling its sunlight through a stone portal onto a rugged dark and twisted wilderness. Here, as the small figures of Adam and Eve are expelled, the exterior of the garden is beset by a mighty convulsion of nature: "a rift opens in the foreground, water plunges into the abyss, a volcano encircled by menacing storm clouds erupts in the distance while a vulture-like bird of prey challenges a ravenous wolf over the carcass of a stag in the lower lefthand corner of the scene."[11]

Cole was greatly influenced by the European landscape artists and their attempt to convey the struggle between nature and civilization. One of his more famous paintings, *View from Mount Holyoke, Northhampton, Massachusetts after a Thunderstorm*, referred to simply as *The Oxbow* (1826), was very much influenced by the French landscape artist Claude Lorraine. In this remarkable work is a dramatic view down into a deep golden valley segmented by a serene bending river running through open pastureland. Dark ominous storm clouds hover in the distance over the landscape signaling both the untamed aspects of nature and its sublimity. Still the pasturelands glow in golden greens and yellows celebrating the taming of the wilderness. Inherent in Cole's art is the notion that the cultivated lands replacing the wilderness could be as beautiful as if not more beautiful than the untamed nature they succeeded. Common to much of his work is the recurrent small figure of an axman gazing on the vast panorama of his handiwork of a cleared wilderness while he leans on his ax.

The Hudson River School helped to inspire the taming of nature, and the settlement of what many referred to as the frontier. It was a time of substantial population migration, particularly to the west. Such imagery encouraged exploration and sanctified alteration of the face of nature along the way. Some Americans, like the adventurer-pioneers, movement from one town to another, or from town to country was a key to their success. Western expansion, however, was primarily an economic quest as opposed to a spiritual one.

The early history of the American west, northwest and southwest is in part a history of ghost towns: the exhaustion and exploitation of resources until the land no longer provided a basis for livelihood, the bleeding dry of mines and oil fields, the over-farming of rich fertile lands. The pioneering ethic was mythologized to cover its true record of violence, environmental destruction, and waste. In the old west, pioneers moved forward, destroying anything or anyone who got in their way. This included the extermination and forced segregation of American Indians and the destruction of native beauty and wildlife. The few living things that were not destroyed were housed in zoos, made part of circuses, or put onto reservations. There was always a price of admission to see the rare American Indian perform his dance or to take a look at the last buffalo. Land was bled dry of its use. And once its use value was extracted, the pioneer-adventurer was free to go on to his next station. Historian Frederick Jackson Turner proposed that the frontier was among the chief influences in shaping the unique character of Americans in that it provided a vast amount of space to which early settlers could escape and move on to greener pastures.[12]

THE EBBING OF COMMUNAL LIFE

Grieving for the lost community has a long and rich history in the development of sociological thought. While both classical as well as more contemporary theorists recognize an ebbing of traditional communal life, few have agreed on the causes of this phenomenon or on what constitutes the proper purpose of community. Still, many observe a deterioration of the traditional, territorially based social arrangements.

For some nineteenth-century social scientists, such as Ferdinand Tönnies, modernity moved like a steamroller—plowing a broad swatch of secular banality through the mystical garden of an organic world. Tönnies, the infamous German social theorist who published his classic work *Gemeinschaft und Gesellschaft* in 1887, is credited with setting a mournful tone in modern community theory.[13] His seminal work on communal loss asserts that traditional social life and familial sentiment were giving way to a more impersonal set of human arrangements characterized chiefly by indifference. The solidarity of the closely knit familial order was being displaced by more calculated relationships predicated on self-interest.

Although Tönnies attempted to be objective in his analysis, there was significant reason to read into his writing a lament—a mourning for primary group arrangements. He saw *Gemeinschaft* as a naturalistic community characterized by a medieval-style familial patriarchy, ties of blood relations, clan arrangements, and collective living. Here there was a collective organic will of social totality predicated on the longing of mother and child to restore their oneness.[14] This persisted in all other communal arrangements. People worked cooperatively and in harmony. *Gesellschaft*, on the other hand, was identified by ubiquitous market relations turning each person into a buyer and seller competing with each other in the marketplace.[15] It was void of mutual cooperation upon which the traditional community had been built.

Emile Durkheim had an even more profound effect on scholarly sociology. His *Division of Labor in Society*, published in 1893 established a duality in community arrangements rivaling that of Tönnies.[16] While Durkheim saw the world shifting from a state of mechanical solidarity characterized by communities with common beliefs, values, customs, religions, and cultural practices to organic solidarity, which emphasized differences and complementary interdependencies, he also saw in this transition a loss of collective conscience—an erosion of shared sentiments and values that united the group morally. Like Tönnies, Durkheim hoped that the state would eventually provide the basis of social cohesion through civic association and national pride.

Furthermore, Durkheim proposed that for this newly emerging organic solidarity to exist, a mere integrated network of complementary activities involving each social unit or organ was inadequate. He espoused a form of social control wherein government would regulate and manipulate the personal affairs of its citizens to promote a new harmony—a new form of social consciousness. Like Rousseau who came before him, Durkheim did not romanticize traditional values. However, he rejected the notion of a social contract. Instead he argued for refining the competitive system and finding ways to make this new solidarity more harmonious and less discordant. This would entail the development of a new rationalistic morality.[17] Such a new morality, however, would be societal. Durkheim viewed community, as characterized by sentiment, as in eclipse.

IMPERSONALITY AND THE LOSS OF COMMUNITY

For many scholars alienation, isolation, and anomie were viewed as consequences of modern urban life. Louis Wirth borrowed extensively from some of the greatest European theorists of his time to develop his portrait of alienated urban existence. Chief among his sources were Ferdinand Tönnies, Max Weber, Georg Simmel, and Emile Durkheim. Wirth had been among the first to translate the work of many German sociologists into English and to introduce these ideas to Americans through his editorship of the *American Journal of Sociology*. In "Urbanism as a Way of Life," he constructed a narrative of urban life that in many ways portends Edward Hopper's *Nighthawks* (1942), *film noir*, and other statements of urban alienation of the late 1930s and early 1940s.[18]

Beginning in the 1950s, American sociologists borrowed more extensively from psychology to explore personality. Wirth of course had already integrated Simmel into his cityscape but avoided what he viewed as the "psychologizing" of urban problems. But beginning in 1950, the Chicago school was in decline. New books were released that helped change the course of community and urban studies. These works corresponded to the increased popularity of the corporate human relations movement of that time. An outstanding example of this was David Riesman's *The Lonely Crowd* (1950).[19]

Riesman's work along with C. Wright Mills' *White Collar* (1953) and William H. Whyte's *Organization Man* (1956) delved into the corporatization of personality. What they found was not very encouraging. Twentieth-century business enterprise generated a tide of conformity and superficiality. The film *The Man in the Gray Flannel Suit*, which was based on the Sloan Wilson novel of the same name, was released in 1956 warning of this white collar malaise. For the most part, Riesman's book borrowed extensively from two European emigres: Erich Fromm and Erik Erickson. Its stated purpose was to explore the character of the newly emerging middle class in the United States. The roots of character had to be traced to early childhood upbringing that was produced not by parents in isolation but as a response to the social system in which they lived.[20] In his study Riesman found an increase in what he termed "other-directed" personality types: shallow, uncertain of self, and longing for personal recognition. Also, he observed in such people a growing indifference to public life. Three forces: capitalism, industrialization, and urbanization made this type a world-wide phenomenon, not simply restricted to the United States.

In the 1970s Philip Slater's *The Pursuit of Loneliness* (1970), Richard Sennett's *The Fall of Public Man* (1976) and Christopher Lasch's *The Culture of Narcissism* (1979) picked up from where Riesman had left off with scathing criticisms of the shallowness of American character. All were in agreement that narcissism best described this emerging condition. All viewed bureaucratic capitalism as an underlying cause. Here the desire to escape commitment, the juvenile quest for control, and the inordinate fear of otherness hastened the decline of healthy diverse communities.

It was Slater's contention that Americans have powerful cravings for community; but they paradoxically have a desire to be left alone. They want to be engaged with their physical and social environment but also want considerable independence from it. Working against the building of viable communities was their fear of losing themselves in otherness. While the desire for community is expressed in the arts, in theater, cinema and novels, individuals pursue loneliness and privacy in their personal lives: private home, gardens, separate rooms, and separate schools. There is a desire to be free from commitment to others, a quest for isolation.

It was Richard Sennett's claim that there is an adolescent craving for homogeneous community, a purified identity based on common values and shared perspectives that undermines the development of authentic community. This quest for sameness expresses a narcissistic fear of otherness and it is strongly evident in the American psyche. Americans crave order and routine while priding themselves on a romanticized notion of their own independence. While many see value in ethnic and racial diversity, the middle class displays an inordinate degree of xenophobia. They work to control and restrict differences and to limit their own choices, in a sense, afraid of their own potential . . . their own freedom:

> Community has become both an emotional withdrawal from society and a territorial barricade within the city. The warfare between psyche and society has acquired a geographical focus, one replacing the older, behavioral balance between public and private. The new geography is communal versus urban.[21]

All of this work reveals a strong internal attachment/separation dialectic identified by object relations theorists. This infantile struggle of rapprochement is played out in the social tension between the extremes of submission and escape. While there is a desire to join into a community of interests, there is also a real fear that commitment will mean abrogation of personal identity or the total loss of self. Often escape is sought in stability and regularity, in homogenization or bureaucratic order; there is an attraction to being a salaried cog in the machine. Critical thought is displaced by a happy consciousness. The social isolation and anonymity of modern life are often confused with freedom and individualism. And in rejecting the need for dependency people deny the potential power they have over their own lives; many come to view themselves as helpless, ineffective, and perhaps even inconsequential.

This tension between submission and freedom, as it relates to community, has classical and neoclassical roots. It is essential to Plato's discussions of the *polis* as well as Jean-Jacques Rousseau's notion of the general will. For both men virtue was a product of democratic community; the glory of the individual could only be achieved by service to society. Virtuosity was incompatible with privacy. For Plato and Rousseau the importance of the group far exceeded the importance of the individual, but this did not mean a denial of individuality. True individualism, the heroic spirit, was measured as service to the community and not by individual acquisitiveness.

DOMINATION, SUBMISSION, AND COMMUNITY

It is in Rousseau's work that we most clearly see the dialectic of modernity. This is the tension between reason and emotion, between thought and feeling, between compliance and revolution. It is in some ways paradoxical that Rousseau can be credited with being a founder of the European Enlightenment, promoting the uncompromised power of reason, while simultaneously becoming a leader of the romantic movement in the arts. He vacillated between extolling the commanding powers of science and celebrating the untamed freedom of nature. He was a leading intellectual, yet he rejected intellectualism. However, he was not alone in experiencing such ambivalence. Such feelings were characteristic of his time. With the decline of feudal society, the old order was giving way to an unchartered course signaling great societal apprehension. Still, Rousseau was much more than a simple product of his environment.

It is obvious from even a casual acquaintance with Rousseau's life that it was replete with feelings of isolation and abandonment. In *The Confessions*, he reveals an emotionally distraught childhood: a mother who died from complications in giving him birth and a watchmaker father who loved him dearly, but abandoned him when Rousseau was only eight years of age. Speaking of his father's lament for his wife: "He seemed to see her again and again in me, but could never forget that I robbed him of her . . . 'Ah,' he would say with a groan; 'Give her back to me, console me for her, fill the void she has left in my heart.'"[22] Rousseau was given into the custody of an uncle and then sent off to boarding school to be taught by the Reverend Lambercier. It was during these formative school years that he slept with the pastor's thirty-year-old sister from whom he received frequent and regular beatings for minor indiscretions.[23] Such beatings were to become commonplace in his youth, and one might even say that he was addicted to them.

> But when in the end I was beaten I found the experience less dreadful in fact than in anticipation; and the very strange thing was that this punishment increased my affection for the inflicter. It required all the strength of my devotion and all my gentleness to prevent my deliberately earning another beating; I had discovered in the shame and pain of the punishment an admixture of sensuality which had left me rather eager than otherwise for a repetition by the same hand. . . .[24]

> My old childish tastes did not vanish, but became so intimately associated with those of maturity that I could never, when sensually aroused, keep the two apart. . . . I never dared to reveal my strange taste, but at least I got some pleasure from situations which pandered to the thought of it. To fall

on my knees before a masterful mistress, to obey her commands, to have to beg for her forgiveness, have been to me the most delicate of pleasures.[25]

Rousseau claimed that traditional bonds of society were chains. Each link was tempered by inequality. For him, community is a dialectic of submission and freedom. It is the very basis for self-awareness and individual development. The core of Rousseau's notion of community is the general will.[26] Through it each individual surrenders all autonomy to the benign state and in turn receives more rights than those given up. Trust is essential to this surrender, as is equality. Unlike those who saw the state as a drag on freedom and a tool of the aristocracy, Rousseau embraced it as a mechanism that might be used for personal liberation. Laws would be the products of this general will, and no one could be above them. The goal of each law was to bring about freedom and equanimity.

Much of this thinking was in line with those ideas advanced by Plato wherein every person had to enter the *polis* as an equal. The particular will of the individual needed to be surrendered to the general will of the citizens. All needed to work for the common good even if it meant acting against private personal interests. Only in this way could individuals build character and achieve virtue.

Abandonment haunted much of Rousseau's life. There is a particular scene in *The Confessions*, which he most lucidly describes; it is a turning point in his life. He is sixteen years old; it is night. He and two friends are coming home to Geneva after an evening of revelry. He had been severely beaten by his master, an engraver, several times in the past when he missed the city's curfew and was locked outside the gates overnight. He had resolved that this would not happen again, but it did:

A mile and a half from the city I heard the sound of the tatoo and increased my pace. Then I heard the drum-roll and ran my hardest. I arrived out of breath and bathed in sweat, my heart pounding. I saw from the distance that the soldiers were at their posts. I ran up and shouted breathlessly. It was too late. When I was twenty paces away I saw them raise the first bridge; I trembled as I watched its dreadful horns rising in the air, a sinister and fatal augury of the inevitable fate which from that moment awaited me.[27]

Rousseau was locked outside the city gates. He would spend the night under the stars and would resolve not to return to Geneva again. He would be free. It was at this point that his life became his own. It was a life filled with wondrous experiences and incredible accomplishments. It was to take him to places he never thought possible. He would write plays, novels, and operas. He would win awards for his insightful prose.

Nevertheless, it was a life punctuated with abandonment . . . from abandoned lovers to his own abandoned children.

In the end he found himself quite paranoid and alone. In his earlier *Discourses* he had promoted the notion of the natural goodness of people, but as he aged he grew increasingly distrustful and cynical. Where he once believed that society was the corrupting influence on the individual's life, now he felt that *only* society could produce goodness. His notion of enforcement of the general will at any price, in the end, was colored by his distrust. He saw the state as a new religion predicated on spiritual morality with a social contract enforced by severe discipline. This was coupled with a pontification of self-denial. For him, totalitarianism might be the price that had to be paid for true community.

At the end of his life we find him secluded from the world, retreating into nature for solace: "So now I am alone in the world, with no brother, neighbor or friend, nor any company left me but my own. The most sociable and loving of men has with unanimous accord been cast out by all the rest."[28] Yet despite what was obviously a severe melancholia, Rousseau had clear insight into the importance of nature and his search for solace:

> Everything is in constant flux on this earth. But there is a state where the soul can find a resting-place secure enough to establish itself and concentrate its entire being there with no need to remember the past or reach into the future, where time is nothing to it, where the present runs on indefinitely but the duration goes unnoticed, with no sign of passing time, and no other feeling of pain, desire or fear than the simple feeling of existence, a feeling that fills our soul entirely as long as the state lasts, we can call ourselves happy, not with a poor incomplete and relative happiness such as we find in the pleasures of life, but with a sufficient, complete and perfect happiness which leaves no emptiness to be filled in the soul. Such is the state which I often experienced on the Island of Saint-Pierre. In my solitary reveries, whether I lay in a boat and drifted where the water carried me, or sat by the shores of the stony lake, or elsewhere, on the banks of a lovely river or stream murmuring over the stones.[29]

It was in his retreat from the world that Rousseau died, some suggesting that he took his own life. Nevertheless, many of his ideas, including his dedication to equality and community were to be taken up by his intellectual heirs, most particularly Karl Marx.

COMMODIFICATION OF SPACE

Although many utopian versions of community came and went neither Plato's nor Rousseau's vision ever saw fruition. Decaying medieval towns that gathered their communitarian character from a commonality of work, religion, and commerce with minor exceptions failed to evolve democratically. With the advent of the industrial revolution and the fall of feudalism, democracy and community became utopian ideals and the subject of pastoral poems, sonnets, and romantic philosophies.

Whereas in premodern society place was a sacred link between time and space—a center of felt value, capitalism segregated these elements and assigned each a distinct exchange value. With the advance of market capitalism came the desanctification of place. Geography was a barrier to be transcended and place no more than commodified space. As Henri Lefebvre suggests: "The commodity world brings in its wake certain attitudes toward space, certain actions upon space and even a certain concept of space."[30] For Lefebvre under capitalism space became a highly fragmented, homogenized, and hierarchial abstraction. Modern community became alienated, hollowed-out, and commodified. The emergence of modern technology diminished the significance of space and place. Place was emptied of transcendental value. Just as the worker assumed the role of a commodity, so did the community in which he or she lived. Land, and eventually community, were factors of capitalistic enterprise. Place was defiled by the reorganization of production.

A few grand experiments were attempted to curtail the onslaught of industrial urban blight and save the worker from his or her slothful nature, but rarely were these designs aimed at achieving democratic community. The plans of Robert Owen and Charles Fourier, met with varying degrees of success; but these "utopias" could not be strongly enough insulated from the forces which had been unleashed by industrial revolution. Such was true of dozens of utopian experiments that flickered in the eighteenth and nineteenth centuries. More radical democratic projects involving worker communes were short-lived and were crushed by reactionary violence.

Following the Paris uprising of 1848, Baron Haussmann under Napoleon's directives worked to ensure that the army could maintain public order over workers by eliminating the narrow streets in poor neighborhoods and clearing away some of the more dilapidated examples of worker housing. Haussman constructed broad expansive boulevards that helped to vitalize commerce and directed the bourgeoisie toward cafes and shopping arcades.

The Paris Commune of 1871 was a proletarian experiment led by laborers who helped to build these thoroughfares as well as women, artists, writers, and other intellectuals. It was a response to the corruption of the Bonaparte Empire, which had entangled France in war, incurred enormous debt and finally succumbed to a humiliating defeat at the hands of the Prussian army. This had led not only to severe economic hardship for Parisian workers, but also to the occupation of their beloved city by German troops. It was to this occupation that Parisians responded with spontaneous rebellion. The Paris Commune, which became a symbol of worker empowerment around the world, was an uprising of the oppressed classes wherein the people took power for themselves, democratically elected a government, formed alliances, and established a progressive public agenda.

With the help of the national guard, the commune fortified itself from threatened attacks of the French regular army which along with the head of state had retreated to Versailles. The people of Paris, who supported the commune, built barricades in the center of the city and patrolled them. More than 160 were erected within the course of a few days, these ranging between five and eighteen feet tall. However, under the direction of Adolphe Thiers, head of the French national government during the period of occupation, the barricades were breeched within a few short months. The French army was marched into Paris. A bloodbath followed whereby close to thirty thousand commune supporters, including many women and children, were killed in the streets. The whole of Paris was in flames.

This slaughter was to have the support of industrialists and financiers throughout Europe. It was to send a clear message. The Paris Commune, had it been a success, might have inspired other workers around the world. In this sense, the more bloody the repression, the greater the violence, the more powerful the message: public space belongs to the bourgeoisie. Without doubt, Paris would be a nineteenth-century symbol of this. The boulevards of the city were to come under the control of the capitalists and would chiefly serve the interests of this new aristocracy. Haussmann's Paris of elegant tree-lined promenades and expansive avenues conveys this message quite clearly.

It was nineteenth-century Paris that became the signifier of modernity. It was a city in which urban renewal would expel the workers and replace their homes with upscale apartments and cafes. But such a move would be met with historic resistance. Lefebvre notes: "One strong aspect of the Paris Commune (1871) is the strength of the return towards the urban centre of workers pushed out towards the outskirts and peripheries, their reconquest of the city, this belonging among other belongings, this value, this *oeuvre* which had been torn from them."[31]

Speculation in real estate was to guide the city. The Paris arcades, which were modeled after the Palais Royal, offered an alternative to the muddy proletarian streets. Glass-enclosed paved passageways stretching for blocks with uniformed double-tiered rows of shops provided shopping opportunities for bourgeois customers. Only luxury goods would be sold here and access would be limited to the upper classes. Domestics, soldiers, beggars, and students would be prohibited admission to many of these. Entry to the arcades would be policed. Walter Benjamin saw these as temples of commodity capitalism promoting a new consumer culture that would mesmerize people quelling any chance for critical thought and revolt.[32] He saw in these arcades the essence of capitalistic modernity and filled notebooks with his own insights and thoughts on them.

Benjamin, a friend of Adorno and Bertolt Brecht, was himself an exile from the Nazis. During World War II, he sought refuge from his native Germany in Paris. A story is frequently told of his fleeing occupied Paris to the Spanish border in 1940 accompanied by the wife of an acquaintance he had made in an internment camp along with a few others. She led him on a winding uphill route across the Pyrenees to Spain. On this long mountainous trip he was carrying a heavy briefcase. She noticed his having to stop every few moments to catch his breath and questioned if the briefcase was necessary. It also appeared that they might have been followed. "It's my manuscript," he supposedly responded. "It is important that it be safe . . . even more important than myself." At the border, however, they were stopped by the Spanish police, who found that their papers were no longer valid. They were then forced to turn back. In total despair, Benjamin took an overdose of morphine and died.

The manuscript he was carrying was somewhat of a mystery since when the police inventoried his belongings they found nothing in the briefcase. However, it is generally assumed that in the briefcase was his unfinished *Passagen-Werk*, or better known in English as *The Arcades Project*. Whether or not this was in the briefcase no one will know for sure, but he supposedly left behind a copy of the manuscript with his friend Georges Bataille in Paris. *The Arcades Project* was a poetic work of impressions of the city. Benjamin integrated into this work his fascination with Baudelaire whom he saw as an icon of urban modernity and his intrigue with fashion and commodity culture. For him, the arcade represented the reenchantment of space through the fetish of commodities:

> They [the arcades] radiated through Paris of the Empire like grottoes. For someone entering the Passage des Panoramas in 1817, the sirens of gaslight would be singing to him on one side, while oil-lamp odalisques offered enticements from the other. With the kindling of electric lights, the irreproachable glow was extinguished in these galleries, which suddenly became more difficult to find—which wrought a blackmagic at entranceways, and peered from blind windows into their own interior. It was not decline but transformation. All at once they were the hollow mold from which "modernity" was caste.[33]

> The arcade is a street of lascivious commerce only; it is wholly adapted to
> arousing desires. Because in this street the juices slow to a standstill, the
> commodity proliferates along the margins and enters into fantastic combi-
> nations, like the tissue of tumors.[34]

This idea of hollowing out space and then filling it with meaning is
the subject of Sharon Zukin's *Landscapes of Power* (1991) and Mike
Davis's *City of Quartz* (1990). Both books were significantly influenced
by Lefebvre and both to some degree are indebted to Benjamin. It is
Zukin's contention that, historically, place was always essential to
market both literally and symbolically, an image supported by
Mumford's discussion of the neoclassical market in *The Culture of Cities*
(1938). Well up until the nineteenth century, merchants and traders
would come from far corners and descend upon an important urban
place or square, most typically one that would have deep cultural or religious significance. Market would frequently constitute a festival. Traders
would come to town with new or important consumables and stay until
their goods were gone. Always the integrity of place would be maintained. While trace elements of this marketplace still exist in major cities
around the world, the modern nineteenth-century market was divorced
from place. Market capitalism comes to the city and trivializes place relegating it to the position of a location commodity or real estate. As markets become more globalized, the significance of place is even further
diminished. Market invades place and consumes it. "The language of
modernism," posits Zukin, "expresses a universal experience of movement away from place, and aspires to submerge or incorporate it into a
larger whole."[35]

Zukin's central assertion is that space is today unmistakably divided
between landscapes of consumption and landscapes of devastation.
Places reliant on production are likely candidates for devastation; they
are forever vulnerable. This is primarily because standardization and
technology of production makes place less consequential. Alternatively,
places of consumption—those connected to finance, real estate development and entertainment—are sites of power wherein "consumer pleasures hide the reins of concentrated economic control."[36]

Today shopping malls and department stores become symbols of
power. Also, they have replaced civic gathering places as arenas of public
life. There is an amalgamation of culture and commerce in shopping
malls. And in fact, the design of the mall has had a pronounced impact
on modern culture. Architectural historian Margaret Crawford notes:

> Today, hotels, office buildings, cultural centers, and museums virtually
> duplicate the layouts and formats of shopping malls. A walk through the

new additions to the Metropolitan Museum in New York with their enormous internal spaces, scenographic presentation of art objects, and frequent opportunities for purchasing other objects connected to them, produces an experience very similar to that of strolling through a shopping mall. The East Wing of the National Gallery of Art in Washington, D.C., designed by I. M. Pei, is even a closer match.[37]

Mike Davis holds up Los Angeles as the quintessential capitalist city—the epitome of commodity culture. Like Zukin, he asserts that the image of the city is more essential than what constitutes its physical composition or its true historical development. Every new landscape of Los Angeles is a fabrication:

> Los Angeles in this instance is, of course, a stand in for capitalism in general. The ultimate world-historical significance—and oddity—of Los Angeles is that it has come to play the double role of utopia and dystopia for advanced capitalism. The same place, as Brecht noted, symbolized both heaven and hell.[38]

The layering-over of history is a leitmotif of Davis's work. He surveys the city and finds it to be a stratified facade of frontier, mission, *noir*, and high-tech. But very little of the imagery associated with the city is real. In essence it has been developed by real estate speculators, movie moguls, aviation industrialists, public relations people, and creative German intellectual leftists who escaped Nazism in the 1940s. "The city," says Davis, "is a place where everything is possible, nothing is safe and durable enough to believe in, where constant synchronization prevails, and the automatic ingenuity of capital ceaselessly throws up new forms and spectacles—a rhetoric, in other words, that recalls the hyperbole of Marcuse's *One Dimensional Man.*"[39]

Perhaps the most pointed of Davis's criticism is the fortification of Los Angeles and the associated privatization of public space. While this phenomenon can not be credited to Los Angeles alone, certainly L.A. must be credited with instituting many innovations. For Davis these include turning numerous public parks and city streets over to the homeless and other outcasts and funneling middle-class pedestrians into the corridors of megastructures and super-malls under the watchful eyes of private police. "The Oz-like archipelago of Westside pleasure domes—a continuum of tony malls, art centers and gourmet strips—is reciprocally dependent upon the social imprisonment of the third world service proletariat who live in increasingly repressive ghettoes and barrios."[40] Parks go derelict, beaches become more segregated, libraries and playgrounds close while several million immigrants in search of the American dream find themselves relegated to limited public amenities.

Throughout the spaces of the city is *de facto* disinvestment and a major shift of public revenues to corporate-defined redevelopment programs. Walls are erected all over Los Angeles to isolate the classes from each other and to particularly provide logistical security to the most wealthy. The surface of the city streets is hardened against immigrants, people of color, and especially the poor. There is what Davis calls the "South Africanization" of spatial relations.[41] Some gated luxury neighborhoods institute passport controls, restricting access to all but home owners and their guests. There is tremendous isolation and fear of otherness that Davis views as constituting the heart of Los Angeles.

URBAN RENEWAL AS A SYMBOL
OF ABANDONMENT

If any event symbolized the planned abandonment of community in American culture, it was the urban renewal programs coupled with the Federal government's policies of suburbanization in the 1950s and 1960s. Los Angeles had taken advantage of these programs in wrestling the central business district away from poor people, immigrants, and people of color. More than 12,000 low income residents were removed from their homes in the early 1950s alone to make the central city safe for new investment and redevelopment.[42]

In the 1940s and 1950s, families of former slaves were directed by economic necessity, organized terrorism, and police power to relocate to the industrial north from the south, a new black diaspora—similar to the western movement of pioneers was to be reenacted. As poor blacks moved north and began to gain some degree of economic equity, private capital took flight, taking with it jobs and the means of survival. The loss of well paying factory jobs coupled with insurance and bank redlining turned once viable but decaying neighborhoods into ghettos—penitentiaries for the poor. The quality of education in these neighborhoods would plummet. Infant mortality rates would reach levels experienced only in third world countries.

Observing profit-making opportunities in such human misery, land speculators joined with public enterprise to develop programs of slum clearance. Such programs had the full backing of the liberal establishment. It was called urban renewal. Understanding the danger that slums represented to the propertied class, tax dollars were used to eradicate any semblance of poor communities and to build housing for the middle class. Bulldozers moved into northern cities, which assisted builders in the purposeful destruction of viable underclass neighborhoods, historic brownstones, and other architectural landmarks.

Dislocated African-Americans and Latinos were either left homeless or were forced into public housing projects where they would come under close surveillance by authorities. In line with Joseph Schumpeter's hypothesis, the force of creative destruction, which he saw as characterizing all of capitalism, was clearly unleashed in the American inner cities.[43] J. John Palen notes:

> The most glaring weakness of urban renewal programs was the displacement of large numbers of low-income families without adequate provision for their relocation. Until criticism built up to a point where it could no longer be ignored, little had been done to rehouse those who were forced to move from a renewal area. It is generally agreed that during the first years of the urban renewal program, residents were dispossessed and ejected from their homes in a fashion that can only be characterized as ruthless.[44]

The destruction of viable but poor neighborhoods was the outcome of much of the urban renewal programs of this era. Jane Jacobs's classic *Death and Life of Great American Cities* became a monument in the 1960s to the havoc wrecked by such programs.[45] She pointed out in her book that old neighborhoods had much to offer cities. They provided residents with a sense of place and they provided the city with a persona—*a soul*.

Herbert Gans's touching study of the loss of an Italian neighborhood in Boston's West End due to urban renewal showed the viability and vitality of poor neighborhoods destined for clearance.[46] Marc Fried, who was research director of Massachusetts General Hospital's Center for Community Studies, conducted a review of the psychological impact that such renewal programs had on this population. For Fried, dislocation brought with it a pathology emanating from loss and expressed in grief. In his review of 250 women who were forced by the city to leave their homes, 46 percent gave evidence of long-term grief reactions. Among the 316 men interviewed, 38 percent had such reactions. Although many of those interviewed felt only casual loss, many were profoundly affected: "I felt as though I had lost everything," "I felt as though my heart was taken out of me," "I lost all the friends I knew," "I threw up a lot," "I had a nervous breakdown" were some of the comments.[47] Short-term impact of dislocation on feelings were even more intense. Fifty-four percent of the women and 46 percent of the men reported "severely depressed or disturbed reactions."[48]

Urban renewal displaced more people than it housed. It worsened the housing conditions of the poor and it substituted unsafe, institutionalized public housing projects for less dangerous low-rise tenements. It sometimes demolished landmarks of significant architectural importance and beauty. Combined with the loss of well paying industrial jobs, urban renewal devastated dozens of urban communities. It created rubble-strewn expanses out of viable neighborhoods in sections of Detroit, Chicago, and New York.

Working together, the public and private sectors eliminated what was left of decent places for poor and working class people to live in the city. In building new museums and civic centers and granting variances and tax abatements, urban governments went to work for speculators and developers promoting higher real estate values through razing of tenements and the erection of luxury housing in formally poor neighborhoods. City officials and developers went into partnership substituting artificial quaintness, generated by planners such as James Rouse, for authenticity, and making any trace of once thriving commercial neighborhoods into counterfeit experiences through what Michael Sorkin has referred to as "the architecture of deception."[49] History becomes an element of the consumer experience—Manhattan's South Street, Boston's Quincy Market, and Baltimore's Harborplace. But what was once public space becomes privatized. The upper middle classes are welcomed back into the city to displace what remained of the poor in neighborhoods targeted by speculators for regentrification. In Manhattan, rents skyrocketed during the 1980s into the late 1990s as SROs were converted into luxury condominiums and many of the most desperate of the poor were turned out onto the streets. And in key cities, these trends have continued into the twenty-first century.

Modern cities are forever transformed by ongoing renewal policies that put money into the hands of private developers and decrease the supply of housing for the poor. The role of federal government in the United States has been minimized, replaced by policies of benign neglect and public housing curtailments. Many government officials collude with wealthy real estate developers and little in the way of new affordable housing has been made available to the poor.

DISPOSABLE COMMUNITIES

There is no escaping the fact that market has claimed dominance over the aesthetic quality of life in America and now in the world. Although the bleaching of American cities of their color and character has been the subject of urban critics from Louis Wirth onward, the actual prosaicness of the cities, according to George Ritzer, has intensified through what he calls a process of *McDonaldization*.[50] Ritzer posits that modern cities lose much of their singularity through the displacement of locally significant retail enterprises with mass-market chains and franchises. Thus Starbucks displaces the street-corner café, Eddie Bauer the local haberdashery, Barnes & Noble the bookshop, and so on. Out of these establishments, just like out of McDonalds, comes a uniformed quality controlled set of merchandise targeted to a bureaucratically processed consumer. Each store, exterior and interior, is a slightly modified prefabrication. Not only does localized urban architecture, which creates a uniqueness of place, yield to mass-produced designs and modular themes, but these uniformed designs repeat themselves converting downtowns into undifferentiated shopping parks and commercial centers.

Exquisite architectural wonders have been targets of the wrecking ball to accommodate urban commercial investment. New York City has been exemplary in this fashion, losing much of its character in the last half of the twentieth century. Among one of its most treasured landmarks was the original Pennsylvania Station on which construction began in 1906 and was completed in 1910. The project was designed by McKim, Mead, and White, whose work was internationally acclaimed. This project in particular was a civic masterpiece built by the Pennsylvania Railroad Company to immortalize railroads. This grand neoclassical structure was designed to replicate the Caracalla Baths in Rome with classical columns and grand cornices at the facade. Internally, the great train concourse was covered with acres of domed glass, arches and vaults mimicking crystal palaces and Parisian arcades. "Until the first blow fell," the *New York Times* wrote on October 30, 1963, "no one was convinced that Penn Station really would be demolished or that New York would permit this monumental act of vandalism . . . we will probably be judged not by the monuments we build but by those we have destroyed."[51]

What seems authentic gives way to the plastic. The Disney take-over of New York's once notorious Times Square in the 1990s is a case in point. Here seedy topless bars, darkened game-arcades, and massive marquees promoting sexually raunchy cinema have given way to a sanitized Las Vegas with oversized exploding signage advertising the GAP, Victoria's Secret, Toys 'R US and Disney's own mediocre movies and theatre productions. Tourists walk the safe streets unhassled by the drug dealers and pimps that were at one time part of the local color. The Disney Store has a central place in this new outdoor entertainment mall. In it is sold Disney-wear and artifacts to promote the symbols of Disneyfication known throughout the world: little stuffed Mickeys, Minnies, Donald Ducks, and Goofeys. Nevertheless, behind this facade of benign consumerism rests a transnational conglomerate, which has its toys and logo-encrested clothing made in third world sweatshops by twelve-year-old children working for pennies an hour to support their families. And should the price of labor rise, Disney is willing and able to take its manufacturing business elsewhere. Like other transnationals Disney recognizes its role in the global economy and its ultimate allegiance to stockholders.

The flow of capital in modern society dictates patterns of community settlement and the nature of community itself. This is not a particularly American phenomenon, but rather a capitalistic one. Today's planned suburban communities are laid out in ways simulating shopping malls. Developers such as Disney and their town of Celebration in Orlando, Florida have been relatively successful in packaging those elements that were used to sell Disney World: cleanliness, security, and the small town pastiche of wholesomeness. In Celebration these things are corporately controlled by one of the most powerful multinationals in the world. But the control is not obvious, it is buried seamlessly in the fabric of the community just as it is in Disneyland and Disney World.

The migratory nature of capital is now a global phenomenon producing enormously disruptive events for communities dependent on industry. Barry Bluestone and Bennett Harrison, in their prophetic *The Deindustrialization of America*, made this point well before the advent of NAFTA.[52] Their book was among the first to describe the collapse of domestic production in the United States. According to Bluestone and Harrison the costs of domestic disinvestment far exceeded the lost wages and diminished productivity: " Workers and their families suffer serious physical and emotional health problems when their employers suddenly shut down operations, and the community as a whole experiences a loss of revenue needed for supporting police and fire protection, schools and parks. Entire cities and towns can be brought to the brink of bankruptcy."[53]

The unique aspect of Bluestone and Harrison's work was that it was the first popular liberal recognition of the local as well as international dynamics of the convulsive flight of capital. The studies that came before it recognized the redistribution of employment and capital flight primarily on a national level. With the global freedom of capital that could purchase labor more cheaply in the developing world, the future for U.S. communities was starting to look extremely grim.

In the 1970s GE and RCA both increased employment worldwide, but reduced employment in the United States. When General Motors closed its plants in the United States, but hired additional workers at its facilities in Spain, it increased its efficiency and its profit. But American communities have suffered the consequences. In 1997 U.S. corporations were investing $95.7 billion abroad where factors of production were cheaper. In 2001, just four years later, that number had reached $132.1 billion.[54] While the American share of manufactured goods exported abroad continues to drop, American corporations have increased their sales abroad and have been able, therefore, to maintain some degree of competitive edge.[55] However, the corporate beneficiaries are not always American, and the profits do not necessarily find their way back into the domestic economy. Local communities, which lose jobs due to relocation decisions, are very hard hit. This is not only true for American communities, but it is also true for communities in the developing world. When the cost of doing business rises, capital gets going. But the impact of new investment on economies can be culturally traumatic. Sociologist Saskia Sassen notes:

> Perhaps the single most important effect of foreign investment in export production is the uprooting of people from traditional modes of existence. It has long been recognized that the development of commercial agriculture tends to displace subsistence farmers, creating a supply of rural wage laborers and giving rise to mass migrations to cities. In recent years, the large-scale development of export-oriented manufacturing in Southeast Asia and the Caribbean Basin has come to have a similar effect (though through different mechanisms); it has uprooted people and created an urban reserve of wage laborers. In both export agriculture and export manufacturing, the disruption of traditional work structures as a result of the introduction of modern modes of production has played a key role in transforming people into migrant workers and, potentially, into emigrants.[56]

CONCLUSION

Community, like family, is a powerful sociological signifier that often identifies the ideological position of its member. In contemporary heterogeneous societies we have many types of families and an almost equal range of communities. While some are grateful to see such a wide variety of family and community types available to us, an equal number lament the passing of a mythical homogeneous world they believed would be around forever, a world in which the bowling team was central to life. While some observers like Robert Putnam can put an impressive assortment of data together as proposed evidence of an inordinate amount of social detachment, there is certainly a generalized sense that things have been changing; and his data surely reveals this.[57]

Putnam and others tend to lay fault for the failure of community in the generation of the 1960s and those who came later. But the abandonment of the territorial community, both literally and figuratively, is an essential part of capitalistic development. The theme of community loss expressed in art and literature chronicles a concrete sociological phenomenon. The filling-in and emptying-out of neighborhoods in modern societies, the building, razing, and rebuilding of homes, stores, and factories and the overall commodification of place contributes to the sense of separation and alienation of people from place.

Between 1947 and 1997, 16 percent to 21 percent of Americans moved each year from their primary place of residence.[58] On an average, the typical American moves eleven times over a lifetime, which is approximately once every seven years. This makes the population of the United States the most mobile in the developed world. It is interesting to note that of those who move at the highest rate are children under five. African-Americans and Latinos have extremely high rates: 19 percent and 23 percent respectively. While educational attainment is related to geographic mobility, high school dropouts have a much higher mobility rate than those who are college educated.

Settlement on a social plane becomes extremely difficult with the constant and continuous uprooting of people. Many find it difficult to claim an allegiance to place and to neighbors under these circumstances. It is also more difficult to establish and continue ties. This is not to argue that the neighborhood fails to remain important to the homeowner or apartment resident, but its significance is in the amenities or commodities it offers to the resident: education, recreation, access to shopping, transportation, place of worship, and the like. The ebb and flow of population into and out of place has led to a weakening of communal social bonds. For many in the U.S., neighborhood has become merely a territorial launch-pad for successive moves into wealthier communities with higher quality amenities. For others it is the opposite.

Thus community still retains a viability today but its functions are significantly less social and integrative than might have once been the case. The propinquitous social neighborhood is still very much alive, and as heterogeneous as it is homogeneous. As urban planner Mel Webber suggested over thirty years ago, electronic technology and communications have made space less important in terms of establishing interest-sharing cohorts. The so-called compression of time has transformed the way people interact with each other and with whom they have come to associate.

Chapter 6

Abandonment of Nature

The abandonment of what we have come to refer to as "nature" was deeply rooted in the sixteenth century—in the rise of science, the emergence of modern capitalism and the ascendancy of the European Enlightenment. Characterized by a bourgeois quest to tame the world's savagery, process its physical resources, and convert them into profitable commodities and conveniences, the machinery of early industrialization desanctified the raw essences of the earth. The justification for its crude exploitation was provided by an austere instrumental reason. For critical theorists such as Adorno, instrumental reason served to alienate nature and naturalness from humankind. The idealistic imagination of classical civilization was forced to give way to mechanistic pragmatism. The surrender of creative intuitive processes to base calculation was the result. While the eighteenth-century romantics responded to these challenges and attempted to reclaim the bygone Dionysian world of primitive sensuality and artistic truth, they eventually became disillusioned in their quest and their work frequently degenerated into escapism and nihilism.

This chapter looks at the domination of nature, its abandonment, and the romantic response. It begins by presenting a model romantic narrative, examining Mary Shelley's life and her story of Frankenstein. Her novel is presented as an early illustration of romanticism's distrust of rationalistic science and its disdain for the crudification of nature. Mary Shelley laid the groundwork in *Frankenstein* for a deeper understanding of the relationship between abandonment of nature and the abandonment of the primal intuitive self. However, in promoting the notion of science at odds with nature, Shelley and other romantics were culpable, intentionally or not, in deepening an illusionary schism between both. Thus, romanticism helped to promote and sustain the nature/civilization dichotomy. In a drive to confront what they viewed as the earth's disenchantment, the romantics commenced construction of a bourgeois escapist aesthetic. They would provide synthetic and parallel realities in which the bourgeoisie could retreat from the world torn apart by capitalistic enterprise.

MARY SHELLEY'S *FRANKENSTEIN*

The fear of abandonment makes a striking appearance in Mary Shelley's novel, *Frankenstein*, and some literary critics suggest that terror of abandonment and personal loss drive most of the novel's central characters, including the monster.[1] There can be little doubt that Mary Shelley's own life was haunted by traumatic childhood separation, guilt, and fear of loneliness.

Her remarkable novel, completed in 1816 when she was only nineteen years of age, was replete with both literal and figurative orphans: Captain Walton, Dr. Victor Frankenstein, and even Elizabeth—"Family histories, in fact, especially those of orphans appear to fascinate Mary Shelley and wherever she can include one in the narrative," note critics Sandra Gilbert and Susan Gubar, "she does so with obsessiveness."[2]

Mary Shelley's own youth is characterized by anxiety relative to parental loss and rejection as well as the sorrows of actual abandonment. Her mother, Mary Wollstonecraft, a major public figure, feminist, and author, died of childbirth complications ten days after giving birth to her. This left the young child with a cold, distant, and often rejecting father, William Godwin. Godwin was also a leading public intellectual whose many philosophical works, including *Inquiry Concerning Political Justice and its Influence on Morals and Happiness* (1793), would inspire a whole generation of young poets and idealists.

As soon as she was able to read, the young Mary Godwin lost herself in the world of books. By the time she was eight years old, she had become a solitary, withdrawn child. Sometimes she would leave home and visit her mother's grave at the St. Pancras Churchyard where she would spend hours reading her mother's works. Sometimes she even slept on the grave overnight. And it was here, at the graveyard, she would rendezvous with her first lover. By the age of sixteen, she escaped an intolerable household, run by her physically abusive stepmother, and went to live with that lover—Percy Bysshe Shelley.[3]

Mary Shelley's entire life reflected deep and profound loss, not only commencing with the loss of her mother, but also ending with the death of her own three children and the tragic early death of her husband. "It is not surprising," wrote Bonnie Reyford Neumann, "that this constant personal grief should have found objective form over and over again in her writings."[4]

Readers can not help but view Mary Shelley as an orphan—an infant abandoned through the death of her mother, a child emotionally abandoned by her father. Like all orphans before and after her, like all children unloved by their parents, she must have felt this very deeply, so deeply that it could arouse in her psyche an image of a murderous monster (herself)—created, rejected, and never loved. This was a monster that was spurned by all whom it knew and attempted to love. This was indeed a cursed progeny. Like the monster of her novel, everything she touched, including her progenitor, would die.

Yet, Mary Shelley, her novel, and her monster, were products of their age—an era marked by rapid change, consumed with the romance of nature in the face of inhuman science and mechanistic industrialization. Much of her work, as well as the work of other artists of her day, displayed an infatuation with history and legend, a romance with the wilderness, ruins, decay, and death, and a disillusionment with the calculating outcomes of science and reason.

Victor Frankenstein represented all that humanity was becoming—the epitome of a new narcissism spurred on by an insatiable desire to appease the intellect, incapable of authentic caring, void of love. Victor Frankenstein was himself a clumsy imitation of life—a new but sorrowful Prometheus who could generate life in a laboratory, yet have no drive to make love to his fiancé. Here was a man who had little sense of the world around him. Victor's "heroic autonomy," his inability to connect to others, was central to this story. According to Harold Bloom, he appeared much less human, less in touch with his own feelings than his monster.[5] The perceptive reader must question Victor's ability to love Elizabeth, the woman he is intended to marry. His controlling demeanor, his compulsivity, his need to ensure his own immortality through this scientific progeny attests to his uniquely modern yet disturbed character. Nevertheless, he was a symbol of his times. The monster he created, of course, was a reflection of himself—an alter-ego so to speak.

In the novel, the monster struggles to connect, to overcome the feelings of loneliness that arose from his creator's rejection of him. There is no real love in the Frankenstein family that holds people to one another. To learn about love, the monster spies on the cottage peasants who express their affections openly and honestly. It is from these peasants that the monster learns the use of words. Looking in on the cottagers he comes to appreciate the arts and music and the joys in living. From them he learns acts of kindness.

Like Adam in Milton's *Paradise Lost* (a book the monster has read and carries about), he is an exile, cast away attempting to reconnect to his master. Throughout his murderous rampage his ultimate aim is to find love. This tragic and, eventually, self-destructive journey leads the creature further and further away from his creator, further alienated from his source of life. Never does the monster come to terms with his own autonomy or realize that his creator is even more alienated and less capable of ever loving than himself. Victor, the maker of this monster, is thus both an orphan and an exile. As a scientist he is exiled from his own humanity, estranged from his family and the beauty in nature that surrounds him.

Mary Shelley uses the German Alpine to ground two very unusual characters. It is an awe-inspiring landscape—the same backdrop used as an inspiration for much of Percy Bysshe Shelley's poetry including his work *Mount Blanc*. Both Victor and the monster tread through the snow-covered mountains on an existential journey to find their own souls. The nature/civilization opposition is magnified by the intensity of nature's beauty and power. The scientist and his creature will come to tragic ends far away in the Arctic's snowy wilderness. The pristine evening snowscape into which the monster is seen disappearing at the novel's end, as he flees the lifeless body of his master, presents the reader with a surrealistic image of the modern individual—one filled with guilt and self-loathing—sailing out to sea on an ice floe with every intention of destroying himself.

The timeless popularity of this tale leaves little doubt that the sentiments expressed in *Frankenstein* resonated with some very real anxieties, the fear of abandonment, loss of feeling due to mechanization and alienation felt by the early nineteenth-century bourgeoise, and still felt today. The novel clearly articulated a growing tension between nature and science. Such tension was reflected on the one hand in the works of Enlightenment philosophers and writers who believed that civilization was predicated on emotionally detached science and that its advance depended on sensual repression. On the other hand, there was a deification of nature on the part of many European romantics.

The ability of science to create, or at the very least imitate, life and wrestle from nature its magical powers, underscored the growing disenchantment of nature and the rise of secularized culture. Along with this disillusionment came intense feelings of alienation and detachment. Such feelings are evident among all the central characters in Shelley's novel, but are most prominently seen in Frankenstein and his creation. The novel's focus on personal feelings of loss and abandonment are not simply reflections of the author's own unconscious childhood sentiments, but also reflect the social malaise of her time. Here in the characters of Elizabeth, Victor, and the monster, anxiety and guilt stemming from feelings of rejection and lovelessness drive them to desperate means to fill a gaping void.

The novel depicted emotional and erotic repression produced by the intellectual, religious, and economic currents of the day. Victor's sexual repression and unresponsiveness is obvious. For some, the monster represented his repressed alter-ego and the outpouring of his violent and lustful urges. Victor spent considerable time in isolation creating what would appear to be a monstrous extension of himself, perhaps best viewed as a masturbatory experience. Trudging through the frigid snows of the Arctic, guilt-ridden and fearful of what he had "unleashed," he would dedicate the latter part of his life in a quest to destroy it .

This novel, therefore, provides the reader with an encoded view of transition from a world of nature to a world of science, from a world of sensuality and emotionality to a world of intellectuality and repression. It combines Gothic romanticism with a modern vision of a science unregulated by humanity to promote an ideology that has at its core a pessimistic view of the civilizing process. This was a view shared by many philosophers and intellectuals of the early nineteenth century. At the heart of this novel is an intense concern with the destructive potential of civilization in its drive to supplant the natural with the synthetic and to entomb human sensuality with its seal of hyperintellectualism.

THE NATURE/CIVILIZATION DICHOTOMY

In contrast, in the seventeenth century, René Descartes took the lead not only in promoting the Enlightenment's view that the world's secrets could be unlocked mathematically, but that mankind held a sacred place in the universe apart from nature. Unlike other animals, which were literally no more than unthinking, unfeeling machines, only men had souls and intellect. Man was deemed to be the master of nature and the only creature capable and spiritually worthy of dominating it. This notion was nothing new. Classical western thought long held the seeds for such a world view. Historically, the Judeo-Christian tradition advanced the idea that all of God's creations, including women, were provided to serve the needs of men.

It was an extension of this patrimonialism that the world was a hostile place, nature was wild, and needed to be tamed. The Enlightenment put a relatively new spin on such thinking. It was through men's reason and intellect (things thought to be absent in other animals and women) that the external wilderness would be dominated and domesticated for the glory of God. Civilization, therefore, was perceived as being at war with nature. It stood in opposition to nature's erraticism. Imperialism and colonialism could serve as instruments of economic avarice, but were also avenues to taming the wild and dark corners of the earth. Although this emphasis on repression ran counter to many other competing beliefs, including both ancient animism and the classical and Eastern religious recognition of a need for balance and harmony with nature, it gained ascendancy because it seemed to justify a burgeoning system of environmental and personal exploitation. Thus, it became the hallmark of a new rationalistic ethos.

During the Renaissance and continuing with the expansion of trade into the seventeenth and eighteenth centuries, western European religious leaders and intellectuals advanced a view that the animal-like passions of humans needed to be quelled in order to maintain and promote the development of civilization. Thus, a barrier had to be erected between one's innate nature and the modern world—between the wild and the tamed. The belief in an internal bestiality and an external environmental one, running parallel to each other, both of which needed to be constrained, was reflected in the dominant intellectual paradigms of early modernity and the Enlightenment. Among the most influential contributors to this model were seventeenth-century British philosophers Frances Bacon and Thomas Hobbes.

For Hobbes, particularly, civilization was a necessary set of controls exercised over virulent human nature. Although one could be forced to take on the external appearance of a rationally acting subject, Hobbes believed that only force could maintain that veneer separating man from the most loathsome of beasts. Similarly, Bacon's *New Atlantis* espoused a futuristic vision of large scale technological mastery over nature and over man himself. Few would ever come close to Bacon in directing their full attention to celebrating nature's conquest and the repression of nature in human beings.

This on-going system of dynamic social control and imposed order seemed to ensure a privileged position for man in the antinatural hegemony. Norbert Elias's work is crucial for a full understanding of how the various measures of control, including modern rules of conduct, were instituted.[6] The purpose of the civilizing process was to insulate man from his volatile, passionate and brutish self and to allow him to identify with the empowered. Not only would the adherence to rules of corporeal conduct become a sign of one's humanity, such would be the measure of where one stood in the stratified order. The closer one was to his animal nature, the lower was one's position in the social and biological hierarchy. The perceived affinity between peasants and the untamed natural world supported this ordering.

Those who worked the soil and worked directly with animals were considered to be closer to nature and so less civilized than those who were further separated from it. The hoards of peasants, or the "rabble," as David Ricardo called them, could therefore be viewed as minimally human. The unrefined, uneducated bumpkins were seen as having much more in common with the farm animals than with the emerging bourgeoisie. Their overt sentimentality, highly charged emotions (emanating from their untempered bodies) needed to be constrained. And the bourgeoisie, desiring to separate themselves from such lower social forms, therefore assumed a vast assembly of affectations and refinements. These were designed to help them identify themselves with court society and the aristocracy. Fashion, particularly, became a method for the bourgeoisie to signify both their separation from the peasantry and the magnitude of their personal enculturation and affluence.[7] It also signaled a distance from nature and the powerlessness of the peasantry.

The civilizing process that helped to launch the Modern Age required suppression of raw emotions associated with kinship to the beasts. It required that feelings be held generally in check. Elias suggests that a substantial outcome of this civilizing process was the removal of sexual relations from public view. At this stage, sexual activity and discussion of it became sequestered. The civilizing process came to associate human sexuality with animal behavior and, therefore, with shame. Even the language of sex became encoded and secretive. Elias notes:

> The process of civilization of the sex drive, seen on a large scale, runs parallel to those other drives, no matter what sociogenetic differences of detail may always be present. Here, too, measured in terms of the standards of the men of successive ruling classes, control grows even stricter. The instinct is slowly but progressively suppressed from the public life of society. The reserve that must be exercised in speaking of it also increases. And this restraint, like others, is enforced less and less by direct physical force. It is cultivated in the individual from an early age as habitual self-restraint by the structure of social life, by the pressure of social institutions in general, and by certain executive organs of society (above all, the family) in particular. Thereby the social commands and prohibitions become increasingly a part of the self, a strictly regulated superego.[8]

With the advent of modernity, the rise of the bourgeoisie and the Protestant Reformation, the middle classes gave great import to making clear distinctions between the natural and the civilized, the erotic and the chaste, the peasant and their own kind. Control over untamed nature, both internal and external varieties, was seen as essential to civilization and progress. And as Freud would later explain in *Civilization and its Discontents, Eros* would be denied and forced into the service of industry.

By the beginning of the eighteenth century all bourgeois social institutions revealed an exaggerated emphasis on rational asceticism and repressed eroticism. And along with this came an emphasis on bureaucratic reason and the ascendancy of private life. In the late eighteenth century, European capitalism forcibly extended its ethos onto rural peasants who were converted into urban factory workers and made into extensions of factory machines. Michel Foucault observed that capitalistic enterprise had led the attack on sex in order to amass the energies needed to run the means of production:

> A principle of explanation emerges after the fact: if sex is so rigorously repressed, this is because it is incompatible with a general and intensive work imperative. At a time when labor capacity was systematically exploited, how could this capacity be allowed to dissipate itself in pleasurable pursuits, except in those—reduced to a minimum—that enabled it to reproduce itself?[9]

While capitalism required the sexual reproduction of labor, it also necessitated the alienation of the worker's erotic passion. The sublimation of libidinal impulses into productive work produced enormous economic benefits for the few who controlled these processes. However, it drained vitality from the worker's life. According to Herbert Marcuse, de-eroticized sex was a critical component of early and late capitalistic development. Not only could erotic energy (detached from sex) be put to use in capitalistic production, it eventually would provide the basis for mass commodity consumption and a culture based upon such consumption. The erotic was to be found external to one's very nature. The worker's life might be bleak and banal, but color and excitement could be purchased just beyond the factory door or office portal. Thus, authenticity was eclipsed by the fetishized market. As noted earlier in this book, Marx had already recognized the power of commodity fetishism in directing the course of modern history.

Many modern artists took aim at these dehumanizing processes. This notion of sexual de-eroticism became a common theme in art. Dadaist Marcel Duchamp's *The Bride Stripped Bare By Her Bachelors* (1923), was a controversial rendering of a dehumanized, industrialized object of sexuality and synthetic organism. In his rendering of foil, glass and metal, the artist projected the degradation and dehumanization of sexual intercourse. The Bride is a meta-machine, capable of no feeling. Art critic Robert Hughes described the work accordingly:

> The Bachelors are mere uniforms, like marionettes. According to Duchamp's notes, they try to indicate their desire for the Bride by concertedly making the chocolate grinder turn, so that it grinds out an imaginary milky stuff like semen. This squirts up through the rings, but cannot get into the Bride's half of the Glass because of the prophylactic bar that separates the panes. And so the Bride is condemned to always tease, while the Bachelors' fate is endless masturbation.[10]

For Hughes, Duchamp's *Bride* is the artist's commentary on the dehumanizing influences of mass production and the artist's own ambivalence toward modernity. Duchamp would eventually abandon art and pursue the life of a reclusive chess player. Yet his Ready-mades, commercially massed-produced insipid commodities to which he would sign his name, gained enormous popularity as symbols of artistic cynicism.

CAPITALISM, NATURE, AND ROMANTICISM

"Man's" role as master of nature is seen in the writings of some of the major proponents of unbridled capitalism. Many of these capitalistic ideologues blended an ascetic Protestant theology with a belief in natural law. Their works reflected an unwavering faith in the mechanical characteristics of free markets, guided by God's laws and man's inherent rationality. Although there has been a significant discussion of Adam Smith's "invisible hand" hypothesis in Chapter One, it is important to reiterate how this iconography was a synthesis of mystical Christianity and a new faith in reason. Inspired by the Enlightenment and strongly influenced by his Scottish Presbyterianism, Smith believed natural laws of cupidity could be put to use to benefit the whole of society. Many other economic theologians, likewise, viewed the world as a product of such natural laws, imposed by God, which quietly and mechanistically regulated supply, demand, commodity pricing, and the value of labor. The economic order was a complex, well lubricated, celestial machine. These notions could certainly be ascribed to the Reverend Thomas Malthus as well as David Ricardo—a broker and financier who converted from Judaism to New Presbyterianism.

The thoughts and writings of Martin Luther and John Calvin had been translated into the philosophy of the classical economists, most of whom expressed disdain for peasants and laborers. David Ricardo and Thomas Malthus both despised laborers and the poor, and saw factory

owners as justified in paying low wages, requiring long hours, and providing horrid working conditions in the name of free markets and commodity pricing. For Ricardo, workers were "rabble" in need of control
and direction and deserving barely a subsistence wage so as to ensure
low reproductive rates and high profits. It was no wonder that these
economists embraced faiths that called for abstinence and repression.
For them, low wages and worker exhaustion would help contain excessive sexual activity. These theorists opposed public assistance and even
personal charity, viewing them as encouraging both lethargy and excessive intercourse, ultimately, at the expense of profit. People and nature
needed to be tamed.

In his classic study entitled *The Domination of Nature*, William
Leiss proposed "the vision of human domination of nature becomes a
fundamental ideology in a social system (or a phase in the development
of human society considered as a whole) which consciously undertakes a
radical break with the past, which strenuously seeks to demolish all
"naturalistic" modes of thought and behavior, and which sets for itself as
a primary task the development of productive forces for the satisfaction
of human material wants. The first social system in the history of civilization in which these tendencies are found," contends Leiss, "is
Western capitalism."[11]

Indeed, western capitalism benefited both directly and indirectly
from an ideology that provided justification and support for the
exploitation and commodification of all the earth's natural resources
including trees, minerals, and animal life. The devastation of the British
forests, the intensive mining of pristine landscapes, the excessive pollution of waterways, oceans and air intensified with the advent of capitalistic development and particularly with industrial capitalism.

Industrial cities supplanted the medieval towns as unskilled labor
displaced craftspeople. Factories and the system of worker exploitation
produced an array of physical degradations and social problems documented in Engels's *Condition of the Working Class in England* (1844).
Air pollution, water pollution, and the spread of inhuman and unsani-
tary working conditions took the lives of tens of thousands in Britain
alone. "The middle classes have made it perfectly clear," noted Engels,
"that they do not consider the workers as human beings and that they
have no intention of treating them in a humane manner."[12]

As industrialization advanced, so did the systematic depletion of the
world's natural resources. The burgeoning population had of course put
pressure on the need for clean air and water; nevertheless, expanding
consumption and profit were prime factors leading to the systematic
depletion of most of Europe's wildlife, mineral deposits, and diverse

vegetation. This held true for the economic plunder of the so-called "New" World as well. The mass felling of virgin forests, the over-hunting of fur-bearing animals such as beaver and fox, the mass slaughter of buffalo and whales led to the extinction, or near extinction, of hundreds if not thousands of species of animals. Unique plants, birds, and vegetation gave way under a purposeful program of land settlement, which aimed primarily at achieving great profit for the few.

Environmental historian, Donald Worster, noted:

> The capitalists and their theoreticians promised that through the technological domination of the earth, they could deliver a more fair, rational, efficient, and productive life for everyone, themselves above all. Their method was simply to free individual enterprise from the bands of traditional hierarchy and community, whether the bondage derived from other humans or the earth. . . . That meant teaching everyone to treat the earth, as well as each other, with a frank energetic self-assertedness, unembarrassed by too many moral or aesthetic sentiments. . . . They must regard everything around them—the land, its natural resources, their own labor—as potential commodities that might fetch a profit in the market.[13]

Conquest and colonization of the underdeveloped world was the next logical step. This is not to suggest that imperialism was solely a product of capitalistic enterprise. Certainly, it had existed long before market capitalism. Modern nation states, established with the help of bourgeois capitalists, however, did provide for its promotion in a drive to expand world markets. Imperial profits helped to fund the industrial revolution and contributed to widespread wealth, creating fertile ground for investments, particularly in British society.[14] Early market capitalism benefited from both imperialistic exploits and slavery in the colonial world through the mercantilist system. With the advent of global capitalism, classical liberalism took hold in Europe to protest and eventually overthrow the mercantile state system it previously helped to establish. With the advent of monopoly capitalism, a process of world-wide accumulation through exploitation became commonplace. Capitalism was able to transport both its methods of production and its machinery of labor exploitation to new lands and, in the process, undermine traditional societies and their intricate social arrangements.

Through use of the nature/civilization duality, European aristocrats and the bourgeoisie justified racism and the exploitation of "savages" in far-off continents. They destroyed their cultures, covered their immodest bodies with western clothing and attempted to infuse them with religious sexual guilt. Thus, a more thorough comprehension of western antagonism toward nature, toward the "savage," and toward the "underdeveloped" or "uncivilized" world is possible only by recognizing that nature often stood as a mirror as well as a metaphor for human sexuality and its expression. As has been previously noted, this battle to subdue nature, to bring it under the civilizing process was an externalization of an internal quest to subdue and deny *Eros*. And the greater the sexual repression, the more intense the civilizing process became. This battle against nature, the battle to restrict, confine and deny it, emanated from anxiety—fear of and disdain for human sexuality itself. Capitalism, guided by the Calvinistic ethos, was both a catalyst for this repression as well as a sanctioned outlet for its expression. Thus, *Eros* was displaced by moral ethos.

By the nineteenth century, capitalism had become the target of those who viewed the natural world as under assault from the forces of ratio-nalistic, scientific, technological, and religious constraint. The nature/civilization duality, wherein redemption could only be achieved through sensual denial, seemingly drained the world of its magic. The spiritual emptiness associated with modernity and the corresponding dismantling of community by the forces of monetary capitalism created in the human condition an aloneness—a sense of alienation. It is this condition to which the romantics responded.

THE POLITICS OF ROMANTICISM

Toward the end of the eighteenth century, just as the manacles of a new social order were being forged in the west, there appeared a fissure in the shackles of repression. A small group of intellectuals, artists, philosophers, poets, writers, and musicians, who were disturbed by the new political and social restraints and who were in search of an outlet for their own creative passions, caused a groundswell of countercultural protest. These individuals created, through their work, something resembling a social and artistic movement, which was later termed European romanticism. At first romanticism was an extension of a crude sixteenth-century sentimentalism in the arts, which focused on feeling above intellect. However, romanticism would later connect sentiment to intellectual imagination. In this new form, art and philosophy directly confronted the Cartesian culture, challenging what they viewed as its spiritual vacuousness.

The peasant, the savage, and the laborer, symbols of a crude, under-development of human intellect to the bourgeoisie, were now enshrined by these artists, such as Pieter Bruegel, who turned the dismal world of art on its head. For the romantic, the shepherd not the tradesman was the exemplar of human dignity and spirituality. It was he and his lover for whom their sonnets were written. It was the pasture, not the city, that was vibrant with color and life. Unbridled nature became the source of artistic and emotional inspiration, a symbol of nature's power in the face of the machine. Organic, communal harmony was viewed as a utopian goal. It appeared that these thinkers and artists were tapping into what has been called a "hunger for wholeness," a need to reconnect with nature and one another.

German writers and philosophers, such as Goethe and later Schelling and Schopenhauer contributed wondrous poems and metaphysical flights of fancy, and helped to inspire the movement's early course, which contributed to the further polarization of nature and civilization. While some romantics embraced modernity and the freedom associated with it, others retreated from it. Their subjects were frequently reactionary ones, harkening back to a more mystical time, casting a warm patina of remembrance over feudalism, ignoring its social abuses and either ignoring or romanticizing its repression. Yet the artificial opposition between nature and civilization was embraced by both factions.

Although the reactionary attributes of romanticism should not be underestimated, romanticism was not simply a reactionary movement in the arts. As Alvin Gouldner noted, it had the potential to be a revolutionary force and provide an opening to the left.[15] However, it was a force that seldom was used for bringing about political change despite its strong critical views of aristocratic rule and its critique of industrialization. After the French Revolution many progressive romantics, who had been inspired by the ideals of individual liberty and equality, turned their backs on the pressing social issues of the day to escape into and seek wisdom only from nature.

Few romantics worked to foster a sense of communal interconnectedness that could be translated into political action. Yet, there was something that seemed liberating and exhilarating in this movement itself—something almost revolutionary. For not only did the romantics foster a Kantian respect for the relation of the self to the phenomenal world, they also stressed the inaccessibility of the human senses to it. For them, science and rationality frequently suffocated individualistic expression. "Art is life," William Blake is supposed to have said, "science is death!"

Although the form, content, and style of work of those associated with romanticism were quite different, and often assumed a nationalistic character, the romantics actually shared much common ground: an emphasis on the dialectic between the individual and the community, a disdain for mechanistic science, an inspiring reverence for nature, and apprehensions over the problems brought about by industrial capitalism.

Many drew their inspiration from common sources including Goethe, Hugo, Voltaire, Rousseau, and Chateaubriand. Some of the intellectual inspiration for British romanticism came from radical thinkers such as William Godwin who inspired a whole generation of romantic writers and poets with images of a new secular order characterized by maximum personal freedom, equality, and communal utopianism.

The idea of the innate rectitude of people (counterposed to the Hobbesian view of humanity's innate brutishness) was a central tenet of Rousseau and those who shared his utopian visions. It remained a cornerstone of romanticism even subsequent to the French Revolution and what was viewed to be its excesses. For many romantics only nature was pure, only the savage was uncorrupted.

Rousseau had frequently used the metaphor of "nature in chains" to represent the shackling of the spirit by the quest for order, the tethering of the heart by the mind. As a major inspiration to the romantic *avant-garde* he crystallized a central image of unbridled human creativity capable of destroying those chains of oppression, capable of creating a new utopian order. He would set the tone for a revolution in social theory that viewed artistic insight as an alternative to scientific understanding.

According to the romantics, one had to look to nature to find the self. And nature was far from tame. It was a cauldron of intense conflict, constantly transforming itself. The insulated intellectual, surrounded by material things, looking at the world through a microscope, never opened people's eyes and hearts to the essence of humanity. For the romantics, only the artist or poet could do this.

Art, therefore, glorified nature in landscapes that reflected its power and majesty. John Constable's naturalistic paintings done in the early nineteenth century are a case in point. The exalted might of the ominous clouded skies at *Weymouth Bay* (1818) are an example of this mystical transcendence. Here and in his other seascapes and landscapes we see, captured in oil, the vibration of air and light, a breeze, the waves, all fleeting phenomena—the radical passage of time and the primal force of nature.

In the early work of romantic landscape artists such as Constable, nature is wild, free, powerful, and unpredictable. Frequently, the artist asks us to merely observe its majesty or feast upon its untamed beauty. These artists appealed to the soul that connected one's basic humanity to the earth. While some focused on the pastoral, and the deep serenity of nature, others depicted nature as unbridled and awe-inspiring—something imposing and threatening. In the fine arts, nature was divided between the peaceable kingdom and the untamed wilderness.

Often nature was portrayed as a destructive force, intensely connected to doom, death, and violence. This is true for the work of British artist John Martin (1789–1854) whose *The Great Days of Wrath* (c. 1853) and other paintings depict cataclysmic doom wherein nature's power is revealed in tidal waves, roaring seas, ice floes, and earthquakes. The landscapes of William Turner (1775–1851), his raw abstractions of nature, captured the imagination. A pioneer in the study of light, color, and atmosphere, he had an almost supernatural ability to depict both the beauty and terror in nature. Turner would eventually help to inspire French Impressionism.

The metaphoric significance of such turbulence in nature may be interpreted in several ways. Of course, the anxiety produced in the middle classes ran high, reflecting the great social and personal instability of this era that was reflected in this art. The unleashing of nature's power frequently expressed rebellion against personal and political constraint, which characterized the nineteenth century. Some artists confronted the secular force of the mechanized factory system with the spiritual power of nature. Beyond this, however, they represented the release of repressed human sexuality in the form of violent storms, crashing waves, and jetting rocks. Nature in romantic poetry and in art was often about human sensuality. The expressive arts provided a means or conduit for its liberation.

Many of Europe's romantics rebelled against the power of industry and science, which dispelled the magic of nature as it tore through pastures, filled rivers with debris, and pumped smoke into the air, darkening the skies. Although they did recognize the sanctity of the individual, they also recognized the sanctity of nature and the destructive powers that challenged it. They condemned the harshness and inhumanity that this new technocratic and rationalistic order brought with it. And as the world became more materialistic, romantic art became less so. It brazenly moved into a realm once only reserved for the mystical and religious—*the sublime*.

To experience the sublime was to be filled with astonishment and awe. Primarily a term used to describe the divine, the mystical, and the exalted, romantic landscape artists captured on canvas images that seemed to overpower the soul, opening up unending vistas of space and sky, lifting the viewer into the realm of the infinite. Denis Cosgrove notes:

> Against the unnatural but apparently "organic" growth of capital whose fertility was apparently greater than that of land, the romantic sublime proclaimed a natural and properly organic intrinsic value located in the soul of the individual—notably the poet or artist—and in the processes and phenomena of the external world, especially those which underlined human insignificance and weakness: barren mountain recesses, storms,

seas and night. Against the dissecting eye and analytical logic of natural science whose understanding of natural processes was increasingly underpinning the new forces of production, the romantic sublime stressed the continued existence of the divine in nature, reasoning by analogy rather than by cause.[16]

American landscape art and, in fact, American nature poetry frequently bore witness to personal struggles *against* nature. Although the majesty of nature is praised, so is the individualistic effort to conquer it. This can be seen in the poetry of Whitman in which he simultaneously praises the glories of the redwoods and the dignity of the axeman. In a similar, perceptibly paradoxical vein it was not beyond the sensibilities of romantic poets to wear furs that came from the massacre of animals for the sake of bourgeois fashionability—enhancing capitalistic profit along the way. Such egocentrism was the hallmark of the romantic era.

Thus, romantics were both progressive and reactionary—espousing the wonders of community while glorifying the oppression of European feudalism, viewing nature as inspirational and leading to truth, yet viewing it as threatening. They frequently promulgated liberal idealism tempered with nihilism and alienation. Romanticism, therefore, never materialized as a true social movement because it was empty of any comprehensive, unified, sustainable philosophy. As noted earlier, it was factional, confused, and contradictory, reflecting a diverse array of bourgeois sensibilities.

It must be credited, however, with helping to bolster the nature/civilization opposition through a renewed emphasis on the Dionysian, stressing the importance of human imagination, subjugation, and domination on a personal level. It created a paradigm of subjectivity that would for years to come confront the soullessness of much of science. Wordsworth and others, with their poetry and art, accused science with having transformed a beauteous world into a laboratory of unrelated studies, void of imagination.

ROMANTICISM AND ENVIRONMENTALISM

It has been proposed that romanticism's overall mystification of nature and its characterization of it as sublime was reactionary. This claim has been expanded by Marxian and neo-Marxian critics such as Georg Lukács and Walter Benjamin as well as more conservative social theorists.[17] Nevertheless, if one looks closely at the work of Coleridge, Shelley, Byron, Wordsworth, and other British romantic poets, one finds some eloquent criticisms of the abuses of early industrialization on the natural environment, and at least a spark of disdain directed toward the fundamental tenets of capitalism itself. Critic H. G. Schenk went as far as to posit that "the spirit of the Romantic Movement struck at the very root of capitalism in a far more uncompromising way than did secularized Socialism or Communism."[18]

Eventually, particularly among the British romantics, there was a turning away from a world wrought with poverty, conflict, and class turmoil, and a general aversion to all materialism. This escapism accelerated after the French Revolution due to what was seen as its excesses and failures. Wordsworth, especially, looked inward to the "mind's eye" for inspiration rather than to follow the dialectical, materialistic struggles going on in the dirty, polluted world around him. In doing this, he developed a creed that the all powerful imagination could dispel political disillusionment and construct a beauty far better than that devised by nature. This is exemplified by *The Prelude* wherein the mind has become "a thousand times more beautiful than the earth."

This escape into imaginative fancy, along with the belief that the imagination could produce a better, more beautiful world than the natural one, did two things. It provided a veil through which the imaginer could soften life's harsh realities and social struggles, and it substituted intellectually synthetic beauty for the authenticity of nature. As critic Jonathan Bate noted: "Imagination is seen as a way of transcending 'this frame of things,' the earth in which we dwell, where revolutions go sour; imagination remains 'unchanged,' it is 'exalted,' 'divine.'"[19] In a sense, the romantics set the stage for intellectual abandonment of the social world by an escape into art, poetry, theater, and the novel. Much of their work was predictive of the imagineering of the late twentieth century produced in the Disney dream factories. Not only had these artists and poets raised their supporters' consciousness related to the importance of beauty and nature, but now they provided an avenue for the middle and working classes to flee from social commitment and the monotony of their day-to-day lives. This was the point in time when privatization became a hallmark of middle-class existence and communal life was abandoned for the chimera of community. Capitalistic societies entered a world of symbolic fantasy.

It becomes obvious that this romantic abandonment of political and communal life diverted attention from important issues that needed to be confronted by the progressive segment of the bourgeoisie. Also, there can be little dispute that the genre that emerged from unsophisticated sentimentalism and gradually took on social and political importance at the beginning of the nineteenth century eventually retreated into a cult of bourgeois aestheticism.

Rarely do we see articulated in the late poetry of Keats or Wordsworth the direct relationship of greed-directed capital to environmental distress and destruction. Instead, such artists provided a means for the socially conscious bourgeoisie to ignore the harsh realities of the cities and the poor who surrounded them. By escaping into the "mind's eye," and deeply into the pastoral, many romantic poets served the interests of the aristocrats and industrialists who preferred keeping the harsh consequences of business and public affairs from affecting what might remain of middle-class sensibilities. They also helped to construct a commodified literature of "escapism," an imaginary highway into an aesthetic world of naturalistic adventure and make-believe. It was the romantic novel, perhaps even more than the poem, that became the last refuge for the naturalistic ideal. And as writers and artists took to their pens and brushes to conserve the world's beauty for the middle classes to procure for their library shelves and hang over their mantels, forests were felled, rivers polluted, and unique species of *flora* and *fauna* were extinguished from the face of the earth. Such was the price of venturing into the world of imagination.

Nevertheless, some supporters of romanticism suggest that without the movement the attack upon the natural environment would have been more ruthless. Although most artists preferred not to engage the powerfully destructive forces directly, their work was inspirational to many who did. In fact, the argument goes, their work inspired generations to come. The romantics established an artistic and intellectual beachhead for the defense of nature in the nineteenth century when the natural environment was undergoing brutal assault from expanding and uncontrolled population as well as from the machinery of development.

Jonathan Bate, in reviewing this period of romanticism, notes that a whole generation of British environmentalists was inspired by the romantic poetry of the early nineteenth century. He particularly defends Wordsworth against the charge that he was counter-revolutionary by showing how his work inspired the establishment of the National Trust in Britain as well as the National Park system.[20] Wordsworth was not only endeared for great naturalistic poetry, but he was also a major social influence who celebrated the direct personal experience of the pristine natural landscape in his *Guide to the Lakes*. This book, which originally appeared in 1835, was to become a regular best-seller that went through a total of ten editions by 1859. According to Bate, it was without a doubt his most widely read work, and Bate suggests that Wordsworth's reputation as a naturalist far exceeded his reputation as a poet in many parts of Great Britain. [21]

The *Guide*'s primary focus was the Lake District in Northern England. In his introduction, the author noted that the book was to be a companion "for the *Minds* of persons of taste, and feeling for the Landscape, who might be inclined to explore the District of Lakes with the degree of attention to which its beauty may fairly lay claim."[22] It was this book, more than any other volume, that claimed a major impact on the conservation movement in Britain. Bate has suggested that this volume, which eventually assimilated essays by botanists, geologists, and essayists helped to move romanticism from the ephemeral back into the material world. And although Wordsworth, himself, was not in the forefront of the eventual battle to protect the natural environment from commodification and degradation, his work contributed greatly to the conservation effort. The Lake District Defense Society, which fought the encroachment of the railroads into the Lake District, and the National Trust for Places of Historic Interest and Natural Beauty, were inspired by the consciousness-raising efforts conducted by poets such as Wordsworth.

The conservation movement was brought about quite differently in the United States. It wasn't until the publication of George Perkins Marsh's *Man and Nature* in 1864 that the preservationist movement gained political and social acceptability in the United States. It was this very same year that Abraham Lincoln signed into law a bill that gave the State of California trusteeship of Yosemite Valley. Frederick Law Olmstead, a young utopian socialist whose efforts were instrumental in securing the preservation of Niagara Falls in New York, acquiring the lands for Central Park in Manhattan, and who was involved in a whole host of other private and governmentally sponsored land-preservation projects, was in the forefront of California's acquisition of Yosemite.[23] Always, such conservation projects ran into great resistance.

Early attempts to deal with the disappearance of the wilderness in colonial America were met with strong opposition from settlers who voiced indignation over the government's denial of people's "God given right" to make money from buying and selling land. Although many people did sympathize with the need to protect and conserve the beauty of nature, the quest for profit took priority over conservation. Therefore, nationalistic conservation movements, particularly in the United States, were forever mindful of the public clamor for economic growth and expansion as well as the need to feed the dreams of proletarians who sought economic salvation in their quest for cheap government lands. Even the preservation of large open tracts of forests or pine barrens in the form of government sponsored parks met with considerable public opposition at first. Virgin forests rapidly disappeared in North America just as they had in Great Britain and France, and just as the rain forests now disappear in the Amazon.

If there was an environmental conscience in America, it was Thoreau. The work of Henry David Thoreau occupied a central place in mid-nineteenth-century environmentalism. His critique of the market system, the mechanization of farming and the unrestrained pillage of the American wilderness were his special targets. His most noted work, *Walden*, dealt with the need to ensure the physical and spiritual survival of the natural environment. For Thoreau, the individual was the guardian, not the possessor, of the natural environment. For him, nature in its rawest of forms could provide for all living necessities. Thoreau could never accept a communally oriented environmentalism, however. His attitude toward industrialization was more conservative than it was progressive as his rugged individualism stood in the way of developing a civic consciousness or even promoting government involvement in the conservation process. Thoreau's work was inspired by an anti-urbanism and a romantic Puritanism—a belief in hard work and sacrifice. Nevertheless, his call to simplify, and his assertion that a quality life could be best achieved in the wilderness were rallying cries of later conservation efforts.

Yet, it wasn't until the late nineteenth century that the steamroller of American industrial and economic progress was slowed by more organized and politically influential efforts. It is noteworthy that the first conservation measures that met with most success were those advocated by business interests seeking to protect fishing and hunting rights, or mineral rights, or to provide inexpensive power for their businesses. It was much later that grass roots environmentalists gained success in pressuring the federal government to preserve national forests, deserts, and mountain ranges. It was only toward the birth of the twentieth century that pragmatic Americans came to recognize that the country's resources were less than inexhaustible.[24] However, preservation of these resources would assume a particularly capitalistic character.

Alison Byerly, a scholar of environmental literature, has suggested that the history of American preservation is elitist—predicated on the bourgeois aesthetic of the picturesque rather than on nature. She proposed that the American wilderness was gradually reduced and circumscribed by economic and political interests until those open vistas that once inspired a sense of the sublime—an overpowering sense of transcendence—were all but gone. The national park preservation, in particular, was fashioned from an aesthetic of the picturesque. "The specific qualities the picturesque aesthetic required from a scene were based on principles derived from painting, not from nature, and hence many parks and gardens needed tasteful 'improvement' in order to conform. The aestheticization of landscape removed it from the realm of nature and designated it a legitimate object of artistic consumption."[25] But the so-called "beautification of nature" was merely a response to its devastation by the forces of capitalistic rapaciousness.

CAPITALISM AND THE COMMODIFICATION OF NATURE

That western landscape painting emerged alongside the European conquest of the globe, the devastation of domestic forests, the mass torture and burning of women as witches, and the brutalization and enslavement of native peoples around the world is no historic coincidence. The landscape, according to geographer Denis Cosgrove, became a way of seeing the world—a perspective vitally connected to the European Empire. The perspective here of the artist was one far removed from the subject. "Landscape painting first emerged as a recognized genre in the most economically advanced, densest settled and most highly urbanized regions of fifteenth-century Europe."[26] According to Jean-François Lyotard, landscape as an art form reflected not only estrangement from the land, but a modern melancholia and personal emptiness.[27]

At the same time, landscapes represented the commodification and parceling of tracts under a new, post-feudal form of land distribution. While historians have disagreed about its specific origin in time, the post-feudal era is in part defined by new land-tenure systems, especially the breakdown of open common lands into smaller privatized tracts.[28] Max Weber proposed that an important and revolutionary aspect of capitalistic land use was initiated in much of Europe, particularly in Britain, beginning in the fifteenth century, lasting well into the seventeenth, and intensifying in the eighteenth century. He labeled this "estate economy."[29] It was then that the medieval system of fiefdom gave way to radical land enclosure. For Weber and others, this alteration of land arrangements reflected the development of capitalism itself, wherein land became a factor of profit-making. Pasturelands, woodlands, and water rights, which were once held in common and open to public access, were now privatized and given back to the lords by kings, who enjoyed ancient title to them, for the purpose of rental, lease, and sale. In England, lands originally cultivated and farmed by peasants were converted into sheep walks and placed into the service of the burgeoning wool and textile industry. Fences and stone walls were erected over what previously were miles of open pastures, hillsides, and valleys.

Enclosure forever altered the relationship of people to the land. The large tracts developed for grain cultivation displaced numerous small family farms. And, while the state imposed protective duties and export bounties to protect this new industry, when these protections were later abolished, the large labor force, which had been used to grow the grain, had to be released. Enclosure caused a major exodus of peasants and displaced tenant farmers and villagers who either starved or were forced to seek work in urban factories. As land was further commodified, it eventually entered into the capitalistic marketplace as an object of speculation. By 1700, nearly half of all cultivatable land had been enclosed.[30] Historian Roy Porter has remarked on some of its later forms:

> In 1716 John Warren, Lord of the Manor in Stockport, simply started selling common land on his own initiative for building and industrial purposes. The one patch of land left as common he set aside as a site for a gaol (*jail*), and some of the profits of enclosure were earmarked to build a workhouse for 170 people, thus anticipating the plight of the people under the enclosure.[31]

Yet, enclosure did not stop there. Environmental historian Murray Bookchin noted that: "From 1800 to 1820 more than three million acres of English countryside were enclosed, an area nearly as large as all the enclosures which occurred during the seventeenth century."[32] Enclosure radically altered the landscape, imposing not only a checker-board pattern over previously open-fields, but also instituting ruler-edged land perimeters, hedgerows, and straight, wide roads.[33]

Capitalism drew upon science and cheap labor to confront nature. Wage labor, paid by task or by day, became common to the peasant way of life. Agriculture was already feeling the impact of the scientific revolution, and crop production had increased significantly by the mid nineteenth century. With burgeoning profits and a surplus of wealth, many in the upper middle classes put science to more aesthetic uses that could help signal their power and social class. Accordingly, inspired by romantic landscape artists, the manipulation of nature was applied to the *flora* of their private estates.

Symbols of wealth and power were important for the emerging bourgeoisie; and, such symbols might be reflected in how their acres of private lands could be cultivated and controlled. With the advancements in technology, botanists could duplicate, simulate, and even enhance the products of nature. Thus, middle-class acquisitiveness and an emerging sense of individualism fused with romanticism to produce what was called the "gardenesque." Cosgrove describes this emergent aesthetic as follows:

It crowded together a bewildering variety of species, many of them exotics, brought from overseas into dense shrubberies: private, romantic, walled enclaves which, in their "precise, scientific, tangible, three dimensional organization" represented an authentically bourgeois style. They were replicated for broader, more public consumption and edification in new municipal arboreta, public parks and gardens.[34]

Cosgrove notes that the gardenesque eliminated the need for landscapes because the eye would now focus on detail, a planting, rather than scan the land. What it did provide was an idealized, controlled form of nature. Nature could be restricted to conform to need. It could be confined to create the allure of "the luxuriance of vegetative life." In this way the gardenesque would diminish the aesthetic need for vast open spaces and substitute for the sublime wilderness an "entirely artificial environment wherein land is irrelevant and natural processes depend utterly on human control."[35]

Likewise, the first private botanical gardens and menageries were representations of both capitalism's ability to both control nature and offer in its place a new aesthetic based on facsimile. Here is a corruption of the aesthetics of romantics such as Turner and Wordsworth, and a very clear symbol of capital's potential. Such bourgeois exhibits were little more than trophies of capitalistic and imperialistic conquest over the world's natural environment, and conspicuous displays of great wealth. The obvious imprisonment of exotic plants and wild animals in these private and, eventually, public gardens and zoos would trigger respect and awe in the proletariat who saw the majesty of nature captured, enslaved, and bent to the desires of human will. Because of the growing uneasiness of some who looked upon such displays as barbarism and who saw parallels between the domination of animals and the domination of labor, zoos began to provide more "naturalistic" settings—settings of concealed bars a hidden barbed wire—a *faux* environment wherein the worker, on a Sunday afternoon, could visit and come face-to-face with a lion or a gazelle and pretend that he and it were both free.

Circuses and rodeos provided escapist entertainment in like fashion. Illusions of history, like illusions of nature, went up for sale. Wild west reenactments staged by such men as Buffalo Bill Cody (who was renowned for his single-handed slaughter of 4,280 buffalo in an eight-month period of 1867 and 1868, and who took pride in having engaged in sixteen Indian fights and a much publicized scalping of a Cheyenne warrior named Yellow Hair) met with receptive audiences in America and Great Britain alike. The conquest and taming of the wild west was promoted by the Cody tableau in which he put on display over one hundred yelling Native Americans, including the aging Chief Sitting Bull. Queen Victoria was said to have seen the show three times.[36]

Conquest became "discovery" in history books. Celebrity biographies white-washed the exploits of vicious men and, particularly, their plunder of nature. Indigenous Americans were relegated to their reservations and their likenesses put on display at museums of natural history. The black bear was confined by hunters and conservationists to its place in the national park. In this new system, all that was truly free and close to nature was made to yield to an invisible but covertly brutal force of industry in the creation of *ersatz* conservation. A rose would become captured forever in glass, and a simulated snow storm sealed in a crystal ball.

If, as previously charged, the romantics provided escapist diversions for the middle classes from the pillage of the wilderness that was all around them, they also can be accused of constructing an artificial world in which people could escape from the meaninglessness of their lives and their own quiet desperation. The artificial worlds they helped to construct could be far nicer places than the actual one, far more exciting, more alive. The synthetic Frankenstein monster, thus, becomes more real that its unnatural maker.

Romantics must be credited with having prepared the way for what Umberto Eco has called hyperreality wherein "the completely real" becomes identified with the "completely fake."[37] In the hyperreal world, absolute unreality is real. As Jean Baudrillard contends in *Simulacra and Simulations*, distinctions between the object and its representation are no longer valid.[38] Wordsworth's "mind's eye" translated the authenticity of nature into symbols and images of an *experience* of nature. Such an experience might be considered more valid than the reality of nature, perhaps more real.

Jean Lyotard has suggested that because of modern capitalism, the sublime has been forced to yield to an objectified and completely commodified world.[39] In this world of commodities the representation of nature is far more malleable and therefore has far greater value than that which it symbolizes. Gertrude Stein's synthetic rose is perfect. And, unlike the actual rose, it will neither decay nor die.

The movement of the romantics into the plane of hyperreality is a consequence of capitalistic enterprise securing a monopoly over materialism. However, even images, including powerful icons of nature, have been forced to take their place as products in the market system. Although the romantics escaped into the imagination, they unwittingly laid the groundwork for its invasion by forces of capitalistic consumerism. The deep-seated hunger for nature brought about by its annihilation by forces of industry could now be fed with a variety of consumer goods, artificial substitutes to satisfy this endless craving.

Sociologist Colin Campbell has suggested that romanticism helped to fashion the bourgeois addiction to consumerism. It imbued its audience with a drive to seek pleasure in a representational world of make-believe.[40] The romantics fed the public's irrational penchant for the different and the new, their need for heroes and glamour in a world drained of its vitality by machines. Campbell goes as far as to suggest that the romantics unwittingly helped to bring about a craving for the new that fueled modern consumerism. In turn, these cravings could be put into the service of a burgeoning fashion industry and a consumer quest for novelty objects and experiences. Fashion, in particular, became a means through which the individual could not only construct a personal identity but also become a representational work of art. Individuals thus became aware of themselves as objects of beauty and this attitude had a major impact on future patterns of consumption.[41] In other words, romantics built castles in the air, consumers occupied them, and capitalists collected the rents.

As Jean Baudrillard explains in *Consumer Society*, commodities take upon themselves the power of signaling objects, possessing both denotation and connotation. Objects displayed in department store windows speak to one another in signifying chains, forming a type of commercial tableau, which powerfully reach out to the imagination of the potential consumer. Values once associated with nature are now associated with a product imbued with the essence of nature. In postmodernity, the images frequently transcend the reality, or are at the very least confused with it. Thus, when one purchases an item she or he also enters a fantastical world wherein each possession is a promise of something else. Each thing seen in a shop window is communicating—conveying an intention to deliver an experience or a feeling. It is clear that The Nature Shop's view of the natural world is quite different from that of the Museum Shop's image of it. Both are selling a select set of images to the customer. In the former, the consumer desires to own the magic of a living wilderness, in the latter its mummified remains allures the buyer.

Today, throughout the shopping malls and in all the cyberspace markets, repressed sensuality is released through the purchase of fetishized products. These, in turn, allow the displacement of threatening erotic drives. In the market system, fantasy is substituted as an aphrodisiac for reality—the mundaneness of everyday life yields to the sublime, which can only be purchased in the market through the franchise of a multinational conglomerate. Nature degenerates into *faux* nature, sex into *faux* sex. This serves the dual role of maintaining a repressed social order—ensuring that all creative forces flow into production—while providing consumption as the only acceptable form of release for these repressed urges. The integrity of each sign is tightly controlled by advertising and the popular media.

Veblen, Marcuse, and Baudrillard have each recognized the power of the market to appropriate meanings that could only be found in nature, and use these to orchestrate the ebb and flow of commodity production and consumption. Marcuse and his notion of "false needs" addressed the compulsive tendency in people to become one with the flow of commodities. He believed people became habituated to a range of commodities that they perceived as compensation for their own alienation and commodification.

For Marcuse, the market enthralls us with its products. It moves us to suspend disbelief much as the romantics did. It is the market's profit-making role to displace nature and provide us with a less erratic alternative, an uncritical understanding of our world.[42] Thus, we are expected to live a life of unfulfilled desires in the natural sense, seeking satisfaction and fulfillment in the artificial world of television, film, the Internet, and the shopping for commodities that these media promote. The sublimation of desire is "desublimated" in the marketplace where products and their purchase take the place of sex. By controlling the cultural signals, including erotic ones, the market directs us through merchandising to the newest sensation. Baudrillard concurs: "Sexuality, which was once repressed, is liberated as a game of signs."[43]

Rachel Bowlby, in her review of the novels of Dreiser, Gissing, and Zola, describes the historic accuracy of Zola's *Au Bonheurs des Dames* published in 1883—the first novel to deal with the legendary *Bon Marché* in Paris. In this novel, Zola shows the department store owner and manager, Octave Mouret, to be purposefully manipulative and seductive in his display of merchandise: fabrics and colors that would not only entice the female customer but arouse in her "new bodily desires." Zola describes Mouret's character as a covert seducer, driven to the conquest of women through his artful displays; yet once enticed, driven to destroy them.[44] Here is both capitalistic merchandising and misogyny rolled into one. We are reminded by Zola and by Bowlby that there is an obvious sensuality one encounters in such stores. Seduction and conquest, subliminal or otherwise, are its primary objectives. Capitalism in the consumer marketplace expresses quintessentially these same goals.

Nature and eroticism, repressed in reality, become the raw materials for merchandising. They are put into the service of the marketplace and are made available only to consumers. The rich semiotics of romanticism was brought into the marketplace and employed to sell products to those who futilely seek sensual fulfillment through their purchases. The destruction of all that is natural, and its eventual conversion into designer lines of consumables, is a logical consequence of a process predicated on mass consumption and labor exploitation. It poses, and promises a cure for, the profound human alienation driven now by repressed emotional needs and longings.

EGO-CENTERED CAPITALISM AND
THE DOMINATION OF NATURE

How is it that people have come to be so separated from one another and from themselves; and why are they so alienated from nature, from the air they breathe, the food they eat, the land upon which they walk? How is it that human beings are so estranged from their bodies, from their sensuality, from their essence? There is considerable speculation that the process of commodification has been instrumental in promoting human separation and detachment of people from their environment and each other; and there is significant indication that human estrangement begins very early in life for those living in advanced capitalistic societies.[45] But how do such very personal experiences connect to the social structure and, particularly, how do they relate to the domination of nature?

One answer has been proposed by the Frankfurt School theorists who devoted a significant portion of their speculative theory examining the connection between feelings of abandonment, engendered by aberrant socialization under capitalism, and the domination of nature. For them, an explanation is to be found both in Marx's ideas on capitalistic exploitation and in Freud's drive theory. The conquest of nature, which was rooted ideologically in the Enlightenment experience, was thus seen as a product of personal insecurities and a need for control.

As noted earlier in this book, these theorists had attacked the Enlightenment as an intellectual and social project that unwittingly worked to impede critical thought and impose a crude and narrow program of reason aimed at conquest and manipulation. Adorno and Horkheimer proposed that Enlightenment philosophers had falsely pitted people against nature in a battle for dominance.[46] The program of modern capitalism emerged from this opposition. Nevertheless, the impact of the material forces of capitalism on the lives of people produced an array of psychological insecurities through a radical rearrangement of the social structure.

Dominance over nature was viewed by the Frankfurt theorists as both a narcissistic and sadistic response to modern anxiety. The roots of nature's domination were both historical and psychological. As William Leiss suggested: "The purpose of mastery over nature is the security of life. . . ."[47] The Frankfurt theorists recognized the power of early childhood experiences under capitalism as producing exceptional insecurities. Even object relations theorists, such as Melanie Klein, suggested that fantasies of domination helped to compensate for fear of separation in early child–parent relations. Klein spoke of this in terms of the "manic defense." Along with this defense came "a sense of omnipotence for the purpose of controlling and mastering objects."[48] Adorno, Horkheimer, Fromm, and Marcuse were to propose that such insecurities were played out not only in the personal arena, but also in the political one. Fascism was the product of such forces. Frankfurt School theorists were proposing, therefore, that the conquest of nature was merely an extensive elaboration of a greater program of domination and conquest that was reflected in modern political economy.

MISOGYNY AND THE RAPE OF NATURE

The association of nature and femininity has a long history in western narrative. When Adorno and Horkheimer wrote *Dialectic of Enlightenment*, they made much of Homer's *Odyssey*. The tale represented not only a metaphor for the centrality of the need for man to separate from nature, but also linked the natural world to eroticism and femininity.

For these Frankfurt theorists, Odysseus ventured away from his safe home in order to develop his autonomy. In doing this, he needed to confront the terrors of nature and its challenge to his independence. He outwitted nature not only by returning home safely, but by denying his own naturalistic tendencies. For instance, tethering himself and his crew to his ship's mast, and plugging their ears with wax signaled his recognition that they all lacked the internal strength to resist the Sirens and their enticingly erotic song—feminine voices that could lead to a disastrous wreck should these men submit to their natural inclinations. For Homer, this temptation represented the call for self-abandonment, and a passion to fuse with nature—to become one with it. Nature takes on a female voice. Here, say Adorno and Horkheimer, is the view of nature as both feminine and evil needing to be subordinated to the libidinal desires of civilized men. They write: "As a representative of nature, woman in bourgeois society has become the enigmatic image of irresistibility and powerlessness. In this way, she reflects *for* domination the pure lie that posits the subjection instead of the redemption of nature."[49]

The domination and devaluation of women quiets deeply held male fears of their own sexuality, and their own estrangement from nature. As Jessica Benjamin has suggested, the desire to dominate (or submit) is essentially erotic.[50] Its origins are found in the earliest issues of intimacy and separation, which have been examined at some length in Chapter 3. The physical and psychological domination of women by men is ultimately due to men's failure to recognize women as similar but separate. The same might be said of men's relationship to nature.

Domination frequently begins with a denial of dependency. This, in a sense, defines masculinity. In the early socialization of boys, for instance, identity formation is thought to occur following separation from their mothers rather than because of boys' attachment to them. According to Nancy Chodorow, boys receive the message from their social environment that to be male means that they must reduce the intensity of their first loving relationship; in fact, they must abandon it altogether. They are required to identify with a male—a father who is frequently more distant, often less emotionally expressive, and usually less nurturing. Such withdrawal is termed "heroic autonomy" and, for Chodorow, represents a form of emotional distancing that is viewed as masculine and valued as such.[51] But inherent in this separation is considerable insecurity.

The values of competition and separation imbued in boys impact on their ability to empathize with others and to respond to the suffering of those who are not like themselves. If a boy is not allowed to see and value aspects of his mother in himself and cannot value these, if he is forced to separate from her and denied the realization that she is part of him as he is part of her, there can be little capacity for him to connect to others or to the natural environment (which mother represents) that surrounds and supports him. Such separation has a cost. Theodore Roszak notes: "there is no question but that the way the world shapes the minds of its male children lies somewhere close to the root of our environmental dilemma."[52] The male denial of maternal femininity and its associated sensuality is thereby translated into a distancing from nature. Historically, the degree of misogyny in society closely corresponds to the level of domination over nature and the repression of sexuality.

Feminist historian and environmentalist Carolyn Merchant has written extensively on the history of the association between misogyny and the male quest to dominate and control nature. She asserts that sixteenth-century Europe had begun with two competing visions of nature. On the one hand, nature was the iconographic "nurturing mother," peacefully providing for human needs. On the other hand, nature was depicted as a wild, violent, destructive, and irascible force. Merchant suggests that not only did the scientific and capitalistic revolutions bring with them a pronounced emphasis on the later image, but the witch trials of the late 1500s ensured currency of this image.[53]

As long as nature was characterized as a life-giving, nurturing force, ethical human behavior required that there could be no acts of violence directed against it. So sacred was the earth and its resources, that miners of classical times and throughout medieval Europe were required to engage in religious rituals prior to entering the earth's womb to remove its minerals. As in Ancient Greece, nature was deemed to be sacred, benevolent, bounteous. But all this was to change. With the Reformation and advancing capitalism came a new agenda for production. Although the drive to control and dominate nature was not new and was long present in the tenets of ancient Judaism, its newest support was found in the work of a host of Enlightenment thinkers and religious reformers. Merchant suggests that Calvinism, to a significant degree, held the seeds of modern misogyny.

John Calvin, John Knox, and other radical reformers concurrently preached the need for the subordination of women and man's destiny to dominate nature. In fact, Merchant asserts that Frances Bacon's misogyny came from his strong Calvinistic upbringing and was reflected in his personal participation in the witchcraft trials. She further suggests that his imagery of nature as a female who needed to be "seduced," "bound into service," "constrained," and "molded," were derived from his oversight of the mechanical torture of women for crimes of witchcraft. Most of their so-called crimes, declares Merchant, were deemed to be sexual. It is her contention that the torture of women in the 1500s was driven by male fears of unrepressed female sexuality. This is supported by the court testimony of the day suggesting that the "carnal cravings" of such women brought them to "copulate with the devil."[54] Some of the most brutal punishments directed against women accused of witchcraft were reserved for crimes involving corporeal debauchery or crimes of conspiring with nature. This reflects Foucault's contention that enormous power lay behind sexual repression in the sixteenth century.

Merchant strongly suggests that capitalism's drive to exploit nature rested at the heart of the matter: "As woman's womb had systematically yielded to the forceps, so nature's womb harbored secrets that through technology could be wrested from her grasp for use in the improvement of the human condition."[55] It is her contention that the degradation of nature frequently was joined to the repression and disempowerment of women, which at the same time reinforced a close affinity of women and nature. Through capitalistic processes nature and women, thereby would become commodified, forced to yield to the demands of productive power. And both would emerge as signifiers of repressed sensuality.

Susan Bordo, a feminist philosopher, shares many of these sentiments. Bordo contends that Cartesian thought radically altered modern epistemology, transforming a feminine cosmology that had characterized medieval life and the Renaissance. Where the earth was viewed as receptive, genitive, and nourishing during this premodern period, the modern scientific impulse was directed toward controlling the earth's "untamedness," commodifying it, and exploiting it. She proposes that Descartes helped to impose what would become a masculine epistemological and ontological framework by emphasizing order, rationality, and objectivity. This escape from the feminine, she suggests, was a reaction-formation on the macro-order deeply rooted in separation anxiety resulting from the disorienting discoveries, events, and inventions of the seventeenth century. The reaction-formation of Descartes and others was an attempt to find security by completely denying the past and attempting to regain control. Misogyny would be an outgrowth of this drive to masculinize the world.[56]

Literary critic Laura Brown, in dealing with the issue of misogyny and the colonial Empire of the early eighteenth-century Europe, suggests that the depiction of women in English literature as both passive objects of control and impassioned signifiers of unrestraint helped to promote mercantilist ideology and its inherent exploitative and commodifying agenda. Feminine imagery was constructed by men. The female body, itself, was fetishized and made part of the fashion system where it would be dressed and undressed, thus reflecting, as Brown suggests, "the sustained tension between nature and art."[57] Women's bodies became signifying objects. Sociologist Ann Game has noted that the commodified woman then came to represent the false opposition of nature, itself—the serene and the dangerous.[58] The schizoid depiction of nature in the works of the romantics was now reflected in the images of women portrayed in fashion magazines. Women were both nurturing and wild, frail and wicked. Such imagery in popular media responded to a larger array of social and economic needs requiring the exploitation of women and their use as signifiers in profit-making enterprises; women came to symbolize society's opposition to nature and its sensual emptiness. The oppression and control of women through manipulation of their imagery parallels the repression and control of nature for the ultimate advancement of profit.

A variety of responses to this manipulation of feminine/nature symbolism has emerged from various feminist enclaves including the romantic ecofeminists and more radical feminist ecosocialists. Where many of the former group often stress in their narratives the acceptance of an inherent affinity between women and nature, the importance of intuition as against science, and the primacy of the body over the intellect, the later group emphasizes the social construction of nature by men for the disempowerment of women through a gendered system of labor exploitation.[59] The location of the feminine in nature, they say, has no more validity than the situation of the masculine *outside* of it.[60]

The coupling of women to nature, according to Donna J. Haraway, was used to separate women from the scientific bases of power and technology. She asserts that domination over women's lives has been embedded in the natural and behavioral sciences and that the knowledge obtained from these fields has been directed toward the control of women rather than their liberation. The alienation of women from the sciences has made their exploitation even more acute. This is especially true, she notes, in the biological sciences. Haraway asserts: "We (women) have challenged our traditional assignment to the status of natural objects by becoming anti-natural in our ideology in a way which leaves the life sciences untouched by feminist needs."[61]

While early industrial capitalism produced an intensity of sexual repression aimed at fostering a greater level of productivity, it concurrently sponsored a greater repression of women. This was simultaneously coupled with a more violent assault against nature in order to maximize production and eliminate women from this fulcrum of power. Thus, historically, women came to signify nature and its exploitation.

CONCLUSION

The environmental crisis that affects the earth: the pollution—contamination, degradation, and death of intricate ecosystems that support life on this planet—is best understood by examining its place in the history of modernity. The modernization of nature might be defined by its degree of alienation and commodification. As nature is converted into products by the machines of industry to be sold in the marketplace, both the producer and consumer become further dissociated from its essence and theirs. Thus, as suggested by Marx, there appears to be a devaluation of nature inherent in its alienation.

These rationalistic, materialistic paradigms, which had their origin in the earliest forms of Enlightenment thought, and which were produced by an array of privatized interests, required objectification of the earth. Only by understanding these structural and systemic forces can there be an understanding of the causes of this environmental crisis.

The postmodern sociologist Jean Baudrillard posited that nature has become dominated essence, nothing more. It is deemed to have value only when commodified and exploited. Yet, the constraint of nature's tumultuousness becomes a metaphor for human oppression. It signals a form of self-domination and a denial of our own ferity. Baudrillard notes: "Everything that speaks in terms of totality (and/or 'alienation') under the sign of Nature or a recovered essence speaks in terms of repression and separation. Everything that invokes Nature invokes its domination."[62] Those who fear it and drive to repress it see in nature the sign of human liberation. It is this liberation that strikes terror in the hearts of many, it is this emancipation that they strive to contain.

Chapter 7

Dark Utopia: Globalization and Abandonment

The fall of the Berlin Wall in November, 1989, symbolized both the demise of shadowy, monolithic communism and the opening up of once restricted markets to the sunny glow of global capital. There was plenty to commemorate as thousands of people gathered at the Brandenberg Gate on the late afternoon and evening of November 9th to celebrate the inevitable reintegration of Germany and the collapse of Soviet totalitarianism. Young people, students, and workers scaled the wall, sang songs, danced around in designer jeans, and played music well into the night. Some began chipping at the wall with pickaxes to get souvenirs that would eventually be sold over the Internet on eBay. But much more than this, the shops in West Berlin received special permission from the government to remain open longer than the legally allowable hours. There seemed to be an orgy of consumerism as hungry shoppers came west. The festivities would last for months.

On the other side of the wall something more sinister was happening. The centrally planned economies were beginning to collapse. Parents began deserting their children in record numbers to go west. Sometimes children would be left unannounced with neighbors and frequently they'd be dropped off at the local orphanage. In East Berlin, governmentally run hospices and orphanages were filled to capacity and overflowing with children by mid-December. Dr. Klaus Rueder, director of the Korczak Home (which was named after a Polish-Jewish physician who had volunteered to accompany children from the Warsaw

215

Ghetto to the Treblinka concentration camps where he and they died), claimed that parents who were abandoning their children were motivated by material greed. Other stern East Berliners on the orphanage staff agreed suggesting that some parents felt that the opportunity to flee west relieved them of familial obligations and social responsibilities.[1]

By 1997 similar abandonments characterized many former Soviet nations. Many adults could not afford to house and feed their own children. With the advent of capitalist "shock therapy" in Russia alone, it was estimated that more than one million children became homeless and many could not be accommodated in state-run institutions. In the city of Moscow there were often between 50,000 and 100,000 children relegated to the streets and another 80,000 in St. Petersburg. There were even some attempts to bring these children into the Red Army, so they could be fed and clothed. Throughout Russia and Eastern Europe childhood illness, delinquency, and sexual aggression became rampant.[2] Lawyers and corrupt government officials successfully brokered U.S. adoptions throughout Eastern Europe and there was some money to be made here in selling white babies. While American child abandonments also surged at this time, they were primarily in poor communities of color, which were undergoing their own domestic shock therapy brought on by the Reagan-Bush social service and food stamp cuts. Thousands of these children from distressed families were consigned to foster care. This was the beginning of a so-called "New World Order."

The utopia of globalization is viewed in this chapter as a process through which the profit-making paradigm displaces all others as the means for constructing change throughout the world. However, this process is seen as a mere extension of an ongoing program of human and environmental exploitation that had as its object the conversion of the earth into a common marketplace.

THE MEANING OF GLOBALIZATION

The origins of modern globalization can be found in both the rise of nation-states and in the advancement of the Enlightenment Project. Historically, globalization was part of a systematic effort to master nature, tame savagery and impose reason on the irrational. Its strategic arsenal included the application of science to organize, dissect, exploit, control, and annihilate radical differences. It was from these interventions that capitalism would emerge as the quintessential paradigm for global mastery and world integration.

Capitalism required the opening up of the globe as a marketplace. In fact, Immanuel Wallerstein suggests that from its very beginning, the aim of capitalism was an integrated world system.[3] His contribution has been his long-standing vision of capitalism as central to the process of globalization. For him, global capitalism has historically promoted a hierarchy of economic space wherein nation-states take their place either in the core, semi-periphery, or periphery. This position determines their material fate.

Globalization has meant different things at different times. In the 1950s it was associated with the progressive notion of world community. The ultimate goal of world community was to weaken the significance of nation-states and their boundaries in order to enhance global peace and cooperation. World governance predicated on some general form of consensus would guide decisions, and nations would move away from protectionistic restrictions directed not only to control the flow of goods and services but also to halt the movement of people across borders. Globalization meant that a sense of oneness would develop, which would enhance communication and significantly free people.[4] Howard Perlmutter views global civilization in this way.[5] For him and others, globalization means a world order with shared values, processes, and structures wherein nations and cultures influence each other. Although he recognizes that this is a lofty goal, he proposes that it is reachable.

Most significant among globalization theories has been that of Anthony Giddens. He views globalization as an extension of modernization, and suggests that it is in one sense defined by the "time-space distanciation." "Globalization," Giddens suggests, "can thus be defined by the intensification of world-wide social relations which link distinct local communities in such a way that local happenings are shaped by events occurring many miles away and vice versa."[6] Inherent here is a sense that remote decisions are being made over which the local citizen has no control. This connects to what he describes as "disembedding" of social relations: separating social relationships from physical propinquity. In fact, it is the stretching of these characteristics around the world that helps to define the process of modernity.[7] Similarly, David Harvey's position on globalization stresses what he calls the "compression of time and space." By this he means both the speeding-up of time over space and the associated collapsing of space to be transcended for purposes of communication and trade. These shifts are brought about by technological advances that alter not only economic relations, but social ones as well.[8]

Today the term globalization has become increasingly murky. As Peter Marcuse suggests: "Politically leaving the term vague and ghostly permits its conversion into something with a life of its own, making it a force, fetishizing it as something that has an existence independent of the will of human beings, inevitable and irresistible."[9] He asserts that this lack of clarity in the use of the word creates several problems chief amongst these is its divorce from capitalism. For Marcuse, globalization is merely an intensification and extension of particular forms of capitalistic relationships "both in breadth (geographically) and in depth (penetrating ever-increasing aspects of human life)."[10] But he also recognizes a clear division in the literature between viewing globalization as product of advancing communications technology and seeing it as a shift in the nature of global capitalism.

Howard Adelman has distinguished between three types of globalization: physical globalization wherein the world is viewed as a unified cohesive entity; normative globalization, in which the principles of modernity become universal as norms; and economic globalization, in which abstract principles are united with the practical production and distribution of goods and services.[11] While the first two types might be best understood as consequences of modernistic expansion including the compression of time and space through technological innovation, the last type dominates modern discourse. But technology, as Zygmunt Bauman suggests, establishes the way for global capital expansion:

> Technologies which effectively do away with time and space need little time to deride and impoverish space. They render capital truly global; they make all those who can neither follow nor arrest capital's new nomadic habits helplessly watch their livelihood fading and vanishing and wonder from where the blight might have come. The global travels of financial resources are perhaps as immaterial as the electronic network they travel, but the local traces of their journeys are painfully tangible and real: "Qualitative depopulation," destruction of local economies once capable of sustaining their inhabitants, the exclusion of millions incapable of being absorbed by the new global economy.[12]

It is the consequences of globalization that need attention, claims Bauman and others.

For Adelman, if any one phenomenon most vividly characterizes the social consequences of globalization, it is the actual disembedding and uprooting of people. Modernity and capitalism set into play wave upon wave of population migration across the face of the globe. As Adelman notes:

> Refugees are the products of modernity. Their plight became acute when the processes of modernity became globalized, when the political system of nation-states first became extended over the whole globe and efforts were made to sort the varied nations of the world into political states.[13]

Psychodynamic theorists, such as Salman Akhtar, have developed important clinical insights into the relationship between refugee status and self-identity. The loss of place, especially the abrupt loss, can be critical to individual psychological development. The loss of place often corresponds, on a symbolic level at least, to the loss of mother, or the loss of nurturance. For the immigrant and the exile, but particularly for the refugee, separation from one's home culture entails a delicate internal process of mourning and adjustment to loss. While moving to a new land can be liberating, it can also be psychologically alienating—especially for many young children. Akhtar draws on the work of object relations theorists and self-psychology to illustrate the psychodynamic processes involved in separation from culture and loss of place.[14]

The growth in the number of global refugees in the last quarter of the twentieth century was to a great extent a product of capital shifts, political turmoil, and structural adjustments imposed on the developing world by the west. Certainly, the refugee population surged at the end of the Cold War reaching record heights. Approximately one percent of the world's population or fifty million people are now refugees: homeless people seeking a safe haven, a place to work or an improvement in their standard of living.[15] At least half of this global refugee population is comprised of children under the age of sixteen.[16]

GLOBALIZATION AND ABANDONMENT

The impact of the free flow of capital around the globe, promoted by both the loosening of governmental restrictions and by neoliberal institutions such as the World Bank and the International Monetary Fund, has had dire consequences for vast segments of the population and has mostly benefited a wealthy few. Bauman notes that 358 global billionaires have combined fortunes in excess of the total income of 2.3 billion of the earth's poorest, or 45 percent of the world's population.[17] By the time one reads this statistic, global inequality will have most certainly worsened. The most significant players, namely transnational corporations and financial institutions, have gained the most. In many instances national governments have become their servants, protectors, and the referees.

In the poorest countries of the world where massive debt incurred in the 1980s and 1990s, strangled the potential for growth and development, western banks and trade organizations imposed strict austerity measures. For many of these developing countries national resources were privatized and budgets were divested of social and economic supports. In Senegal, as an example, the government was obligated to remove subsidies on food—driving prices out of range for most consumers.[18] The

nation was forced to cut public employment and to divest itself of bank-
ing, tourism, and other businesses. While citizens were forced to pay a
premium on gasoline, wheat flour, and utilities, the country was coerced
into opening its markets to cheaper and more competitive goods wrecking havoc with its own domestic industries and products. User fees were
added to health clinic visits; the per capita expenditures on health
dropped twenty percent. Education also suffered as school fees were
added; the beginning school age was moved from six to seven years of
age and there was a rash of teacher lay-offs. In her study of Senegal in
the mid to late 1990s, Carolyn Somerville notes:

> The structural adjustment program may have benefited some Senegalese,
> but for the vast majority it has torn apart families; wounded a generation
> of youth devoid of any hope for the future; exacerbated existing poverty;
> contributed to growing ills such as drug and alcohol use and abuse, juve-
> nile delinquency, and prostitution; led to growing insecurity due to the
> rise of violence; accelerated rural–urban migration; turned traditional
> values upside down; and increased political apathy, as many feel that the
> government does not care about them.[19]

Zygmunt Bauman quotes from Le Monde diplomatique:

> In the cabaret of globalization, the state goes through a striptease and by
> the end of the performance it is left with the bare necessities only: its
> powers of repression. With its material basis destroyed, its sovereignty and
> independence annulled, its political class effaced, the nation-state becomes
> a simple security service for the mega-companies.[20]

In Senegal the situation went from bad to worse as its currency was
devalued. Rioting broke out in the city of Dakar with mob violence
directed against the police; the university went on strike. Toward the
end of the 1990s thousands of Senegalese made their way from rural
areas to Dakar. Finding no way to earn a living there, many came to
New York City to set up stalls and sell merchandise on the streets.[21]

The flow of refugees from rural areas into cities and from poorer
nations into the wealthier ones is not solely the result of economic displacement or structural adjustment; politics, technology, cultural perse-
cution, and to some extent natural disasters certainly enter into this
formula. However, as Adelman has indicated, although the Hutu/Tutsi
conflict in Rwanda had a long history dating back to the expulsions of
the Tutsi people in the late 1950s and early 1960s, the IMF and World
Bank structural adjustments imposed on that struggling nation in the
1980s ordering a cut in domestic programs and civil service helped to
bring about one of the most violent events of the latter part of the twentieth century.[22] While no one lays this bloodshed at the feet of these

western mechanisms of globalization, one cannot overlook the culpability of such policies in helping to disrupt vast sectors of the world's population despite announced intentions to do otherwise.

In the last half of the nineteenth century the number of world refugees mushroomed. Adelman suggests three primary reasons for this: the legalized protection of refugee status under the Geneva Convention; the ease of access to transportation; and economic crises occurring in developed states just as globalization and automation reduced the need for unskilled labor.[23] It was the United Nations statute establishing the Office of the U.N. High Commander for Refugees in 1950 and the subsequent 1951 Geneva Convention Relating to the Status of Refugees that helped to establish a means of both understanding and treating the global phenomenon of massive population migrations. These rules came into effect to address the destabilizing consequences of World War II. In an effort to impose humanitarian standards throughout the world, states were assigned responsibilities for this growing cohort of migrants seeking refuge.

However, as Saskia Sassen has noted, although the 1952 Convention established the universal right for people to leave a nation, it remained silent on the right to enter another. Thus, while the right of refugees to flee and not to be forcibly returned is established in international law, the Convention remains silent on the right to asylum. And while some nations formally recognized this right to asylum, the collapse of the Soviet Union marked a rescindment of these obligations.[24] Just as states were lifting restrictions on the flow of capital across borders, there were tighter controls placed over the flow of people across these same boundaries. In many instances this led to war and bloodshed. In other instances it led simply to economic exploitation. It was possible for the U.S. to open its doors to Cubans fleeing the conditions of poverty and human rights oppression in Cuba, but the same rights were refused to darker-skinned Haitians attempting to flee the political terrors and dire poverty in their own land where political leaders were propped up by U.S. foreign policy and where American corporations were exploiting workers on a daily basis. This link between corporate globalization and political repression has become evident in relations between the wealthy western nations and the poorer states to the south and east.

Neoimperialism was very much a part of the NAFTA agenda as jobs were moved south from the United States to Mexico and tighter border restrictions were simultaneously imposed to prevent Mexicans from coming north, literally locking them into an economic prison. This pattern was reproduced across the poorest areas of the Caribbean, Central and South America. Modified versions of this appeared in Asia, Africa, and the Middle East. Global sweatshops sprung-up guarded over by armies and police. Restrictions were placed on union organizing. The radically uneven distribution of global development has created grave political and social problems and has helped direct the flow of people from rural areas to towns and from towns to big cities. Many people cross borders or move into and out of cities in search of work no matter how marginal it might be. The expulsion of ethnic groups and so-called ethnic cleansing, more often rooted in the competition for scarce resources than racism, have been reactions to a perceived threat to a group's economic status.

The sense of economic insecurity and vulnerability have been central to capitalistic development around the world. The business cycles that have been associated with modern capitalistism wreck havoc with the vast majority who are ill prepared for economic recession. The global transformation of local economies, undermining traditional ways of life, and furthermore undermining international political stability, has also promoted a deepening sense of anxiety.

Abandonment is essentially connected to the processes of globalization in several important ways. The structural undermining of local economies that are culturally based is an essential feature of neocolonialism and transnational exploitation of labor. The uprooting of peasant populations from the status of tenants through the selling of the lands on which they have worked for countless generations emulates the radical displacements produced by the earliest postmedieval enclosures. Such structural conversions of indigenous economies have led not only to greater poverty but to familial disintegration. As Michael Parenti notes:

> Hundreds of millions of Third World peoples now live in destitution in remote villages and congested urban slums, suffering hunger, disease, illiteracy, often because the land they once tilled is now controlled by agribusiness firms that use it for mining or for commercial export crops such as coffee, sugar, beef, instead of beans, rice and corn for home consumption.[25]

> . . . in countries like Russia, Thailand, and the Philippines, large numbers of minors are sold into prostitution to help desperate families survive. In countries like Mexico, India, Columbia and Egypt, children are dragooned into health-shattering, dawn-to-dusk labor on farms and in factories and mines for pennies an hour, with no opportunity for play, schooling or medical care.[26]

CHILDREN AS REFUGEES

Abandonment has become a vehicle for survival. That the number of abandoned children grows during times of severe economic austerity is a natural and inevitable consequence of fiscal crises and curtailments of social service supports. According to reports of the United Nations and Amnesty International, more than 100 million children are now living and working on the streets of cities around the world. Many of these young people are the products of domestic, social, and economic crisis brought on both directly and indirectly by structural adjustment. Although a few have family connections, most have been orphaned or abandoned and can be found sleeping in doorways, under bridges, or in abandoned buildings. Children engage in work ranging from peddling fruit, cigarettes, and trinkets to shoe shining, petty theft, or prostitution.

Vânia Penha-Lopes has discussed at length the brutal murders of street children in Brazil in the early 1990s.[27] The most infamous incident occurred in July 1993 where forty-five children were sleeping in the doorway of the Candelária Church in Rio de Janeiro. It was then that hooded off-duty police officers fired on the children killing seven of them and injuring many others. More than seven thousand poor children and adolescents were murdered in Brazil between 1988 and 1991, and many more missing children have died but have not been accounted for. This social-cleansing is frequently unofficially condoned by local businessmen and government officials who see such young people as bad for business. Penha-Lopes notes:

> While the number of youth has been increasing, at least partly due to the rampant economic recession that has created 65 million poor in a country of fewer than 150 million inhabitants, it is worth noting that the majority of street children—including those described above—are Black and mulatto. . . .[28]

> The murders of street youth in Brazil must be seen as a result of the complex relation between extreme economic inequality, racism, and impunity. Economic inequality leads a large proportion of the population to absolute poverty and very few opportunities for gaining full employment. Racism attaches itself to poverty to make a large category of Brazilians even more vulnerable.[29]

The abandonment of children is as concrete an outcome of capitalism today as it was in the eighteenth and nineteenth centuries. Child refugees not only must experience the separation from home and all that this entails, but often must undergo an early separation from immediate family. This frequently leads to problems in social and emotional development.[30] The processes of socialization are radically interrupted. Children under the age of ten are three times more likely than adults to experience some form of post-traumatic stress disorder as a result of their refugee status.[31] Children constitute the largest age group in refugee camps around the world. In many instances children are abandoned in these camps by parents hoping that their children will be better cared for there.[32]

ABANDONMENT OF LABOR

The rapid movement of capital over national borders has posed an immense challenge to organized labor. While capital was moving with less velocity, it was possible for labor to unionize in local areas. However, with the acceleration of capital flow and the change in the nature of work, it has become exceedingly difficult for labor even to organize. This is not to say that capital has just recently become globalized or that the type of work that people do has remained static. But the global dispersal of productive capital has moved rapidly. With advances in technology and the internationalization of financial institutions, rapid assembly of the factors of production has become increasingly effortless.

Globalization has provided greater opportunities for flexibility of both financial capital and labor. This combination of flexibility and mobility has enabled employers to exert pressure on labor to conform. Frances Fox Piven has suggested that deindustrialization strategies in core states in the 1980s and 1990s were combined with policies aimed at undermining social welfare services that once had given people a slight sense of security. The restructuring of work went on unimpeded as jobs moved to periphery states and real work was converted into contingent labor. A new reserve army of labor was amassed consisting of involuntary part-time workers, millions of former public assistance recipients and a cadre of hungry people in the developing world clamoring for jobs.[33]

Stanley Aronowitz and William DiFazio have envisioned what they call "the jobless future."[34] They provide good evidence to indicate that high-tech, knowledge-based economies characterized by postfordist flexible specialization have led not only to the crudification of work, but present a threat to the culture of full-time, paid employment:

> All the contradictory tendencies involved in the restructuring of global capital and computer-mediated work seem to lead to the same conclusion for workers of all collars—that is, unemployment, underemployment, decreasingly skilled work, and relatively lower wages. These sci-tech transformations of the labor process have disrupted the workplace and workers' community and culture. High technology will destroy more jobs than it creates. The new technology has fewer parts and fewer workers and produces more product. This is true not only in traditional production industries but for all workers, including managers and technical workers. . . . [35]

Kate Bronfenbrenner has argued that the flight of capital across borders has posed a real threat to workers' abilities to collectively bargain everywhere.[36] In the United States, even though the American economy experienced the greatest expansion in its history in the last decade of the twentieth century, workers were feeling more unsure about their economic futures than they were during the 1980–1991 recession. Bronfenbrenner's research indicates that persistent worker insecurity has been essentially a function of the extent and frequency of capital mobility. "The specter of capital mobility and the economic insecurity it engenders," posits Bronfenbrenner, "has served to constrain both wages and union activity in a period of tight labor markets."[37] Her study has found that employers' threats to move a plant or an administrative function to another country were endemic throughout those instances in the United States where collective bargaining or labor organizing were taking place.

On a global level this fear of abandonment threatens the very livelihood of workers as they are coerced into bidding-down wages. Frequently, threats to abandon connect to deep-rooted separation issues that individuals often confront in other aspects of their lives. Most workers in the United States are only a paycheck away from homelessness. Loss of one's job signals a removal of the primary means to sustain oneself. But the volatility of the global marketplace itself, the dangers inherent in the instability of currencies and investments around the world, creates a climate of anxiety that goes beyond the lowest line worker and finds a place in a culture of insecurity. Social planner Peter Marris refers to this as part of the "politics of uncertainty," driven by individualism and heightened competition rather than interdependence and cooperation.[38]

In response to this anxiety people build walls around themselves. Bauman notes:

> The preoccupation with personal safety, inflated and overloaded with meanings beyond its capacity due to the tributaries of existential insecurity and psychological uncertainty, towers yet higher over all articulated fears, casting all other reasons of anxiety into yet deeper shade. Governments may feel relieved: no one or almost no one would press them to do something about things which their hands are much too small and feeble to grasp and hold. No one would accuse them either of remaining idle and doing nothing of relevance to human anxieties when watching daily documentaries, dramas, docudramas and carefully staged dramas disguised as documentaries, telling the story of new improved police weapons, high-tech prison locks and burglar and car-theft alarms, short sharp shocks administered to the criminals, and valiant security officers and detectives risking their lives so that the rest of us may sleep in peace.[39]

The separation anxiety—a fear of being abandoned by those who appear to hold one's economic and social well-being in their hands—is greatest in those societies in which individualism is emphasized above communal values, where independence is revered and interdependence held in contempt. It is in such societies that we tend to observe a real disdain for the poor and needy, especially among men who have been pushed into premature autonomy from early childhood.

WOMEN AND GLOBALIZATION

The systematic exclusion of women from most of the benefits of global development, and the disproportionate burden of globalization's adverse effects upon them, speaks to the intrinsic gender bias of this process.

Under the patriarchal system of capitalism women have always been relied upon for marginal and cheap labor. Thus, women have been pushed into the position of supplemental or contingent workers—a reserve army of labor. A history of women in labor reveals that even in industrially developed societies wherein women were allowed to participate in the formal job sector, they were usually relegated to those positions that were least lucrative and more ancillary than those of men. Throughout the world women earn between twenty-five and seventy percent less than men for the same work. In times of economic boom, contingency work was maximized and during depressions and recessions it was contracted. With the advent of increased globalization this has not changed and in fact probably has worsened. In that most of the productive work done around the world is completed by women in the informal sector, including cottage or home work, women occupy the most vulnerable positions as workers, receive few or no benefits, and are saddled with both unpaid domestic service including child care and with this so-called paid supplemental work. Where women are forced into factory work their treatment is generally deplorable.

Women between the ages of 15 and 22 constitute nearly ninety percent of the sweatshop workforce around the globe and are involved in the production of goods ranging from clothing to computer components. Globalization and transnational agribusiness has pushed many women from tenant farming into Free Trade Zone factory employment where they work upward to sixty hours per week and are routinely laid-off when it's discovered that they are pregnant. Throughout Mexico and Latin America *maquiladora* industries sprang to life in the 1980s and 1990s, harvesting young peasants, mostly young women, to work in factories assembling clothing to be sold in major department store chains under major brand names. In such factories, often surrounded by barbed-wire fences and armed security guards, wages are kept low and productivity high. Shanty towns of corrugated tin huts often house these workers whose lives are shortened by a lack of running water, poor sanitary conditions, and rapid spread of infectious diseases. This model has become a symbol of global capitalism around the world. It has been favored throughout South East Asia. When factories shut down, as some did with the Asian financial crisis in the mid-1990s, women and young girls are frequently pushed into lives of prostitution.

Globalization has not done much to liberate women from the repressive patriarchal systems around the world. In fact, there seems to be evidence that as the rhetoric of internationalism increases, many of the most disenfranchised nations are turning with renewed vigor toward religious fundamentalism, which traditionally denies women full participatory rights as well as rights over their own bodies. This is especially true in the poorest parts of Africa, Eastern Europe, and the Middle East. Women constitute nearly seventy percent of the world's poor; they have the highest illiteracy rate and are significantly less educated than men.

Saskia Sassen, who describes globalization in terms of unbundling of traditional concepts of territory associated with nation-states, has proposed that a new global pluralism is emerging that might allow alternative ways through which women can more fully participate in the newly configured world. Her work emphasizes what she refers to as the valorization and devalorization of types of work.[40] She stresses the importance of women as immigrant service workers in global cities and the significance of these cities as platforms of global capital.

While traditional perspectives on globalization emphasize both the power of the state and the advances in technology at the upper circuits of capital investment, she contends that the essence of this process, its very basis, is structured by local constraints, including the composition of the workforce, worker cultures, and political cultures. She sees this dependence as a hidden vulnerability of powerful male elites.

Sassen views immigrant women in a particularly optimistic light. She notes major employment inroads have been made in recent decades, but also recognizes that women are essential players in such areas as community development and small-scale service businesses. Sassen sees great potential in the informal economy, not simply marginalization. This is particularly so in major global cities where male elites monopolize the more valorized positions.

With the unbundling of territoriality brought about with globalization, Sassen makes a case for the development of international law as being a possible locus of liberation. Since women are restricted by regressive codes of nation-states, human rights law offers opportunities for further progress. However, this issue will center around how much powerful nation-states are really willing to relinquish. Enforcement has continued to be one of the central problems here.

THE PRIVATIZATION OF THE EARTH

The idea of privatization, which has been an essential component of a program of structural adjustment imposed by advanced capitalist nations upon economically weaker ones, requires that everything of value becomes subject to private ownership—a notion that would have been distasteful even to Adam Smith. But this veneration of the private, and more particularly, its elevation to a position of reverence by the forces of global capital reveals itself as purely ideological inversion of a slave morality. In classical Greek society, what separated the realm of the private from public life was law. The private arena was characterized by slavery and injustice; there were no rights there, and no equality. Public life of the *polis* was a society of equals. The Athenian *polis* attempted to combine democracy with aesthetics, commitment, and civicism. Virtue emerged here; virtuosity was incompatible with privacy.

The new privatism is void of public good and civic culture. Globalization has little to do with creating a progressive cosmopolitanism; rather it has as its agenda the promotion of the interests of the few most powerful transnationals through grants of special privileges and trading rights. However, corporate globalization led by planners from the World Trade Organization, the IMF, and the World Bank has met with a significant extent of resistance around the world. Coalitions of students, workers, environmentalists, farmers, and feminists have combined their efforts in an attempt to resist this program of international conquest and universal exploitation.

When the European Union imposed restrictions on the importation of hormone-treated beef from the United States, America responded with high tariffs on such items as Roquefort cheese. The power of the United States to inflict its standardized, bioengineered foods upon the rest of world led many small farmers abroad to target U.S. companies as symbols of economic hegemony. In France the reaction has been fierce. In the town of Millau in southern France, Jose Bove, who heads a group called the Peasants' Confederation, led an attack on a construction site for a new McDonald's restaurant with crowbars, sledgehammers, wrenches, and screwdrivers. For Bove and other French businessmen McDonald's has come to represent the

American drive to impose its substandard, homogenized food upon the rest of the world and at the same time to impose its values and tastes on others.[41] More than half of McDonald's profits come from its overseas operations.[42]

British social theorist John Gray has argued that although there are many forms of globalization, there is a growing tendency to equate the current variety with the spread of an American form of capitalism—one with no social consciousness and little sense of responsibility for the damage it inflicts upon the earth and its population.[43] Furthermore, he insists, this anti-social brand of market economics is driving out the other models that are more suitable for sustainability. Gray notes:

> A global free market is the Enlightenment project of a universal civilization, sponsored by the world's last great Enlightenment regime. The United States is alone in the late modern world in the militancy of its commitment to this Enlightenment project. At the same time, in the strength and depth of fundamentalist movements it contains, America confounds Enlightenment hopes for modernity.[44]

Still, while capitalistic globalization celebrates postfordist innovation and the glow of an ever-expanding transnational consumerism, there is another side of globalization—a darker one that reaches deeply into the hearts and lives of those who sense a real connection to the earth. It is a globalization of exiles and refugees, of tortured political prisoners and child laborers; it is the plight of exiled artists and intellectuals. It is expressed in the lives of children and adults caught between danger at home and the loss of identity, trapped between cultural isolation and marginalization. This is a globalization of world hunger in the face of a vast accumulation of wealth by a few; it is the globalization of refugee camps and postcolonial *maquiladoras*.

Such globalization is not one process but many processes. It is expressed in the lives of children and adults caught between danger at home and the loss of identity, trapped between cultural isolation and marginalization; it is expressed, too, in the poetry of despair of refugees, in waves of people struggling to survive. This estrangement is reflected in the words of Chilean poet and writer Pablo Neruda:

> *It is the hard cold hour of departure, the hard cold hour*
> *which the night fastens to all the timetables.*
>
> *The rustling belt of the sea girdles the shore.*
> *Cold stars heave up, black birds migrate.*
>
> *Deserted like the waves at dawn.*
> *Only tremulous shadow twists in my hand.*

Oh farther than everything. Oh farther than everything.
It is the hour of departure. Oh abandoned one!

—From *A Song of Despair*, (1924)

Those people and lands abandoned represent the tragedy of globalization and the dashed hopes for a world of equity and justice. As time
speeds up, as the world becomes smaller, the distance between the fortu-
nate and the destitute grows greater.

THE HAPPY FACE OF GLOBALIZATION

The happy face of globalization is not difficult to find in the mainstream media owned by multinational conglomerates. For those promoting it, it means a respect for diversity, an opening up of the world to
principles of democracy; it entails advanced technology leading to easier
living and a utopia of global consumerism. It means affluence for all.
David Rothkopf, a past director of Kissinger Associates notes:

> The drivers of today's rapid globalization are improving methods and sys-
> tems of international transportation, devising revolutionary and innovative
> information technology and services, and dominating the international com-
> merce in service and ideas . . . major U.S. telecommunications companies
> including giants like Motorola, Loral Space & Communications, Teledesic
> (a joint project of Microsoft's Bill Gates and cellular pioneer Craig McCaw),
> offer competing plans that will encircle the globe with a constellation of
> satellites . . . Technology is transforming the world. . . . Satellites carrying
> television signals now enable people on opposite sides of the globe to be
> exposed regularly to a wide range of cultural stimuli . . . Middle Eastern
> leaders have cited CNN as a prime source of even local news.[45]

Western "progress" is an essential component of this brand of globalization. Rothkopf asserts:

> Critics of globalization argue that the process will lead to a stripping away
> of identity and a blindly uniform, Orwellian world. On a planet of 6 bil-
> lion people, this is, of course, an impossibility. More importantly, the
> decline of cultural distinctions may be a measure of the progress of civi-
> lization, a tangible sign of enhanced communications and understanding.[46]

In his broad ranging treatment of globalization, *The Lexus and the
Olive Tree, New York Times* journalist Thomas Friedman contends that
the most important feature of globalization is free-market capitalism:
"the more you let market forces rule and the more you open your economy to free trade and competition, the more efficient and flourishing

your economy will be."[47] It is Friedman's contention that globalization is new, it's a revolution involving a shift in power from the state to the private sector.[48] Still, in understanding this power shift as one from democratically elected governments serving the people to a cadre of business executives serving themselves, he has difficulty comprehending why people find globalization so distasteful.

One of the more interesting aspects of the book is the myriad of anecdotes that are intended to be revelatory. One story that was truly revealing was about Martin Indyk, the former U.S. Ambassador to Israel. It was on a day serving as Ambassador that Indyk was asked to help open the first McDonald's in Jerusalem. He was given a McDonald's logo-encrested cap to wear. The restaurant was filled with customers and media when a young teenager made his way from the crowd and inquired if he were the ambassador and, if so, if he would sign an autograph for the young man.

As Indyk was obliging him, the boy said: "Wow, what's it like being the ambassador from McDonald's going around the world opening McDonald's restaurants?" Stunned, Indyk looked at the youth and said: "No, no. I'm the American Ambassador, not the ambassador from McDonald's."[49]

Many protesters around the world have seen McDonald's not only as an icon of America, but as a symbol of global homogenization and even imperialism. By 1998, McDonald's had the majority of its restaurants located outside of the United States with most of its profits coming from the non-American market.[50]

THE RESPONSE TO GLOBALIZATION

The responses to globalization have varied significantly. In many cases where western ideotypes are injected into traditional societies through media conglomerates there is little resistance offered up against them. Values associated with western capitalism are often admired. Certainly, materialism and ruthlessness are essential to much of American cinema. Many non-westerners, however, see the American brand of commercialism threatening a way of life and incubating another. The reorganization or elimination of social and cultural institutions is a common fear. Kinship configurations when met with demands of globalized capital often shift, and instead of globalization offering a safe-haven, some suggest that it has led to greater insecurity and greater domestic violence.[51] As Rothkopf and other neoliberals

appear to suggest, this must mean that the weaker cultural elements
have given way to the superior ones.

Throughout the world, fundamentalist groups have strengthened
their opposition to what they perceive as an attack against traditional
ways of life. This is especially true in areas where globalization has created an intensification of unemployment, poverty, and political repression and where people have a sense of being voiceless, ignored, and
marginalized. Connected to many of these movements, including the
U.S. militia movement in the American Midwest, has been some of the
crudest forms of racism. As Bauman notes: "Neo-tribal and fundamentalist tendencies, which reflect and articulate the experience of people on
the receiving end of globalization, are as much legitimate offspring of
globalization as the widely acclaimed 'hybridization' of top culture—the
culture at the globalized top."[52]

At another level, the response to globalization has been an amazing
degree of grassroots organizing and coalition building, greater than that
reflected in the Vietnam era demonstrations. With the help of the
Internet, fax machines, digital cameras, and cellular phones tens of thousands, and sometimes upward of a hundred thousand people and more,
assemble in cities around the world to make their voices heard. Broad
coalitions of trade union people, church groups, indigenous peoples,
women's rights groups, AIDS activists, human rights advocates, students, professors, and political environmentalists rally at demonstrations
from Seattle to Genoa, but also at much less publicized ones. The movement is now transnational. They do not oppose globalization, but rather
target the negative consequences associated with it. The Editors of the
Monthly Review note:

> What makes this new era of protest so distinctive is that it is aimed not so
> much at the state (as in the sixties) but at global corporations and interna-
> tional economic institutions, and thus raises fundamental issues about class
> power and international solidarity with third world workers. . . . It also
> demonstrates the capacity of labor, environmentalist and other left forces
> to act in tandem when confronted by the commonly perceived threat of a
> globalizing economy.[53]

While corporate-controlled media often find it expedient to portray protesters as irresponsible troublemakers who oppose progress, lumping
them together as Friedman has done with reactionary fundamentalists, a
Harris poll taken shortly after the Seattle protests showed that 52 percent
of Americans were sympathetic to the concerns of the protesters.[54] Most
observers seemed to understand that these people are not Luddites; they
have better command of the new technology than do most of the aging

corporate leaders and politicians who promote globalization. Just as the unionists and suffragettes at the beginning of the twentieth-century; and just like the peace activists of the early 1900s were not protesting modernity, these new progressive coalitions have been demonstrating against state cronyism, and the multinational juggernaut aimed at dividing up the world at the expense of workers and the environment.

Nevertheless, the transnational dynamics of the protest movement seems staggering. In Genoa in the summer of 2001, not only did Italian social democrats join forces with anarchists and old line communists, but also in attendance were thousands of French, Canadian, and British farmers, American small business people, Zapatistas from Mexico, and a host of protesters from Africa, the Middle East, Latin America, Eastern Europe, Norway, Germany, and Australia—tens of thousands of people from almost every corner of the earth who because of advanced technology were connected to one another but also could comprehend the destructive consequences of such technology put into the service of human exploitation and greed. The numbers arriving for the G8 protest was astonishing, but many more were turned away at airports, train stations, and bus depots, never having a chance to set foot in Genoa. Los Angeles police were brought in to train Italian police in crowd-control procedures. The Italian government tightened its control limiting the location and numbers allowed to assemble and incarcerated thousands.[55] During the protests, Carlo Guiliani was shot twice in the head by police and backed over by the police jeep when he threatened to fling a fire extinguisher at the police vehicle. The *New York Times* story on the demonstration featured two large photos—one of a gun pointed at Guiliani's head from the inside of the police vehicle and another of his body under the jeep. Underneath this story is a photograph of Laura Bush posing in front of the Tower of Pisa. The caption there reads "Laura Bush Enjoys Globalization's Lighter Side."[56] Guiliani is now the very first casualty in a conflict that is bound to continue into the future.

Thomas Friedman refers to such students and workers as "flat earth advocates." Speaking about the Seattle protests he notes: "What's crazy is that protesters want the WTO to become precisely what they accuse it of already being, a global government. They want it to set more rules—their rules, which would impose our labor and environmental standards on everyone else."[57] He further notes:

> . . . strongest backlash against globalization comes not from the poorest segments of the population . . . but from the 'used-to-bes' in the middle and lower middle classes who found a great deal of security in the protected communist, socialist and welfare systems. They have seen the walls of protection around them coming down, as they have seen the rigged

games in which they flourish folded-up and as the safety nets under them
shrink, many have become mighty unhappy . . . these downwardly mobile
groups have the political clout to organize against globalization.[58]

In point of fact large numbers of Americans and Europeans appear to fit
very well into this category of the downwardly mobile thanks to the loss
of jobs, lowering of living standards, and the virtually unrestrained interests of capital, which so-called globalization strategies have let loose.
Given the volatility of market capitalism, and its inherent harsh cycles,
one may venture to guess that this is among the reasons why the majority of Americans do not have faith in the globalization process—especially those people who work to support themselves and find their jobs
always in jeopardy.[59] With pensions of working-class people (those who
have them) tied-up in a highly mercurial stock market and medical care
costs largely determined at the discretion of profit-making HMOs and
pharmaceutical companies, and with lobbyists working with lawmakers
to restrict liability for the most dissolute of profiteers and polluters,
elected officials are now dismantling the last of governmentally managed
social security programs, creating for working-class people an intensified
climate of vulnerability.

The so-called War on Terrorism has become a convenient means of
diverting anxiety and resources away from the broad and very unsettling
economic concerns while providing a surrogate target to which the
working class can be more safely directed. At the same time, such a
target can change by the hour. Drawing public attention away from the
capitalistic threat to day-to-day economic survival has always been a
function of the tabloid press. The growing police state has been brought
on by very real fears and promoted by the media.

The popular media has done little other than to sing the praises of
globalization and promote the fear of global terror. Many are already
integrated into the web of transnational profits and are linked to the
anti-terrorism-industrial complex. Their future accumulations depend
on these trends continuing. Media expert Robert McChesney has shown
that with the deregulation of media ownership and the privatization of
television in lucrative Asian and European markets eight transnationals
dominate systems of production and distribution throughout the
world.[60] McChesney notes:

> With the hypercommercialization and growing corporate control comes
> an implicit political bias in media content. Consumerism, class inequality
> and individualism tend to be taken as natural and even benevolent,
> whereas political activity, civic virtues and anti-market activities are mar-
> ginalized. The best journalism is pitched to the business class and suited to

its needs and prejudices; with a few notable exceptions, the journalism reserved for the masses tends to be the sort of drivel provided by media giants on their U.S. television stations. This slant is often quite subtle. Indeed, the genius of the commercial-media system is the general lack of overt censorship. As George Orwell noted in his unpublished introduction to *Animal Farm*, censorship in free societies is infinitely more sophisticated and thorough than in dictatorships, because "unpopular ideas can be silenced, and inconvenient facts kept dark, without any need for an official ban."[61]

Students, environmentalists, workers, and others come to learn about the downside of globalization from the alternative media—often at local teach-ins or workshops, sometimes from the alternative press, pirate radio, movement newspapers, and most certainly the Internet. The Independent Media Center, a collective of media organizations and hundreds of journalists from around the world, provides outlets for information and news related to the environment, women's rights, AIDS activism, the labor movement, and a whole range of other issues not generally covered in the commercial press. Then, of course, each large activist organization, in this day of Web and desktop printing, has its own magazine. While these media often get the word out, traditional channels of distribution are blocked to them. However, many activists are on the cutting-edge of new technologies themselves and work creatively to capitalize on what is still left of accessible cyberspace.

IDENTITY AND RESISTANCE

Fragmentation and alienation inherent in processes of globalization have provided obstacles to the development of a sense of authenticity in modern life. The consumer culture associated with late capitalism undermines efforts to establish a coherent sense of self. As Marcuse noted, the unfathomable depth of the global market darkens the prospect of escape from its expansive influence. But it is the space between dominance and resistance that provides an opportunity for an authentic self to emerge.

On a theoretical level, Manuel Castells offers some interesting insights here. For him, power relations form much of the basis of personal identity and reflexivity.[62] He perceives two major categories of identity: those identifying with the dominant power and those viewing themselves as outside of it. To this he adds three forms of identity building: legitimizing identity—that which is inherent in the established dominant power base and maintained through its control of social institutions; resistance identity—generated by those who are marginalized and devalued or stigmatized by the logic of domination and who build "trenches of resistence" on the basis of difference; and project identity—which seems to be a second stage of resistance identity in which people move out from the common trenches of resistance to directly challenge the hegemony. It is these later two that open the door to radical social change.

Castells sees resistance identity as the most important type of identity building—one that leads to the formation of projects of "collective resistance against otherwise unbearable oppression."[63] Such identity can be derived from a sense of marginalization, alienation, or abandonment, but needs to proceed from a sense of self. Castells views mere resistance identity as only reversing the value judgment against the excluded while maintaining the boundaries dictated by the most powerful. The fundamentalist stance against globalization is a case in point. It resists change rather than engineers it. It seeks refuge in destruction of the new and salvation in the myths of the past. It is the advanced stage of project identity that challenges the existing hegemony through the creation of what Alain Touraine has called "subjects."[64] Castells uses this to mean "the collective social action through which individuals reach meaning in their experience."[65] Here identity is not individualistic, but rather collective—gained through prolonged collective resistance, perhaps through an oppressed identity, and then taken to the streets and brought home by transforming the existing power structure—opening it up, not closing it down. If there is hope, it rests in the trenches of resistance, in the marginalized, and in the drive for revolutionary projects.

Notes

INTRODUCTION

1. Raymond Williams, *The Sociology of Culture* (New York: Schocken Books, 1981).

2. James Murray, H. Bradley, eds. *Oxford English Dictionary*, vol. I (Oxford: Clarendon Press, 1989).

3. John Boswell, *The Kindness of Strangers: The Abandonment of Children in Western Europe from Late Antiquity to the Renaissance* (New York: Pantheon Books, 1988), pp. 24–25.

4. Ibid., pp. 92–94.

5. *The Random House Dictionary of the English Language, The Unabridged Edition*, ed. by Juss Stein (New York: Random House, 1967), pp. 2–3.

6. Robert Nisbet, *Sociology as an Art Form* (New York: Oxford University Press, 1976), pp. 42–67.

7. Denis Cosgrove, *Social Formation and Symbolic Landscape* (Totowa, NJ.: Barnes & Noble, 1984), pp. 13–16.

8. Sharon Zukin, *Landscapes of Power: From Detroit to Disney World* (Berkeley: University of California Press, 1991), p. 17.

9. Georg Lukács, *History and Class Consciousness: Studies in Marxist Dialectics* (Cambridge, MA.: MIT Press, 1971), pp. 157–158.

10. See Zygmunt Bauman, *Modernity and Ambivalence* (Cambridge: Polity Press, 1992).

CHAPTER ONE: CAPITALISM, ABANDONMENT, AND MODERNITY

1. Meghnad Desai, "Capitalism," in *A Dictionary of Marxist Thought*, ed. T. Bottomore (Cambridge, MA.: Harvard University Press, 1983), pp. 64–67.

2. Adam Smith, *An Inquiry into the Nature and Causes of the Wealth of Nations*, 2 vols., ed. R. H. Campbell, A. S. Skinner and W. B. Todd (NewYork: Oxford Press, 1976), Book I Ch. VII, vol. I, pp. 72–75.

3. Albert O. Hirschman, *The Passions and the Interests: Political Arguments for Capitalism Before Its Triumph* (Princeton: NJ.: Princeton University Press, 1977), pp. 14–15.

4. Ibid., pp. 17–19.

5. J. Salwyn Schapiro, *Condorcert and the Rise of Liberalism* (New York: Harcourt & Brace, 1934).

6. See Karl Marx's discussion of this in *Das Kapital*, vol. I, ed. F. Engels, trans. S. Moore and E. Aveling (New York: International Publishers, 1967), p. 362.

7. Quoted in Hirschman, *op. cit.*, p. 108.

8. Ellen Meiksins Wood, *The Origin of Capitalism* (New York: Monthly Review Press, 1999).

9. Robert Nisbet, *Sociology as an Art Form* (New York: Oxford University Press, 1976), p. 57.

10. H. G. Schenk, *The Mind of the European Romantics* (New York: Oxford University Press, 1979), pp. 25–26.

11. Karl Polanyi, *The Great Transformation: The Political and Economic Origins of Our Time* (New York: Farrar and Reinhart, 1944).

12. See Alan MacFarlane's *The Origins of English Individualism: The Family, Property and Social Transition* (Oxford: Blackwell, 1978). Also see Rodney Hilton's critique of MacFarlane in "Individualism and the English Peasantry" in *New Left Review*, March–April (120), 1980, pp. 109–112, and Stephen White and Richard Vann "The Invention of English Individualism: Alan MacFarlane and the Modernization of Pre-modern England," in *Social History*, vol. 8 (2), 1983, pp. 345–363. One should also read Alasdair MacIntyre, "After Virtue and Marxism: A Response to Wartofsky," Inquiry, vol. 7 (2–3), July 1984, pp. 253–254. But for an excellent overview of the debate see Peter McMylor, *Alasadair MacIntyre: Critic of Modernity* (London: Routledge, 1994), pp. 77–108.

13. Fredric Jameson, *The Political Unconscious: Narrative as a Socially Symbolic Act* (Ithaca, New York: Cornell University Press, 1981).

14. William C. Dowling, *Jameson, Althusser, Marx: An Introduction to the Political Unconscious* (Ithaca, New York: Cornell University Press, 1984), pp. 19–38.

15. David Levine, "Production, reproduction, and the proletarian family in England 1500–1851," in *Proletarianization and Family History*, ed. David Levine (London: Academic Press, 1984), p. 89.

16. Max Weber, *The Spirit of Capitalism and the Protestant Ethic* (1905), trans. T. Parsons (New York: Charles Scribner's Sons, 1958).

17. Karl Marx, *The Poverty of Philosophy*, trans. N. Utina (New York: International Publishers, 1982), p. 34.

18. Erich Fromm, *Escape from Freedom* (1941) (New York: Avon Books, 1965), pp. 80–81.

19. Max Weber, *op. cit.*

20. Max Weber, *op. cit.*

21. Christopher Kendrick, *Milton: A Study in Ideology and Form* (New York: Methuen, 1986).

22. Joseph Schumpeter, *The Theory of Economic Development*, 3rd ed. (Cambridge, MA.: Harvard University Press, 1951).

23. Herman Kellenbenz, *The Rise of the European Economy: An Economic History of Continental Europe from the Fifteenth to the Eighteenth Century* (New York: Holmes & Meier Publishers, 1976), p. 25.

24. Olwen H. Hufton, *The Poor of Eighteenth Century France: 1750–1789* (Oxford: Clarendon Press, 1974), p. 17.

25. Robert Heilbroner, *The Worldly Philosophers: The Lives, Times and Ideas of the Great Economic Thinkers* (New York: Simon and Schuster, 1961), p. 19.

26. Friedrich Engels, *The Condition of the Working Class in England* (Stanford, CA.: Stanford University Press, 1968), p. 110.

27. John Boswell, *The Kindness of Strangers The Abandonment of Children in Western Europe from Late Antiquity to the Renaissance* (New York: Pantheon Books, 1988), p. 15.

28. Ibid., pp. 15–16.

29. Ibid., p. 19.

30. Hufton, p. 350.

31. Gertrude Himmelfarb, *The Idea of Poverty: England in the Early Industrial Age* (New York: Vintage Books, 1985), pp. 100–144.

32. Polanyi, pp. 77–79.

33. Shari L. Thurer, *The Myths of Motherhood: How Culture Reinvents the Good Mother* (New York: Houghton Mifflin Co., 1994), pp. 178–179.

34. Philip Cushman, *Constructing the Self, Constructing America: A Cultural History of Psychotherapy* (New York: Addison-Wesley, 1995), p. 96.

35. Roy Porter, *English Society in the Eighteenth Century* (New York: Penguin Books, 1982), p. 147.

36. Engels, p. 325.

37. Ibid., p. 329.

38. See Michèle Barrett and Mary McIntosh, *The Anti-Social Family* (London: Verso, 1991).

39. There is of course controversy regarding the origin of the nuclear family. While Frederich Engels' *The Origin of the Private Family, Private Property and the State*, trans. by E. B. Leacock (New York: International Publishers, 1972) used evidence from anthropologist Lewis Morgan to show that the private, nuclear family arose with the advent of capitalism, and Philippe Ariés' *Centuries of Childhood: A Social History of Family Life*, trans. by Robert Baldick (New York: Vintage Books, 1962) provides some evidence that not only confirms this but proposes that childhood was not even considered a distinct phase of life until modern times, other theorists such as Peter Laslett in his book *The World We Have Lost* (London: Methuen, 1972) attempt to refute this. But the controversy still rages. Most of the debate focuses on research methods. A wonderful discussion of this disagreement can be found in Shari Thurer's *The Myths of Motherhood: How Culture Reinvents the Good Mother* (New York: Houghton Mifflin, 1994), pp. 81–223. Much of this controversy seems to be broken down along political lines. But it is safe to say that the nuclear family does not appear in any sizable way until the advent of capitalism in the west.

40. Karl Marx and Friedrich Engels, *The Communist Manifesto* (Middlesex: Penguin Books, 1967), p. 82.

41. Ibid., pp. 120–21.

42. Robert Hollinger, *Postmodernism and the Social Sciences* (London: Sage Publications, 1994), pp. 21–25.

43. Rajani Kannepalli Kanth, *Breaking with the Enlightenment: The Twilight of History and the Rediscovery of Utopia* (Highlands, NJ.: Humanities Press, 1997), p. 130.

44. Emile Durkheim, *Suicide* (1897), trans. J. Spaulding and G. Simpson, ed. and intro. George Simpson (New York: The Free Press, 1951), p. 256.

45. Wilhelm Reich, *The Mass Psychology of Fascism* (1946) (New York: Farrar, Straus & Giroux, 1970).

46. Fromm, *op. cit.*, pp. 157–230.

47. Paul A. Robinson, *The Freudian Left: Wilhelm Reich, Geza Roheim and Herbert Marcuse* (New York: Harper & Row, 1969), p. 46.

48. Alex Callinicos, *Against Post Modernism: A Marxist Critique* (Cambridge: Polity Press, 1989).

49. Zygmunt Bauman, *Modernity and the Holocaust* (New York: Polity, 1991), p. 17.

50. Ibid., p. 8. Quoted from Henry Feingold "How Unique is the Holocaust?" in *Genocide: Critical Issues of the Holocaust*, ed. Alex Grobman and Daniel Landes (Los Angeles: The Simon Wiesenthal Centre, 1983), pp. 399–400.

51. Marshall Berman, *All That Is Solid Melts Into Air* (New York: Penguin Books, 1988).

52. Matei Calinescu, *Five Faces of Modernity: Avant-Garde, Decadence, Kitsch* (Bloomington: Indiana University Press, 1977) , p. 41.

53. Michael Hardt and Antonio Negri, *Empire* (Cambridge, MA.: Harvard University Press), p. 75.

54. Anthony Giddens, *The Consequences of Modernity* (Stanford, CA.: Stanford University Press, 1990), p. 139.

55. Ibid., p. 139.

56. Anthony Giddens, *Modernity and Self-Identity: Self and Society in the Late Modern Age* (Stanford, CA.: Stanford University Press, 1991), pp. 10–34.

57. David Harvey, *The Condition of Postmodernity: An Enquiry into the Origins of Cultural Change* (Oxford: Basil Blackwell, 1989), p. 205.

58. Giddens, *op. cit.*, p. 18.

59. Ibid., pp. 181–202.

60. Anthony Giddens, *Modernity and Self-Identity: Self and Society in the Late Modern Age*, p. 46.

61. Anna Yeatman, "A Feminist Theory of Social Differentiation," in *Feminism/Modernism*, ed. L. J. Nicholson (London: Routledge, 1990), pp. 285–286.

62. Hollinger, *op. cit.*, pp. 1–56.

63. Blaise Pascal, *Pensees*, introd., T. S. Eliot (New York: Dutton Paperbacks, 1958), no. 72.

64. A. O. Lovejoy, "On the Discrimination of Romantics," (1924) reprinted in H. M. Abrams, ed., *English Romantic Poets: Modern Essays in Criticism* (New York: Oxford University Press, 1960).

65. Barbara Johnson, "1820 Alphonse de Lamartine Publishes Méditations poétiques: The Lady in the Lake," in *A New History of French Literature* ed.

Denis Hollier (Cambridge, MA.: Harvard University Press, 1989), pp. 627–632.

66. Ibid., p. 629.

67. See Carolyn Merchant, *The Death of Nature: Women, Ecology and the Scientific Revolution* (San Francisco, CA.: Harper & Row Publishers, 1980).

68. Mario Praz, *Romantic Agony* (New York: Meridian Books, 1960).

69. Daniel Dervin, "Abandonment: A Dominant Pattern in the Development of Creative Writers, Philosophers and Scientists Since the Seventeenth Century," *Journal of Psychohistory*, vol. 15 (2), 1987 (Fall), pp. 153–187.

70. Gustave Flaubert, *Madame Bovary* (1857), trans. M. Marmur (New York: Penguin Books, 1964), p. 79.

71. Ibid., p. 200.

72. Ibid., p. 279.

73. Ibid., p. 77.

74. Colin Campbell, *The Romantic Ethic and the Spirit of Modern Consumerism* (New York: Basil Blackwell, 1987).

75. Ibid., pp. 175–176.

76. Mario Vargas Llosa, *The Perpetual Orgy*, trans. H. Lane (New York: Farrar, Straus, & Giroux, 1986), p. 139.

77. Fredric Jameson, *The Political Unconscious Narrative as a Symbolic Act* (Ithaca, NY.: Cornell University Press, 1981), p. 184.

78. Berman, *op. cit.*, p. 36.

CHAPTER 2: ABANDONMENT AND SOCIAL THEORY

1. Robert Nisbet, *Sociology as an Art Form* (New York: Oxford University Press, 1976).

2. Georg F. W. Hegel, *Phenomenology of Spirit*, trans. by A. V. Miller with analysis of text and foreword by J. N. Findlay (New York: Oxford University Press, 1977).

3. Hegel, p. 119.

4. Robert Solomon, *From Hegel to Existentialism* (New York: Oxford University Press, 1987), p. 8.

5. Hegel, pp. 104–110.

6. Hegel, p. 110.

7. Hegel, pp. 8, 111–119.

8. Hegel, pp. 136–138.

9. Søren Kierkegaard, *The Concept of Dread*, trans. by W. Lowrie (Princeton, NJ.: Princeton University Press, 1957).

10. Kierkegaard, pp. 37–46.

11. Kierkegaard, pp. 68–72.

12. Karl Marx, *Economic and Philosophic Manuscripts*, trans. and ed. M. Milligan (Moscow: Foreign Languages Publishing House, 1956).

13. Karl Marx, *Das Kapital*, vol. I, trans. S. Moore and E. Aveling and ed. F. Engels (New York: International Publishers, 1967), pp. 71–83.

14. Karl Marx, *Economic and Philosophic Manuscripts*, pp. 67–84.

15. Sigmund Freud, *Civilization and Its Discontents* (New York: W. W. Norton, 1961), pp. 21–27.

16. Sigmund Freud, *Beyond the Pleasure Principle*, trans. J. Strachey (New York: Bantham Books, 1967), pp. 32–38.

17. Sigmund Freud, "Three Essays on the theory of Sexuality," in *The Standard Edition of the Complete Psychological Works of Sigmund Freud*, vol. 7, trans. and ed. James Strachey (London: Hogarth Press, 1953), p. 125–245.

18. Sigmund Freud, "Mourning and Melancholia," in *The Standard Edition of the Complete Psychological Works of Sigmund Freud*, vol. 14, 1947, pp. 237–258.

19. Sander Gilman, Helen King, Roy Porter, G. S. Rousseau, and Elaine Showalter, *Hysteria Beyond Freud* (Berkeley: University of California Press, 1993).

20. Erich Fromm, *Escape From Freedom* (New York: Avon Books, 1969).

21. Wilhelm Reich, *The Mass Psychology of Fascism*, trans. Vincent Carfagno (New York: Farrar, Straus & Giroux, 1970).

22. Theodor Adorno, Else Frenkel-Brunswick, Daniel J. Levinson, and R. N. Sanford. *The Authoritarian Personality* (New York: W. W. Norton and Company, 1982).

23. See, for instance, Richard Sennett, *The Uses of Disorder* (New York: Vintage Books, 1970) and Christopher Lasch, *The Culture of Narcissism* (New York: Warner Books, 1979).

24. Fromm, *op. cit.*, pp. 208–230.

25. Herbert Marcuse, *One Dimensional Man: Studies in the Ideology of Advanced Industrial Society* (Boston: Beacon Press, 1964).

26. Herbert Marcuse, *Eros and Civilization: A Philosophical Inquiry into Freud* (Boston: Beacon Press, 1966), pp. 78–96.

27. Georg Lukács, *History and Class Consciousness: Studies in Marxist Dialectics*, trans. by R. Livingstone (Cambridge, MA.: MIT Press, 1971).

28. Herbert Marcuse, *Eros and Civilization* (Boston: Beacon Press, 1955).

29. Jean-Paul Sartre, *Existentialism*, trans. Bernard Friedmann (New York: Philosophical Library, 1947), p. 34.

30. Madan Sarup, *An Introductory Guide to Post-Structuralism and Postmodernism* (Athens, GA.: The University of Georgia Press, 1989), p. 115.

31. Robert Hollinger, *Postmodernism and the Social Sciences* (Thousand Oaks, CA.: Sage Publications, 1994), p. 79.

32. Charles Lemert, "The Uses of French Structuralism in Sociology." In Georg Ritzer, ed., *Frontiers of Social Theory: The New Syntheses* (New York: Columbia University Press), pp. 230–254.

33. Jacques Derrida, *Writing and Difference* (Chicago: University of Chicago Press, 1978).

34. Zygmunt Bauman, *Intimations of Postmodernity* (London: Routledge, 1992), p. 101.

35. The semeiotics of this are best illustrated in Christopher Jencks' reference to the dynamiting of the Pruitt-Igoe public housing projects in St. Louis on July 15, 1972 (see *The Language of Postmodern Architecture*, New York: Rizzoli, 1977)—illustrating not only an abandonment of the poor and a tearing-down of a prize-winning modernist Corbusierian design that had been built as a visionary response to poverty in the early 1960s, but the end of modernism, itself. This symbol has been revisited by several discussants of postmodernity including David Gordon in *The Postmodern Condition* (1989) and Charles Lemert in "The Uses of French Structuralisms in Sociology," in *Frontiers of Social Theory*, ed. G. Ritzer (1990).

36. Fredric Jameson, "Postmodernism or the Cultural Logic of Late Capitalism," in *New Left Review*, 146, 1984, pp. 53–92.

37. Jacques Lacan, *The Language of Self*, trans. A. Wilden (Baltimore, MD.: The Johns Hopkins University Press, 1976).

38. Jean Baudrillard, *For a Critique of the Political Economy of the Sign* (St. Louis, MO.: Telos Press, 1981).

39. Fredric Jameson, *The Cultural Turn* (London: Verso, 1998), pp. 1–2.

40. Douglas Kellner, *Critical Theory, Marxism and Modernity* (Baltimore, MD.: The Johns Hopkins University Press, 1989), pp. 167–175.

41. Ben Agger, *The Discourse of Domination: From the Frankfurt School to Postmodernism* (Evanston, IL.: Northwestern University Press, 1992), p. 295.

42. Max Weber, *The Protestant Ethic and the Spirit of Capitalism*, trans. by T. Parsons (London: Unwin Hyman, 1989).

43. John Boswell, *The Kindness of Strangers* (New York: Pantheon Books, 1988), p. 15.

CHAPTER THREE: PSYCHOLOGY OF SEPARATION AND LOSS

1. For example: Timothy Bright, *A Treatise of Melancholie* (1586); André Du Laurens, *A Discourse of the Preservation of Sight, of Melancholike Diseases, of Rheumes. And of Old Age* (1599); Thomas Wright, *The Passions of the Mind*; Thomas Adams, *Diseases of the Soul* (1616).

2. Wolf Lepenies, *Melancholy and Society*, trans. Jeremy Gaines and Doris Jones (Cambridge, MA.: Harvard University Press, 1992).

3. Ibid., p. 11.

4. Quoted in Wolf Lepenies, *op. cit.*, p. 64. From Johann Georg Zimmermann, *Solitude Considered, with Respect to Its Influence upon the Mind and the Heart*, trans., J. B. Mercier (London, 1796).

5. Ibid.

6. Ibid., pp. 123–124.

7. Ibid., p. 124.

8. Michel Foucault, *Madness and Civilization* (New York: Vintage Books, 1988), pp. 117–158.

9. Ibid., p. 124.

10. For example: Russell Jacoby, *The Repression of Psychoanalysis: Otto Fenichel and the Political Freudians* (New York: Basic Books, 1983) and Paul Robinson, *The Freudian Left: Wilhelm Reich, Geza Roheim and Herbert Marcuse* (New York: Harper & Row, 1969).

11. Lepenies, *op. cit.*, p. 124.

12. Eli Zaretsky, *Capitalism, the Family and Personal Life* (New York: Harper & Row, 1976), p. 99.

13. Frederich Engels, *The Origin of the Family, Private Property and the State* (New York: International Publishers, 1972), p. 121.

14. Richard Sennett, *The Fall of Public Man: The Social Psychology of Capitalism* (New York: Vintage Books, 1974), p. 179.

15. Engels, *op. cit.*, pp. 94–146.

16. Sigmund Freud, "Inhibitions, Symptoms, and Anxiety: Addendum C: Anxiety Pain and Mourning," (1926) reprinted in *Essential Papers On Object Loss,* ed. Rita Frankel, trans. James Strachey (New York: New York University Press, 1994), p. 59.

17. René Spitz, *The First Year of Life: A Psychoanalytic Study of Normal and Deviant Development of Object Relations* (New York: International University Press, 1965); William Goldfarb, "Effects of Psychological Deprivation in Infancy and Subsequent Stimulation." *American Journal of Psychiatry,* No. 102 (1945), pp. 18–55; Margaret Mahler, "Certain Aspects of the Separation-Individuation Phase" *Psychoanalytic Quarterly,* No. 32 (1963), pp. 1–14.

18. Melanie Klein, "The Origins of Transference," in *The Selected Melanie Klein,* ed. Juliet Mitchell (New York: The Free Press, 1986), p. 206.

19. Jay R. Greenberg and Stephen A. Mitchell, *Object Relations in Psychoanalytic Theory* (Cambridge, MA.: Harvard University Press, 1983), p. 158.

20. W. R. D. Fairbairn, "Schizoid Factors in Personality," in *An Object-Relations Theory of Personality,* ed. W. R. D. Fairbairn (New York: Basic Books, 1941), pp. 3–27.

21. Jay R. Greenberg and Stephen A. Mitchell, *op. cit.*, p. 190.

22. D. W. Winnicott, *Deprivation and Delinquency,* ed., Clare Winnicott, Ray Shepherd and Madeleine Davis (London: Routledge, 1997).

23. John Bowlby, *Attachment* (New York: Basic Books, 1971); *Separation: Anxiety and Anger* (New York: Basic Books, 1975); *Loss: Sadness and Depression* (New York: Basic Books, 1981); *A Secure Base* (New York: Basic Books, 1988).

24. John Bowlby, *A Secure Base*, p. 30.

25. Erik Erikson, *Childhood and Society,* Second Edition (New York: W. W. Norton, 1963), p. 247.

26. John Bowlby, *A Secure Base*, p. 147.

27. Yi-Fu Tuan, *Landscapes of Fear* (New York: Pantheon Books, 1979), pp. 19–20.

28. The Brothers Grimm, "Hansel and Gretel," *Grimm's Fairy Tales*, trans. E. V. Lucas, Lucy Crane and Marian Edwards (NewYork: Grosset and Dunlap), 1945.

29. See Ernst Pawel, *The Nightmare of Reason: A Life of Franz Kafka* (New York: Farrar, Straus, & Giroux, 1984), p. 18.

30. Else Frenkel-Brunswik, "Parents Childhood, Sex, People and Self As Seen Through the Interviews," in *The Authoritarian Personality*, ed. Adorno et. al. (New York: W. W. Norton,1950), p. 257.

31. Philippe Ariès, *Centuries of Childhood: A Social History of the Family* (New York: Vintage Books, 1962), pp. 33–49.

32. Sennett, *op. cit.*, p. 94.

33. Daniel Dervin, "Abandonment: A Dominant Pattern in the Development of Creative Writers, Philosophers and Scientists Since the Seventeenth Century," *Journal of Psychohistory*, Fall 1987, vol. 15 (2), pp. 156–157.

34. Patrick F. Quinn, *The French Face of Edgar Poe* (Carbondale: Southern Illinois Press, 1957), p. 73.

35. J. Gerald Kennedy, *Poe, Death and the Life of Writing* (New Haven: Yale University Press, 1987), p. 91.

36. Ibid., p. 95.

37. From the artist's personal manuscript (T 2759) in the Munch Museum Archives and cited in Reinhold Heller *Munch His Life and Work* (Chicago: University of Chicago Press, 1984), pp. 14–15.

38. Erik H. Erikson, *Childhood and Society* (New York: W. W. Norton & Co., 1963).

39. Ibid., p. 249.

40. Ibid., p. 250.

41. Marcelle Marini, *Jacques Lacan: The French Connection*, trans. Anne Tomiche (New Brunswick, NJ.: Rutgers University Press, 1992), p. 24.

42. Ibid., pp. 47–53

43. Karen Horney, *New Ways in Psychoanalysis* (New York: W. W. Norton & Co., 1966), p. 90.

44. Ibid., p. 98.

45. Ibid.

46. Ibid.

47. Dorothy Dinnerstein, *The Mermaid and the Minotaur: Sexual Arrangements and Human Malaise* (New York: Harper and Row, 1976).

48. Ibid., p. 95.

49. Nancy Chodorow, *The Reproduction of Mothering: Psychoanalysis and the Sociology of Gender* (Berkeley: University of California Press, 1978).

50. Ibid., pp. 11–39.

51. Gwendolyn Stevens and Sheldon Gardner, *Separation Anxiety and the Dread of Abandonment in Adult Males* (Westport, CT.: Praeger, 1994).

52. Judith Butler, *Gender Trouble: Feminism and the Subversion of Identity* (New York: Routledge, 1990).

53. Jessica Benjamin, *The Bonds of Love: Psychoanalysis, Feminism, and the Problem of Domination* (New York: Pantheon Books, 1988).

54. Ibid., p. 6.

55. Ibid., p. 7.

56. Ibid., p. 19.

57. Ibid., p. 63.

58. Jonathan Bloom-Feshbach and Sally Bloom-Feshbach, *The Psychology of Separation and Loss: Perspectives on Development, Life Transitions and Clinical Practice* (San Francisco: Jossey-Bass Publishers, 1987).

59. Daniel L. Buccino, "The Commodification of the Object in Object Relations Theory," *Psychoanalytic Review* 80(1) Spring 1993, pp. 123–134.

60. Ibid., p. 127.

61. Ibid., p. 128.

62. C. Fred Alford, *Narcissism: Socrates, the Frankfurt School and Psychoanalytic Theory* (New Haven: Yale University Press, 1988).

63. Marion Toplin, "The Borderline Patient," in *Advances in Self Psychology*, ed. A. Goldstein (New York: Gilford Press, 1980).

64. Otto Kernbeig, *Object Relations Theory and Clinical Psychoanalysis* (New York: Jason Aronson, 1976).

65. Colin Murray Parkes, *Bereavement: Studies of Grief in Adult Life* (New York: International Universities Press, 1972).

66. David Frisby, *Fragments of Modernity* (Cambridge, MA.: MIT Press, 1986), p. 62.

CHAPTER FOUR: FRAGMENTATION AND ABANDONMENT OF CONSCIENCE

1. Carl Schorske, *Fin-de-siècle Vienna: Politics and Culture* (New York: Knopf, 1979), p. xix.

2. Eugene Lunn, *Marxism and Modernism: An Historical Study of Lukács, Brecht, Benjamin and Adorno* (Berkeley: The University of California Press, 1884), p. 34.

3. Herbert Read, *Art Now: A History of Modern Painting and Sculpture* (New York: Harcourt Brace, 1937), pp. 58–59.

4. Malcolm Bradbury and James McFarlane, eds., *Modernism: A Guide to European Literature 1890–1930* (New York: Penguin Books, 1976), p. 25.

5. Ibid., p. 26.

6. Adam Smith, *Lectures on Jurisprudence*, ed. by R. Meek, D. Raphael, and P. G. Stein (Oxford: Oxford University Press, 1978), p. 539.

7. Max Weber, *Economy and Society*, ed. by G. Roth and Claus Wittich (Berkeley: The University of California Press, 1978), p. 224.

8. Ibid., p. 224.

9. David Frisby, "Preface to the Second Edition," in Georg Simmel, *The Philosophy of Money* (London: Routledge, 1978), pp. xvi–xlii.

10. Georg Simmel, *op. cit.*, pp. 65–66.

11. Ibid., p. 66.

12. Ibid., p. 449.

13. Ibid., p. 451.

14. Lee Congdon, *The Young Lukács* (Chapel Hill, NC.: The University of North Carolina Press, 1983), p. 85.

15. Ibid., pp. 3–11.

16. Georg Lukács, History of Class Consciousness: Studies in Marxist Dialectics (Cambridge, MA.: MIT Press, 1971), pp. 83-223.

17. Ibid., p. 84.

18. Ibid., p. 87.

19. Ibid., p. 88.

20. Ibid., p. 88.

21. Ibid., p. 89.

22. Ibid., p. 91.

23. Ibid., p. 93.

24. Ibid., p. 99.

25. Ibid., pp. 110–149.

26. Ibid., pp. 111–121.

27. Friedrich Nietzsche, *The Antichrist*, Book 1. 11 in *The Portable Nietzsche*, ed. and trans. Walter Kaufmann (New York: Viking Press, 1968), p. 577.

28. Alasdair MacIntyre, *After Virtue, Second Edition* (Notre Dame, IN.: University of Notre Dame Press, 1984), pp. 43–47.

29. Ibid., pp. 256–278.

30. Lukács, *op. cit.*, p. 99.

31. Erving Goffman, *The Presentation of Self in Everyday Life* (New York: Avon Books, 1959), p. 253. (Also, see MacIntyre's critique in *After Virtue op cit.*, pp. 32, 35).

32. Ibid.

33. Philip Manning, *Erving Goffman and Modern Sociology* (Stanford, CA.: Stanford University Press, 1992), p. 44.

34. Lukács, p. 74.

35. Lawrence Beesley, *The Loss of the S.S. Titanic* (New York: Houghton Mifflin Co., 1912), pp. 81–82.

36. Leo Gurko, *Joseph Conrad: Giant in Exile* (New York: Macmillan Co., 1962), pp. 7–15.

37. Fredric Jameson, T*he Political Unconscious: Narrative as a Socially Symbolic Act* (Ithaca, NY.: Cornell University Press, 1981), pp. 211–212.

38. Herbert Marcuse, *Eros and Civilization* (Boston: Beacon Press, 1966), p. 94.

39. Herbert Marcuse, *One-Dimensional Man* (Boston: Beacon Press, 1964), p. 12.

40. Ibid., p. 5.

41. Ibid., p. 79.

42. Jürgen Habermas, *Toward A Rational Society* (Boston: Beacon Press, 1970), p. 112.

43. Martin Heidegger, "The Question Concerning Technology," in *Basic Writings from Being and Time (1927) to The Task of Thinking (1964)*, ed. David Farrell Krell (San Francisco, CA.: Harper and Row, 1977), pp. 282–317.

44. Andrew Feenberg, *Critical Theory of Technology* (New York: Oxford University Press, 1991), p. 189.

45. Zygmunt Bauman, *Modernity and The Holocaust* (Ithaca, NY.: Cornell University Press, 1989), p. 26.

46. Peter Berger, Brigitte Berger, and Hansfried Kellner, *The Homeless Mind: Modernization and Consciousness* (New York: Vintage Books, 1974).

47. Ibid., p. 27.

48. Ibid., p. 28.

49. Ibid., p. 34.

50. Robert J. Lifton, *The Nazi Doctors: Medical Killing and the Psychology of Genocide* (New York: Basic Books, 1986).

51. Stanley Milgram, *Obedience to Authority* (New York: Harper & Row, 1969), pp. 145–146.

52. Bauman, *op. cit.*, p. 160.

53. Erich Fromm, *Escape from Freedom* (New York: Avon Books, 1941).

54. Lynn S. Chancer, *Sadomasochism in Everyday Life* (New Brunswick, NJ.: Rutgers University Press, 1992).

55. C. Wright Mills, *The Sociological Imagination* (New York: Oxford University Press, 1977), p. 171.

56. Ashley Montagu and Floyd Matson, *The Dehumanization of Man* (New York: McGraw Hill, 1983), p. 10.

57. Donna Haraway, *Simians, Cyborgs, and Women: The Reinvention of Nature* (New York: Routledge, 1991), p. 51.

58. Jane Flax, "Political Philosophy and the Patriarchal Unconscious: A Psychoanalytic Perspective on Epistemology and Metaphysics,"in *Discovering Reality: Feminists Perspectives on Epistemology, Metaphysics and Philosophy of Science*, ed. S. Harding (Dordrecht: Reidel,1983).

59. Bauman, *op. cit.*, p. 174.

60. Ibid., 175.

61. Ibid., pp. 198–199.

62. Ibid., p. 199.

63. Zygmunt Bauman, *Imitations of Postmodernity* (London: Routledge Press, 1992), p. xxii.

64. Alasdair MacIntyre, *After Virtue*, second edition, (Notre Dame, IN.: University of Notre Dame Press, 1984), p. 227.

65. Ibid., p. 228.

66. J. B. Schneewind, "The Misfortunes of Virtue," Ethics, 101 (1990), pp. 43–63.

67. For a fuller discussion see Athol Fitzgibbons, *Adam Smith's System of Liberty, Wealth and Virtue: The Moral and Political Foundations of The Wealth of Nations* (Oxford: Clarendon Press, 1995).

68. Louis Althusser, "Ideology and Ideological State Apparatuses." In *Lenin and Philosophy and Other Essays* (London: New Left Books, 1971).

69. Gilles Deleuze and Félix Guattari, *Anti-Oedipus*, trans. R. Hurley, M. Seem and H. Lane (London: Athlone, 1984), p. 262–270.

CHAPTER FIVE: ABANDONMENT OF COMMUNITY

1. George Hillery, Jr., "Definitions of Community: Areas of Agreement," *Rural Sociology*, vol. 20., 1955, pp. 779–791.

2. Robert Edwards, "Exile, Self, and Society," in Maria-Ines Lagos-Pope, ed., *Exile in Literature* (London: Associated University Presses, 1988), pp. 16–17.

3. Ibid., p. 15.

4. Edward Shils, "Center and Periphery," in *The Constitution of Society* (Chicago: University of Chicago Press, 1972), pp. 93–94

5. Paul Tabori, *The Anatomy of Exile: A Semantic and Historical Study* (London: Harrap, 1972), pp. 43–45.

6. Jeffrey Sammons, *Literary Sociology and Practical Criticism: An Inquiry* (Bloomington: Indiana University Press, 1977), pp. 16–38.

7. Frances Claudon, *The Concise Encyclopedia of Romanticism* (Secaucus, NJ.: Chartwell Books, 1980), pp. 54, 76–77.

8. Jack J. Boies, *The Lost Domain: Avatars of Earthly Paradise in Western Literature* (Lanham, MD.: University Press of America, 1983), p. 1.

9. Ibid., p. 2.

10. Leo Marx, *The Machine in the Garden* (New York: Oxford University Press, 1964), pp. 9–10.

11. Ellwood C. Parry III, *The Art of Thomas Cole: Ambition and Imagination* (Cranbury, NJ.: Associated University Presses, 1988), p. 77.

12. Frederick Jackson Turner, *The Frontier in American History* (New York: H. Holt and Company, 1920).

13. Ferdinand Tönnies, *Community and Society*, trans. Charles P. Loomis (New York: Harper and Row, 1963).

14. Ibid., p. 40.

15. Ibid.

16. Emile Durkheim, *The Division of Labor in Society*, trans. W. D. Wells (New York: The Free Press, 1984).

17. Durkheim, *The Division of Labor in Society*, pp. 337–340.

18. Louis Wirth, "Urbanism as a Way of Life," *American Journal of Sociology*, 44, July 1938.

19. David Riesman, *The Lonely Crowd: A Study of the Changing American Character* (New Haven: Yale University Press, 1950).

20. Ibid., p. 4.

21. Richard Sennett, *The Fall of Public Man: On the Social Psychology of Capitalism* (New York: Vintage Books, 1974), p. 301.

22. Jean-Jacques Rousseau, *The Confessions*, trans. J. M. Cohen (New York.: Penguin Books, 1953), p. 19.

23. Ibid., pp.25–26.

24. Ibid., p. 27.

25. Ibid., p. 28.

26. Jean-Jacques Rousseau, *The Social Contract*, trans. Maurice Cranston (New York: Penguin Books, 1968).

27. Rousseau, *The Confessions*, p. 49.

28. Jean-Jacques Rousseau, *Reveries of the Solitary Walker*, trans. P. France (London: Penguin Books, 1971), p. 27.

29. Ibid., pp. 87–88.

30. Henri Lefebvre, *The Production of Space* (New York: Oxford University Press, 1991), p. 341.

31. Henri Lefebvre,"Industrialization and Urbanization," in *Writings on Cities*, trans. and ed. E. Kofman and E. Lebas (Oxford: Blackwell Publishers, 1996), p. 76.

32. Richard Wolin, "Walter Benjamin's Failed Messianism," *The New Republic On Line*, January 19, 2000: www:thenewrepublic.com/012400/wolino12400.

33. Walter Benjamin, *The Arcades Project*, trans. H. Eiland and K. McLaughlin (Cambridge, MA.: The Belknap Press, 1999), p. 874.

34. Ibid., p. 42.

35. Sharon Zukin, *Landscapes of Power from Detroit to Disney World* (Berkeley: University of California Press, 1991), p. 11.

36. Ibid., p. 5.

37. Margaret Crawford, "The World in a Shopping Mall," in *Variations on a Theme Park: The New American City and the End of Public Place*, ed. Michael Sorkin (New York: Hill and Wang, 1992), pp. 29–30.

38. Mike Davis, *City of Quartz* (New York: Vintage Books, 1992), p. 18.

39. Ibid., p. 86.

40. Ibid., p 227.

41. Ibid., p. 228.

42. Ibid., p. 123.

43. Joseph Schumpeter, *Capitalism, Socialism and Democracy* (New York: Harper and Brothers, 1962), p. 83.

44. J. John Palen, *The Urban World, 4th edition* (New York: McGraw Hill, 1992), p. 276.

45. Jane Jacobs, *The Death and Life of Great American Cities* (New York: Vintage Press, 1961).

46. Herbert Gans, *The Urban Villagers: Group and Class in the Life of Italian Americans* (Glencoe, IL.: The Free Press, 1962).

47. Marc Fried, "Grieving for a Lost Home," in *The Urban Condition*, ed. Leonard Duhl (New York: Basic Books, 1963), p. 152.

48. Ibid.

49. Michael Sorkin, *op. cit.* "Introduction," p. xiv.

50. George Ritzer, *The McDonaldization of Society* (Thousand Oaks, CA.: Pine Forge Press, 1993).

51. Quoted in Nathan Silver, *Lost New York* (New York: Crown Publishers, 1967), p. 38.

52. Barry Bluestone and Bennett Harrison, *The Deindustrialization of America*, (New York: Basic Books, 1982).

53. Ibid., p. 11.

54. Bureau of Economic Analysis, "International Investment Data—U.S. Direct Investments Abroad—Capital Outflows" (2002).

55. Robert Reich, "Who Is Us?" *Harvard Business Review*, January–February 1990.

56. Saskia Sassen, *Globalization and its Discontents* (New York: The New Press, 1998), p. 41.

57. Robert D. Putnam, *Bowling Alone: The Collapse and Revival of American Community* (New York: Simon & Schuster, 2000).

58. *Population Bulletin*, vol. 53, no. 3, September 1998.

CHAPTER SIX: ABANDONMENT OF NATURE

1. Barbara Johnson, "My Monster/Myself," in Harold Bloom, ed., *Modern Critical Interpretations: Mary Shelley's Frankenstein* (New York: Chelsea House Publishers, 1987), pp. 55–66.

2. Sandra Gilbert and Susan Gubar, "Horror's Twin: Mary Shelley's Monstrous Eve," in *Modern Critical Views: Mary Shelley*, ed. Harold Bloom (New York: Chelsea House Publishers, 1985), p. 120.

3. Bonnie Reyford Neumann, *The Lonely Muse: A Critical Biography of Mary Wollstonecraft Shelley* (Saltzberg: Institute for English and American Studies, University of Saltzberg, 1979), pp. 4–44.

4. Ibid., p. 3.

5. Harold Bloom, "Introduction," in *Modern Critical Interpretations*, p. 4.

6. Norbert Elias, T*he Civilizing Process: The Development of Manners*, trans. Edmund Jephcott (Oxford: Blackwell, 1994).

7. Fred Davis, *Fashion, Culture and Identity* (Chicago: University of Chicago Press, 1992).

8. Elias, *op. cit.*, p. 154.

9. Michel Foucault, *The History of Sexuality: An Introduction*, trans. Robert Hurley (New York: Vintage Books, 1990 [1978]), pp. 5–6.

10. Robert Hughes, *The Shock of the New* (New York: Alfred Knopf, 1980), p. 55.

11. William Leiss, *The Domination of Nature* (New York: George Braziller, Inc., 1972), pp.179–180.

12. Frederich Engels, *The Condition of the Working Class in England*, trans. W. O. Henderson and W. H. Chaloner (Stanford, CA.: Stanford University Press, 1958), p. 331.

13. Donald Worster, "The Vulnerable Earth: Towards a Planetary History," in *The Ends of the Earth: Perspectives on Modern Environmental History*, ed. Donald Worster (Cambridge: Cambridge University Press, 1988), p. 11.

14. Herman Schwartz, *States Versus Markets: History, Geography and Development of the International Political Economy* (New York: St. Martin's Press, 1994), pp. 85–86.

15. Alvin W. Gouldner, *The Coming Crisis of Western Sociology* (New York: Avon Books, 1970), p. 115.

16. Denis Cosgrove, *Social Formation and Symbolic Landscape* (Totowa, N.J.: Barnes & Noble Books, 1984), p. 230.

17. See for instance Eugene Lunn, *Marxism & Modernism: An Historical Analysis of Lukács, Brecht, Benjamin and Adorno* (Berkeley: University of California Press, 1984) as well as Robert Nisbet, *Sociology as an Art Form* (New York: Oxford University Press, 1976).

18. H. G. Schenk, *The Mind of the European Romantics* (New York: Oxford University Press, 1979), p. 26.

19. Jonathan Bate, *Romantic Ecology: Wordsworth and the Environmental Tradition* (London: Routledge, 1991), p. 3.

20. Ibid., pp. 47–49.

21. Ibid., p. 47.

22. Ibid., p. 43. (Quoted from *Guide to the Lakes, The Fifth Edition*, 1835, ed. E. de Sélincourt [Oxford, 1906, repr. 1977]).

23. Albert Fine, *Frederick Law Olmstead and the American Environmental Tradition* (New York: George Braziller, 1972).

24. Charles R. Koppes, "Efficiency, Equity, Esthetic: Shifting Themes in American Conservation," in Donald Worster, *op. cit.*, p. 231.

25. Alison Byerly, "The Uses of Landscape," in Cheryll Glotfelty and Harold Fromm, eds. *The Ecocentrism Reader* (Athens, GA.: University of Georgia Press, 1996), p. 53.

26. Cosgrove, *op. cit.*, p. 20.

27. Jean-François Lyotard, *The Inhuman* (Stanford, CA.: Stanford University Press, 1991), pp. 182–190.

28. Alan MacFarlane, *The Culture of Capitalism* (Oxford: Basil Blackwell, 1987), pp. 192–196.

29. Max Weber, *General Economic History*, trans. Frank Knight and intr. Ira Cohen (New Brunswick, N.J.:Transaction Publishers, 1992), pp. 84–88.

30. Roy Porter, *English Society in the Eighteenth Century* (New York: Penguin Books, 1982), p. 226.

31. Ibid., pp, 226–227.

32. Murray Bookchin, *The Limits of the City* (New York: Harper Colophon Books, 1974), p. 57.

33. Porter, *op. cit.*, p. 229.

34. Cosgrove, *op. cit.*, pp. 236–237.

35. Ibid., p. 237.

36. Rupert Croft-Cooke and W. S. Meadmore, *Buffalo Bill: The Legend, the Man of Action, the Showman* (London: Sidgewick and Jackson, 1952).

37. Umberto Eco, *Travels in Hyper Reality: Essays*, trans. William Weaver (New York: Harcourt Brace Jovanovich, 1983), p. 7.

38. Jean Baudrillard, *Simulacra and Simulations* trans. Paul Foss, Paul Patton, and Philip Beitchman (New York: Semiotext, 1983), pp. 1–13.

39. Lyotard, *op. cit.*, pp. 97–101.

40. Colin Campbell, *The Romantic Ethic and the Spirit of Consumerism* (Oxford: Basil Blackwell, 1987).

41. Ibid., p. 200.

42. Herbert Marcuse, *One Dimensional Man* (Boston: Beacon Press, 1964).

43. Jean Baudrillard, *The Mirror of Production*, trans. Mark Poster (St. Louis, MO.: Telos Press, 1975), p. 146.

44. Rachael Bowlby, *Just Looking: Consumer Culture in Dreiser, Gissing and Zola* (New York: Methuen, 1985), pp. 70–71.

45. Ralph Metzner, "Psychopathology of Human-Nature Relationships," in *Ecopsychology: The Voice of the Earth*, eds. Theodore Roszak, Mary Gomes, Allan Kanner (San Francisco, CA.: Sierra Club Books, 1995), pp. 64–65.

46. Max Horkheimer and Theodor W. Adorno, *Dialectic of Enlightenment* (New York: Continuum Publishing, 1996).

47. Leiss, *op. cit.*, p. 163.

48. Melanie Klein, "The Psychogenesis of Manic-Depressive States," in Juliet Mitchell, ed., *The Selected Melanie Klein* (New York: The Free Press, 1987), p. 133.

49. Horkheimer and Adorno, *op. cit.*, pp. 71–72.

50. Jessica Benjamin, "Master and Slave: The Fantasy of Erotic Domination," in Ann Snitow, Christine Stansell and Sharon Thompson, eds. *Powers of Desire: The Politics of Sexuality* (New York: Monthly Review Press, 1983), pp. 280–299.

51. Nancy Chodorow, *The Reproduction of Mothering: Psychoanalysis and the Sociology of Gender* (Berkeley: University of California Press, 1978), pp. 173–176.

52. Theodore Roszak, *The Voice of the Earth* (New York: Simon & Schuster, 1992), p. 242.

53. Carolyn Merchant, *The Death of Nature: Women, Ecology & the Scientific Revolution* (New York: Harper and Row, 1980), p. 2.

54. Ibid., pp. 35–43.

55. Ibid., p. 169.

56. Susan Bordo, "The Cartesian Masculinization of Thought," in *The Flight to Objectivity: Essays on Cartesianism and Culture* (Albany: State University of New York Press, 1987), pp. 97–118.

57. Laura Brown, *Ends of Empire: Women and Ideology in early Eighteenth Century Literature*, (Ithaca, New York.: Cornell University Press, 1993), p. 120.

58. Ann Game, *Undoing the Social: Towards A Deconstructive Sociology* (Toronto: University of Toronto Press, 1991).

59. Mary Mellor, "Ecofeminism and Ecosocialism: Dilemmas of Essentialism and Materialism," in Ted Benton, ed., *The Greening of Marxism* (New York: The Guilford Press, 1996), pp. 251–265.

60. Kate Soper, "Feminism, Ecosocialism and the Conceptualization of Nature," in *The Greening of Marxism*, ed. T. Benton (New York: ilford, 1996), p. 269.

61. Donna J. Haraway, *Simians, Cyborgs, and Women: The Reinvention of Nature* (New York: Routledge, 1991), p. 8.

62. Baudrillard, *op. cit.*, p. 55.

CHAPTER SEVEN: DARK UTOPIA: GLOBALIZATION AND ABANDONMENT

1. William Tuohy, "Lonely Yule for Deserted Children," *Los Angeles Times*, December 18, 1989.

2. David Carpenter, "Many Homeless Kids Fend for Themselves in Moscow," *Detroit News*, April 21, 1997.

3. Immanuel Wallerstein, "Patterns and Perspectives of Capitalist World-Economy," in I. Wallerstein *The Politics of World-Economy* (Cambridge: Cambridge University Press, 1984), p. 18.

4. Louis Wirth, "World Community, World Society and World Government: An Attempt at a Clarification of Terms," in *Louis Wirth on Cities and Social Life*, ed. Albert J. Reiss (Chicago: University of Chicago Press, 1964), pp. 319–332.

5. Howard Perlmutter, "On the Rocky Road to the first Global Civilization," *Human Relations*, vol. 44, no. 9, 1991, pp. 897–1010.

6. Anthony Giddens, *The Consequences of Modernity* (Stanford, CA.: Stanford University Press, 1990), p. 64.

7. Ibid., pp. 64.

8. David Harvey, *The Condition of Postmodernity* (Oxford: Basil Blackwell, 1989), pp . 201–239.

9. Peter Marcuse, "The Language of Globalization," *Monthly Review*, vol. 52, no. 3, July/August 2000, pp. 23–27.

10. Ibid., p. 24.

11. Howard Adelman, "Modernity, Globalization, Refugees and Displacement," in Alastair Ager, ed., *Refugees: Perspectives on the Experience of Forced Migration* (London: Pinter, 1999), p. 86.

12. Zygmunt Bauman, *Globalization: The Human Consequences* (New York: Columbia University Press, 1998), pp. 74–75.

13. Adelman, *op. cit.*, p. 90.

14. Salman Akhtar, *Immigration and Identity* (New York: Jason Aaronson, 1990).

15. Alastair Ager, "Perspectives on the Refugee Experience, in Ager, ed., *op. cit.*, p. 1.

16. Fred Ahearn, Maryanne Loughry, and Alastair Ager, "The Experience of Refugee Children," in Ager, ed., *op. cit.*, p. 215.

17. Bauman, *op. cit.*, p. 70.

18. Carolyn Somerville, "Confronting Economic Crisis, Structural Adjustment, and Devaluation in Dakar, Senegal," in *Globalization and Survival in the Black Diaspora: The New Urban Challenge*, ed. Charles Green (Albany: State University of New York Press, 1997), pp. 26-38.

19. Ibid., pp. 33–34.

20. "Sept pièces du puzzle néoliberal: la quatrième guerre mondiale a commercé," *Le monde diplomatique*, August, 1997, pp. 4–5. Quoted by Zygmunt Bauman, *op. cit.*, p. 66.

21. Sommerville, *op. cit.*, pp. 34–35.

22. Adelman, *op. cit.*, p. 97.

23. Ibid., p. 95.

24. Saskia Sassen, *Globalization and its Discontents: Essays on the New Mobility of People and Money* (New York: The New Press, 1998), p. 7.

25. Michael Parenti, *Against Empire* (San Francisco, CA.: City Lights Books, 1995), p. 12.

26. Ibid., p. 12.

27. Vânia Penha-Lopes, "An Unsavory Union: Poverty, Racism and the Murders of Street Youth in Brazil," in Charles Green, *op. cit.*, pp. 149–168.

28. Ibid., p. 150.

29. Ibid., p. 163.

30. Ahern, Loughry and Ager, *op. cit.*, p. 217.

31. Ibid., p. 222.

32. Ibid., p. 222.

33. Frances Fox Piven, "The New Reserve Army of Labor," in *Audacious Democracy: Labor, Intellectuals, and the Social Reconstruction of America,* eds. Steven Fraser and Joshua B. Freeman (Boston: Houghton Mifflin Co., 1997), pp. 106–118.

34. Stanley Aronowitz and William DiFazio, *The Jobless Future: Sci-Tech and the Dogma of Work* (Minneapolis: University of Minnesota Press, 1994).

35. Ibid., p. 3.

36. Kate Bronfenbrenner, "Uneasy Terrain: The Impact of Capital Mobility on Workers, Wages and Union Organizing," *A Report Submitted to the U.S. Trade Deficit Review Commission, September 6, 2000* (Cornell, NY.: New York State School of Industrial and Labor Relations, Cornell University, 2000). Executive Summary.

37. Ibid.

38. Peter Marris, *The Politics of Uncertainty: Attachment in private and public life* (London: Routledge, 1996).

39. Bauman, *op. cit.,* p. 119.

40. Sassen, *op. cit.,* pp. 81–100.

41. Thomas Sanction, "Super Fries Saboteur," *Time,* vol. 154, no. 23 December 6, 1999.

42. Georg Ritzer, *The McDonaldization of Society* (Thousand Oaks, CA.: Pine Forge, 2000), p. 4.

43. John Gray, *False Dawn: The Delusions of Global Capitalism* (New York: The New Press, 1998).

44. Ibid., p. 100.

45. David Rothkopf, "In Praise of Cultural Imperialism?" *Foreign Policy,* no. 107, Summer 1997, pp. 42–43.

46. Ibid., p. 41.

47. Thomas L. Friedman, *The Lexus and the Olive Tree* (New York: Farrar, Straus & Giroux, 1999), p. 8.

48. Ibid., p. 274.

49. Ibid., pp. 309–310.

50. Ritzer, *op. cit.,* pp. 7–8.

51. Marc Pilisuk, "The Hidden Structure of Contemporary Violence," *Peace and Conflict: Journal of Peace Psychology,* vol. 4, 3, 1998, pp. 197–216.

52. Bauman, *op. cit.,* p. 3.

53. The Editors, "Toward a New Internationalism," *Monthly Review*, vol. 52, no. 3, July/August 2000, p. 3.

54. William Tabb, "After Seattle," *Monthly Review*, vol. 51, no. 10, p. 5.

55. "Genoa Police Unit Trained by LAPD," (Rome) *Reuters*, 13 August 2001.

56. David Sanger, "Italian Protester Is Killed by Police at Genoa Meeting," *New York Times*, July 21, 2001.

57. Thomas Friedman, "Senseless in Seattle," *New York Times*, op. ed., 1 December, 1999.

58. Friedman, *The Lexus and the Olive Tree*, p. 274.

59. William Tabb, *op. cit.*

60. Robert W. McChesney, "The New Global Media," *The Nation*, vol. 269, no. 18, November 29, 1999, p. 11.

61. Ibid., pp. 14–15.

62. Manuel Castells, *The Information Age: Economy, Society and Culture Volume II: The Power of Identity* (Malden, MA.: Blackwell Publishers, 1997), p. 7.

63. Ibid., p. 9.

64. See Castell's translation of Touraine, *op. cit.*, p. 10.

65. Ibid., p. 10.

Index